ISBN: 978129005977

Published by:
HardPress Publishing
8345 NW 66TH ST #2561
MIAMI FL 33166-2626

Email: info@hardpress.net
Web: http://www.hardpress.net

CAVE ADSVM

EX·LIBRIS
WILLIAM·JARDINE
1903 CAPE TOWN

Thomas Laidlaw

21st Jany 1858

LODGINGS OF MARY QUEEN OF SCOTS

G. B.

THE

HISTORY AND ANTIQUITIES

OF

ROXBURGHSHIRE

AND

ADJACENT DISTRICTS,

FROM THE MOST REMOTE PERIOD TO THE PRESENT TIME.

BY ALEXANDER JEFFREY,

AUTHOR OF THE "GUIDE TO THE ANTIQUITIES OF THE BORDER," &c.

VOL. II.

LONDON:
J. F. HOPE, 16, GREAT MARLBOROUGH STREET
1857.

PREFACE.

In presenting to the public the second volume of the History and Antiquities of Roxburghshire, the author, while acknowledging with gratitude the kindness and encouragement with which he has been honoured since the commencement of the work, has to express regret at the long period which has elapsed since the publication of the first volume. The preparation of a work of the kind, requiring scrupulous accuracy and fidelity, is of itself a laborious task; but, when added, as in the present instance, to heavy professional duties, only a few can appreciate the severity of the toil.

The work was intended to have been confined to two volumes, but the author had not proceeded far with the present volume when he found it impossible to condense the materials within such limits, and do anything like justice to the subject. He has therefore been induced to extend the work to another volume, and the doing so, he hopes, will meet the approval of the public. The third volume will embrace the districts of Kelso, Melrose, Hawick, and Liddesdale ; the civil and ecclesiastical history of the shire; its agriculture, roads, and railways; its botany and zoology; notices of the eminent men who have been born or lived in the county ; with a full account of the gipsy tribes inhabiting the Scots border. It is expected that the third volume will be ready for publication by the end of next year.

As the author is anxious that the work should be complete as well as accurate, he has to entreat all those possessed of any information tending to illustrate the history of the shire, or of families connected with it, to communicate the same to him, without loss of time, in order that it may be used in the third volume. He has also to request those who may have noticed any errors in the volumes already published, to let him know, that the matter may be inquired into, and, if wrong, corrected in the forthcoming volume.

A copious general index of every circumstance in the work will be given in the third volume.

A. J.

Jedburgh, Nov. 1, 1857.

CONTENTS OF VOL. II.

CHAPTER I.

OF ITS NAME—ESTABLISHMENT AS A SHIRE—ITS OTHER JURIS-
DICTIONS, REGAL AND BARONIAL.

CHAPTER II.

OF THE BURGH AND CASTLE OF ROXBURGH.

THE

HISTORY AND ANTIQUITIES

OF

ROXBURGHSHIRE, &c.

CHAPTER I.

OF ITS NAME——ESTABLISHMENT AS A SHIRE——ITS OTHER
JURISDICTIONS, REGAL AND BARONIAL.

THE *scyre* or division of Roxburgh undoubtedly
derived its name from the burgh and castle which
occupied the rocky peninsula formed by the junction of the rivers Tweed and Teviot, but the exact
period when the name was imposed has not been
satisfactorily ascertained. I am inclined to think
that it was conferred on the castle during the end
of the eleventh or beginning of the twelfth century,
by the Anglo-Normans, who had at that early
period found their way to the pleasant banks of
the Tweed, and the soft margins of the Teviot.

B

The name first appears in the writs of David, the youngest son of Malcolm, who, at the death of his brother Edgar, in 1106, had assigned to him as his appanage all the country to the south of the firths, excepting Lothian, which at that time comprehended all the territory lying on the north of the Tweed along the Forth to the Avon on the north-west, while his elder brother, Alexander I., reigned as king over the country to the north of the firths, or Scotland proper. In the early charters it is spelled *Rokesburg*,* *Rokeburc*,† and in several records, Rokeburg, Rokesburg, Rocheburh, Rockeburh, Rogesburgh, Rogysburgh, Rokisburgh, Rokysburgh, Rokesburch, and Rocheburch.‡ In later writs the name is spelled in a variety of ways, and occasionally with an *x*, as Roxburgh, but in all the form of the word is intended to describe a fortress on a rocky promontory, or a castle situated among rocks. Camden, while treating of the locality, says—" This castle was anciently called ' Marchidun,' from its standing on the Marches." Fordun calls it " Marchimond," Bœce and Bellenden " Marchmond," and others call it " Markin."

---

* Nicholson's Hist. Lib., 363-4 ; Smith's Bede, 764 ; Lib. of Kelso.

† Inquisition of David, 1116 ; Dalrymple's Collection, 348.

‡ Chron. Mail. ; Lib. of Mail. ; Lib. of Dryburgh ; Lib. of Kelso ; Records in Rymer ; Symeon Dunelm. ; Register of Glasgow ; Origines Parochiales.

On Camden's statement, Chalmers remarks that his intimation is not warranted by the fact, as the place was not situated on the Marches.* I rather think that the statement by the learned Camden is correct, and properly describes the locality in both ancient and modern times. At the present day, Roxburgh may with propriety be described as upon the Marches, between the two kingdoms. The border line is not above three miles from the castle, and the same boundary has existed since 1020. In the troublous times of the Edwards and Henrys, the castle was usually described as " on the Marches." In a writ, dated 1405, by which King Henry appointed commissioners to treat for peace with Scotland, he directed them to inquire into the bounds of the lands and possessions assigned by the treaty " to his Castle of Roxburgh on the Marches."† The name would also describe the place at a much earlier period. When the Saxons came in upon the British people, about the middle of the fifth century, they occupied all the north side of the Tweed, which was then called " Lothian," and the Romanized Gadeni lived on the south of that river. The Tweed would thus be at that day the March between the two peoples, and the castle, standing on the margin of the river, would be described as standing on the

---

* Caledonia, vol. ii. p. 67.   † Rotuli Scotiæ, vol. ii. p. 174.

Marches. It was so described during the beginning of the twelfth century. Simeon of Durham,
in recording the visit paid by John, Cardinal of
Crima, Legate of Pope Honorius, to the Scottish
king, in the year 1125, to determine the controversy touching the primacy of York over
the Scottish Church, says, "He came by the
river Tweed, which bounds Northumberland and
Lothian, in a place which is called Roxburgh."*
But I am inclined to think that the original name
of the place was "Marcidin," and intended to
describe a fortress situated on cliffs in the middle
of waters. It is probable that the native people
had a *din* or fort on this eminence, which was
afterwards taken possession of by the Romans
when they entered upon the district, and being
a favourable position they built upon it a castle,
described by the native inhabitants as the towering fortress in the midst of the waters. On the
Romans leaving the country, the strength would
be known as the fortress upon the Marches; and
when the Anglo-Normans arrived, it got the appel-

---

* "Pervenit apud fluvium Tuedam qui Northumbriam
et Loidam determinat, in loco qui Rocheburch vocatur."
Simeon of Durham lived about the year 1164, and is
supposed to be the author of the continuation of Turgot's
History of the Church of Durham. Chron. Mail., 165;
Wilkins's Concilia, 407; Lord Haile's An., 65; Sim. Dun.,
252.

lation under which it makes its first appearance in the charters and other writs. Although the ancient grandeur of the castle is now defaced, and the towers fallen, the ruins convey to the mind the impression of its exceeding strength in former days, and its claim to be called the " towering fortress." The ruins and the eminence on which the castle stands still tower nearly fifty feet above the surrounding plain.

The true date when the district was divided and erected into a sheriffdom is not known. It is, however, certain that the division could not have existed earlier than 1097. The Celtic people had no charters, and they had no sheriffdoms. Both were equally odious to them. They strenuously opposed the use of records, and they resisted the appointments of sheriffs. It is thought that at first the term *scyre* applied only to parishes, and did not import a division of land placed under the regimen of a *sheriff*. But as the Saxon people gained power they gradually introduced sheriffdoms, and at the termination of the Scoto-Saxon period, in 1306, the salutary rule of the Anglo-Norman law prevailed throughout nearly all Scotland. We may thus see the causes which led to the change of the ancient customs of the country, and which produced frequent revolts.

When the line of Celtic kings ended with Donal-bane, Edgar, the son of Malcolm, with

Margaret, an Anglo-Saxon princess, succeeded. He gained his crown by an Anglo-Norman army, furnished by William Rufus, and commanded by his unclc. His education and experience induced him to follow the customs of England in the administration of his kingdom, rather than the customs and manners of Scotland. Still, during his reign there is not to be found any reference to sheriffs. The charters of his brother and successor, Alexander I., are almost equally barren, although the term *scyre*, as applied to parishes, occasionally occurs. On David I. succeeding to the territory on the south of the firths, the sheriff, as a law officer, makes his appearance. In the foundation charter to the Abbey of Selkirk, Odard, the sheriff of Babenburgh,* appears as a witness; and it is to be presumed that other parts of the district were also under the charge of sheriffs, although the fact does not appear in those early writs. After Alexander's death, in 1124, David became king of the whole land, and as such endeavoured to introduce into Scotland the rule which was productive of so much good in England. As king, he is found addressing writs to the Sheriff of Rokesburgh.†

Dalrymple's Collection, p. 405.

† Writs among the Charters of Coldingham, preserved in the Treasury of Durham.

The first sheriff that can be traced with certainty is Gospatrick, the owner of Nether Crailing, and whose family rose to great eminence in another part of the district. A person named JOHN, the son of ORM, appears also acting as sheriff about the same time. He was probably the proprietor of Hownam. Orm was the possessor of Over Crailing, now called Crailing Hall, and it is said conferred his name on Ormston on the Teviot, near to where the Cayle joins its waters with that river. Orm is a witness to several charters of King David, Earl Henry, and Malcolm IV.* It may be inferred that the office of sheriff was conferred upon him by reason of his intimacy with the king, and that the settlement at the mouth of the Cayle was the consequence of his appointment to the sheriffship.

The next sheriff that is noticed is GERVASE RIDEL. He is mentioned in a charter of David as "Vicecome de Rokesburch."† This eminent person was a witness, with Hugh Morville the constable and others, to the Inquisitio Davidis, in 1116, and is thought to be the head of the ancient house of Riddell in this county, and Cranstown

---

* He is witness to a grant of the Church of Old Roxburgh to the Church of Glasgow. David Olifard, Gilbert de Umframville, Richard de Morville, Walter de Ridel, and others, are also witnesses.

† Dalrymple's Collection, 382, 384.

Riddell in Mid-Lothian.   In Northumberland, a family of the same name have long existed.   The first grant which the family of Gervase Ridel obtained in this district was the manor of Primside, near Yetholm.   From the age of Gervase when he died, and the great esteem in which he was held, it is probable that he filled the office of sheriff for many years.

Owing to the misfortunes which followed the battle of the Standard, the death of David, and the brief reign of his grandson, Malcolm IV., the notices of the sheriffs who ruled the district during that period are scanty, and the same thing may be said of the earlier part of the reign of William the Lion, who succeeded to the throne in 1165.   On the king being made a prisoner by a band of York-shire barons, the castles of Roxburgh, Jedburgh, Berwick, Edinburgh, and Stirling were delivered up as part of the purchase for the liberty of their inconsiderate king.   On a formal restitution of the kingdom being made by Richard, the English king, in December, 1189, the castles above mentioned were restored, and the land marks as they were at the time of William being made a prisoner.

About 1159, HERBERT MACCHUSWEL was sheriff.[*] He granted the Church of Macchuswel to the

---

* Lib. of Kelso, p. vi.

monks of Kelso. The founder of the family in this county is thought to be Unwyn, who is one of the witnesses to the Inquisition of David. He received a grant of land on the Tweed in the proximity of the castle of Roxburgh, on which he erected a dwelling, and conferred upon it his own name Macchuswel—the modern Maxwellheugh. From a branch of this family the Scottish Maxwells are descended. WALTER CORBET seems to have been the next sheriff; at all events it is certain that he acted in that capacity in 1199.* In 1202 Bernard de Hauden was sheriff;† he seems to have succeeded Corbet. The sheriff was son of Brien, an Anglo-Norman who came into Scotland during the reign of William the Lion, from whom he got Hauden on the banks of the Tweed. The family afterwards assumed the name of Hauden or Haldane. Bernard seems to have been in high favour with William the Lion. The family were also owners of Kirk Yetholm. A John de Macchuswel held the appointment in 1225. In 1235 Adam of Baggot was sheriff.‡ He is supposed to be a son or grandson of Herbert. One of that name is buried in Melrose Abbey in 1241.§ Another Bernard de Hauden is thought to have followed Macchuswel, and

* Register of Paisley, pp. 254, 255.
† Lib. of Kelso, pp. 174, 175.   ‡ Ib. p. 321.
§ Arbroath Charter, p. 94. Dalrymple's Collection, 405; Chron. Mail., 206.

who was probably a grandson of the sheriff Bernard of 1202. The next sheriff noticed is NICHOLAS, son of Fulco de Sules, one of the lords of Liddesdale, and one of the wisest and most eloquent men of the kingdom. He died at Rouen in 1264.* The family held the office of King's butler.† After the death of Sules, Hugh de Abernethy, who held possession of the lands of Rule, is found acting as sheriff in 1264.‡ He seems to have been succeeded in the office by a person named THOMAS CAUER.§ Thomas Randolph appears next. In 1266 he witnessed a charter by Robert France in favour of the monks of Kelso.‖ In 1285 HUGH DE PERESBY held the office. This gentleman signs as a witness, along with Thomas of Ercildun, the Rymer, to a charter granted by one of the Haigs of Bemerside in favour of the monks of Dryburgh.¶ In the presence of this sheriff Hugh of Bluden appeared, and resigned his lands to the monks of Kelso.**

After the death of Alexander III., the first sheriff found acting is WILLIAM DE SULES, one of

---

* Scotichronicon, lib. x. c. 18.

† Register of Glasgow, pp. 13, 15 ; Lib. de Mail., pp. 214, 284; Raines' North Durham, app. p. 16.

‡ Compota Camerar., vol. i. p. 46.　　§ Ib. vol. i. p. 42.

‖ Lib. of Kelso.

¶ Lib. of Kelso, p. 180 ; Nisbet's Heraldry, i. 134 ; Dryburgh chart.

** Ib. ; Lib. of Mail.

the family of Lydal.* On Edward of England obtaining the dominion of the kingdom by intrigue and violence, Walter Tonk was appointed by him to the charge of the castle and county of Roxburgh, in May, 1296.† In 1305 the same king issued an ordinance placing the district under a military government, with instructions that the lieutenant in command should keep in his own hands the castles of Roxburgh and Jedburgh, and govern the shire without the aid of a sheriff. During the war of independence, the castle and sheriffdom remained in the hands of Edward till 1312, when the castle was surprised by the gallant Douglas, who soon afterwards freed the whole of Teviotdale from the English, except Jedburgh and a few other places. By the order of King Robert Bruce the defences of the town were destroyed, and the castle was put under the charge of Bernard de Hauden, to whom he granted a duty for the keeping thereof.

At the peace of Northampton in 1328, the castle of Roxburgh as well as all Teviotdale were relinquished by the English king in favour of Bruce. About this time Henry de Baliol was sheriff.‡ At the death of this truly great man

---

* Compota Camerar., vol. i., pp. 71, 72.
† Ordinance of Edward, in Ryley, 505.
‡ Compota Camerar., vol. i., p. 14.

Edward claimed all Teviotdale, which had been delivered to him by Edward Baliol, and five years afterwards he appointed GEOFFREY DE MOUBRAY sheriff of Roxburgh.* He also acted as one of the justiciary. John de Bourdon appears in 1334 as *chamberlain* of the county. A few years afterwards, the same king appointed WILLIAM DE FELTOUN, who was at the time sheriff of Northumberland, to act as sheriff of Roxburghshire, and it is thought he held the office till 1343. As sheriff he granted, in April, 1338, a charter of confirmation to the monks of Dryburgh of a burgage tenement situated in the King Street of Roxburgh, between the tenement of John Flecher and that of " Emma Kenilis wife," and which belonged to Hutred the baker.† Mr. Chalmers, in noticing this transaction, states that the sheriff who granted the confirmation was William de Seton, a sheriff of David II., and remarks that " the sheriff seems to have acted officially in this transfer, though it appears not by what authority." But this state-

---

* Rymer's Fœdera, vol. ii., p. 889.

† Lib. de Dryburgh, No. 313, 314, 315, 316. Feltoun acted as sheriff in other transfers in the burgh about the same time. Amongst the witnesses thereto we observe the names of Thomas, the abbot of Melrose, John, the abbot of Jeddewod, Robert de Maneris, constable of the castle of Norham, Thomas de ·Rydell, Richard of Rutherfurd, John Burnard of Farnington, Allan of Myndrum, one of the aldermen of Roxburgh, and many others.

ment is incorrect, as the Scottish king had no
sheriff in Teviotdale after the death of Bruce till
1343. There was a necessity for the sheriff William de Feltoun acting in the transfer, as the lands
conveyed were at the time in the possession of the
king of England, and without his sanction the
grant could not have availed the brotherhood of
Dryburgh. No doubt William de Feltoun had the
authority of his master for what he did. The
sheriff was of the family of Feltouns, of West
Matfen in Northumberland, and of considerable
note in that county during the reigns of Edward
II. and III.

In 1343, Sir ALEXANDER RAMSAY of Dalwolsey
got the appointment of sheriff as a reward for his
gallantry in taking the castle from the English.
But this appointment sorely displeased the knight
of Liddesdale, Sir William Douglas, warden of the
West Marches, who, by bravery and perseverance,
expelled the English from Teviotdale. He thought
that he had the best right to be sheriff of the
county he had freed, and while Ramsay was wait-
ing in the church at Hawick, before the meeting
of his court, he was seized by Douglas and carried
prisoner to Hermitage Castle, where he was starved
to death.* Instead of hanging him over the gate

* Sir William Douglas was styled the knight of Liddesdale, and flower of chivalry. He was the bastard son of the
good Sir James Douglas.

of his castle for the atrocious act, the weak David appointed him as successor to the sheriff whom he had murdered. For about thirty-eight years the English king had the appointment of the sheriffs. The first person he made sheriff was the celebrated COUPLAND, who took David prisoner at the battle of Durham. He was sheriff in 1347.* Coupland held the sheriffship in Northumberland from 1350 to 1355. In 1349 HENRY KERR was sheriff. It seems that when the English king got possession of Teviotdale, he generally placed it under the rule of his sheriff of Northumberland. WILLIAM KARES-WELL succeeded Coupland.† He was the husband of Isobel countess of Mar, widow of Donald the 12th Earl, and as such received the appointment. It appears that the lady claimed the sheriffship of Roxburgh and the custody of Selkirk Forest, on the ground that these offices belonged hereditarily

---

* Coupland was celebrated among the men of Northumberland as the valiant knight. Wallis's History, pp. 415, 416 ; Ayloff's Calendar, 108.

† Kareswell is thought to have been of a family of that name who possessed a portion of the territory of *Astenasdane* (Hassendean) during the twelfth and thirteenth centuries. Symond de Cressewill swore fealty to Edward I. in 1296: Ragman's Roll, p. 126. May not this tenement have been named after one of the early settlers, Kerr or Carswell, in the same way as Macchuswell denoted the villa or dwelling of Macchus? The sheriff seems to have had right to the barony of Roberton, and appears to have been lord of Kenback.

to the family of her late husband; for we find, in September 1334, Edward III. issuing a writ to his sheriff of Roxburgh to make inquiry into her rights, and in 1347 the same king ordered Coupland to deliver up to her husband the castle of Roxburgh, and the sheriffship of the county, which he found to be part of her heritage, to be held as by her ancestors.* Although the fact does not clearly appear in what way the lady's ancestors had right to the offices claimed, it is at least certain that the return to the writ referred to, satisfied the English king that the claim to the government of the castle and county, was made in conformity with the laws of Scotland.

By a covenant made at Roxburgh in 1346, Edward bound himself to govern Roxburgh, Selkirk and the forest of Selkirk, Tweedale, Weedale, and Lauderdale, according to the laws and customs used in the time of King Alexander.† He also was bound to appoint sheriffs who would administer the laws in a just and easy manner.‡ At her death in 1348, Kareswell was appointed guardian of her property, including the sheriffship of the county.§ In 1355 Edward appointed HENRY DE PERCY

---

* Rymer iv. 622, 635.

† Acta Parl. Scot., vol. i., MS. notice prefixed, p. vi.   ‡ Ib.

§ Chalmers, vol. ii. p. 983, on the authority of the Douglas Peerage, p. 160, states that the Countess Isobel was a daughter of Sir Alexander Stewart of Bonkil.   Her husband, the

sheriff.* In 1359 RICHARD TEMPEST was sheriff under the same king.† COUPLAND seems to have been again appointed to the office of sheriff, for in 1364 we find the English king appointing ALAN DEL STROTHER in room of Coupland deceased.‡ He also succeeded Coupland in his office of sheriff of Northumberland. The family of the sheriff possessed the Barony of Kirknewton in Glendale, and furnished sheriffs for Edward III., for many years. From the names of various places in the neighbourhood of Roxburgh, it may be inferred that the family had considerable possessions in this district. It is probable that Alan and Henry Strothers were sheriffs for at least nine years. In 1376 THOMAS DE PERCY obtained the office from King Edward in room of Alan Strother.§ The English family of GREY also supplied the castle of Roxburgh with a governor and the county with a sheriff. Sir ROBERT UMFRAMVILLE was also for a time sheriff. When Teviotdale was cleared of the English in 1379, chiefly through the skill and valour of Wiliam, the first Earl of Douglas and nephew of the good Sir James, HENRY DE PERCY DE ALNWICK, Earl of Northumberland, was sheriff both of

---

twelfth Earl of Mar, was elected Regent of Scotland at the death of Randolph in 1332, and who fell at the battle of Duplin in the same year.

* Rotuli Scotiæ, vol. i. p. 781.   † Ib. vol. i. pp. 842, 843.
‡ Ib. vol. i. p. 880.   § Ib. vol i. p. 978.

Northumberland* and Roxburghshire under Richard II. After that period the office of sheriff followed the fortunes of the Lords of Jedburgh Forest. When their star was in the ascendant a Douglas or one of the friends of the house filled the office. Accordingly in 1396, Sir Wm. Stewart of Jedforest, a relation of the Douglas, appears as sheriff.† The sheriff, it is said, was the son of John Stewart of Jedforest by a daughter of Turnbull of Minto, and the grandson of a son of Sir John Stewart of Bonkyl, that was slain at the battle of Falkirk in 1298. The sheriff was a gallant warrior and chivalrous knight. He was taken prisoner in 1402 at the celebrated battle of Homilden in Northumberland, and was tried and executed under the illegal directions of Henry Percy, the sheriff of the English king and the Hotspur of Shakespeare. The mangled limbs of Stewart were exposed on the gates of York. It is not unlikely that the sheriff's, being one of the chief leaders of the brave men of Teviotdale under the Douglas, influenced the decision of Hotspur to such an unworthy and lawless deed as the execution of a prisoner taken in battle.

In 1398 George, Earl of Angus, the half-brother of Isobel, the Countess of Mar, was infeft by a James Sandilands in the lands of Cavers, and on King

---

* The Hotspur of Shakespeare.

† Wynton's Chron. ii. pp. 401, 402 ; Fordun, ii. 433 ; Caledonia, vol. ii. p. 98, foot note.

Robert III. confirming the deed, he at the same time granted to the earl the office of sheriff of the county and keeper of the Castle of Roxburgh.* At his death in 1402 the same Isobel of Mar, who appears to have been in possession of the lands of Cavers, conveyed the same and the office of sheriff, without the consent of the king, to Archibald, Earl of Douglas.† The king not only refused to confirm the deed, but conferred the lands and office of sheriff on his relative Sir David Fleming of Biggar, as a reward for his loyalty and truth. The Douglases enraged that Sir David should have presumed to solicit or accept lands and office to which they claimed a right, he was assassinated at Langherdmanston by a son of the Earl of Douglas.‡ The act was just a repetition of their conduct to Sir Alexander Ramsay. The causes were alike, and the atrocity of the acts was equal.

---

* Robertson's Index, 139, No. 7. In 1388 James was Earl of Douglas and Mar, and Lord of the Barony of Cavers. The lands formed a portion of the territory granted by a grateful king to a faithful subject by the Emerald Charter, in 1325. From that period till 1455 the successors of the good Sir James held the lands.

† Robertson's Index, p. 148, No. 26. Isobel was only daughter of William, first Earl of Douglas, by his first marriage with Margaret, afterwards Countess of Mar. Isobel became Countess of Mar at the death of her brother James, second Earl of Douglas, and fifteenth Earl of Douglas and Mar.

‡ Wynton, ii. 413. Caledonia, vol. ii. p. 99, foot note.

Like David II., Robert III. was forced to pass over the murder as a common event.

The lands and office were next conveyed to Archibald Douglas, said to be a bastard son of James, second Earl of Douglas, and from whom the family of CAVERS is descended.* In May, 1425, the sheriff of Teviotdale witnessed a charter of James I.† He also witnessed several charters of the Earl of Douglas in 1430 and 1433.‡ While he was sheriff he, along with several others, swore, on the part of the Scottish king, to the observance of the truce for nine years.§ His son William succeeded to the office.‖ One of the sheriff's daughters married Kerr of Altonburn, the founder of the House of Roxburgh.¶ Another daughter was married to Ainslie of Dolphingston. Archibald his son succeeded to the lands of Cavers and the office of sheriff, and in 1457 was appointed to preserve the peace on the borders.** William Douglas, his son, was the next sheriff. In 1482 he appeared before the lords, complaining against Walter Turnbull of Gargunnoch.†† By the first parliament of James IV., held in 1488, Archi-

---

* Nisbet's Heraldry, i. 29; Crawford's Peerage, 413 ; History of the House of Douglas, p. 93.

† Douglas' Baron. 278.   ‡ Douglas' Peerage, 592.
§ Rymer x. 695.   ‖ Douglas' Peerage, 592.
¶ Douglas' Baron. 300.   ** Rymer, ii. 597.
†† Rob. Parl. Record, 286.

bald, Earl of Angus, was appointed sheriff. He was also sheriff of Selkirk, Peebles, and Lanark.*

In 1529 JAMES DOUGLAS of Cavers was sheriff. In July of that year he appeared before the Lords of Council, and became surety for James Douglas of Drumlanrig, that he should remain in the castle of Edinburgh during the pleasure of the king, under the penalty of a thousand pounds.† Two years after his name appears among the barons and lairds of Roxburgh, who found surety to the king for not doing their utmost diligence to fulfil their bonds.

In June, 1575, the sheriff was present at the battle of the Redswyre, and, according to the ballad‡—

" Brought the Douglas down,
Wi' Cranstane, Gladstain, good at need,
Baith Rewle Water and Hawick town."

In 1591 James Douglas was sheriff. During that year he appeared before the Privy Council, and became surety for Walter Turnbull of Bedrule under the pain of a thousand merks.§ It was to this sheriff that the warrant was intrusted for the apprehension of Sir John Ker of Hirsel, in May, 1593. He was also sheriff in June, 1600, and enacted himself in the Justiciary Court as cautioner

---

* Acts of Parliament, vol. ii., p. 108, &c.
† Pitcairn's Criminal Trials, vol. i. pp. 142-7.
‡ Border Minstrelsy, p. 72.   § Pitcairn's Criminal Trials.

for Sir John Cranstown of that ilk, and Mr. William Cranstown.* In the following year he was examined as a witness on the trials of the Turnbulls, charged with rioting in the market-place of Jedburgh, and the slaughter of several persons therein.† Two years afterwards the sheriff was amerciated in one thousand merks before William Borthwick, justice-deputy.‡ The Earl of Roxburgh appears for a short time as sheriff during pleasure. In 1642 William Douglas held the office. About 1669 the DUKE of MONMOUTH, who married Anne, the heiress of Buccleuch, was appointed sheriff, and shortly after the lands in Dumfriesshire belonging to him were annexed to Roxburghshire.§ But in 1690 Sir William Douglas is again found in possession of the ancient office. He was present with the *posse comitatûs* at the final pulling down of the beautiful old church of Hassendean, and which, according to tradition, was opposed by the whole commons of the district. For the part the sheriff took on that occasion, the crowd of persons assembled invoked the judgment of Heaven, and in reference to which Leyden sings‖ :—

---

* Pitcairn's Criminal Trials.

† Ib. It is curious to notice that the sheriff seemed to be ignorant of the person of his own clerk of court.

‡ Ib.   § Acts of Parliament.

‖ Scenes of Infancy.

> "Then circles many a legendary tale
> Of Douglas' race foredoomed without a male
> To fade unblest, since in the churchyard green
> Its lord o'erthrew the spires of Hazeldean."

On the heritable jurisdictions being taken away in 1747, Archibald Douglas claimed £10,000 as compensation, and was allowed £1,666 13s. 4d. Previous to the abolition of these offices, there were thirty-three sheriffs and stewards in Scotland. Of these, nine held the office during pleasure, four for life, and twenty hereditary.

The object in passing the statutes abolishing these jurisdictions was to make an efficient provision for the regular administration of justice by the king's judges. The king then appointed professed lawyers to the office, with what were supposed at the time adequate salaries, but which are found not to meet the requirements of the present day. At that epoch GILBERT ELLIOT, the son of Lord Minto,* was appointed the first sheriff-depute of Roxburghshire. His commission is dated 18th March, 1748, and the certificate of his having qualified by taking the oaths to government bears date at Edinburgh, the 25th of the same month.† He was sheriff for five years. William Scott of Woll was next appointed, on 4th December, 1753, as interim sheriff, by warrant of the Lords of Council and Session.‡   In April, 1754, Walter Pringle

---

* A Lord of Session.   † Sheriff Court Record.   ‡ Ib.

was appointed, and filled the office till his death in 1769.* Patrick Murray of Cherrytrees was appointed sheriff in July of same year.† On the 5th of December, 1780, William Oliver of Dinlabyre obtained the appointment, and on the 12th day of May, 1807, his son, now William Oliver Rutherfurd of Edgerston, was appointed sheriff, and which office he now holds. By a recent statute the counties of Roxburgh and Selkirk have been conjoined, and on a vacancy occurring in either sheriffdom, the sheriff of the other will be sheriff of the united sheriffdom.

It is thought that the sheriff was one of the earliest appointments of our Scoto-Saxon kings, and at the least equal in point of antiquity to that of *justiciar*. The justiciary was the supreme judge under the crown, and held justice *aires* in various parts of his district, at which the king was often present. On William the Lion ascending the throne, he appointed justiciaries for all Scotland: two for the country to the north of the Forth, and one for the south thereof. When the state of the district permitted, the court was held at Jedburgh, occasionally at Roxburgh and Hawick. A court of justiciary sometimes sat at Selkirk and Lauder, but the principal seat of the *aire* was at Jedburgh, where in early times the kings resided,

---

* Sheriff Court Record.   † Ib.

and it was the place where the armies assembled. When the district was in the power of the English king, it was generally put by him under military government. There is evidence, however, of the supreme criminal court of England—the King's Bench—sitting for a time at Roxburgh.

By the old laws of the realm the sheriff was bound to hold courts after the space of forty days.* At the court of the sheriff, all barons, knights, freeholders, stewards of bishops, abbots, and earls, were bound to attend under the penalty of the king's unlaw, which, by a law of King Malcolm, was fixed not to exceed the sum of sixteen shillings, to the sheriff-clerk two shillings, "and to his *serjand, an colpondach,* or thirty pennies."† One of the duties of the sheriff was to cause the laws to be published, read, and proclaimed in his court, to be kept and observed by the people. He was also empowered to enter the courts of all prelates, earls, and barons, and others having power of holding courts, and delivering to them copies of the laws for publication, that no man might be ignorant thereof.‡ The sheriff was bound to attend the courts of bishops, abbots, earls, barons, and freeholders, who could not hold their courts without intimation to the sheriff. It was his duty

---

* Laws of King David.   † Laws of Malcolm, c. ii.
‡ Statutes of Robert II.

also to swear in twelve leal and honest men in each burgh within his territory to see that the laws were obeyed in the town.* His presence was also necessary in every baron court of " battle, water or iron," to give validity to the proceedings.† When the king entered his district the sheriff had to give personal attendance, and could not depart without leave asked and obtained under the pain and unlaw of eight cows.‡

In criminal matters the powers of the sheriff were in ancient times great. In cases of slaughter committed within the sheriffdom, he had power to gather the lieges and pursue the slayer with sound of horn. If found with red hand, justice was done by the sheriff before the sun set, and if not found with the blood upon him, forty days were allowed to elapse. In the event of the slayer fleeing to a girth or sanctuary—of which nearly all the great abbeys had grant of girth—the sheriff called upon the master thereof, and put the slayer to the knowledge of an assize, whether the slaughter was of sudden quarrel or forethought felony. If the former, the slayer was returned to the girth; and if the jury found that the slaughter had been intended, death was the punishment. When theft was not followed by way of dittay, it was compe-

---

* Statutes of Alexander.　† Ib.
‡ Laws of King David : Rob. ii.

tent for the sheriff, with the private party com-
pearing, to punish the thief with death, and in
that case all the moveable goods were declared to
belong to the sheriff. The sheriff was also enjoined to punish with death " all witches, sorcerers,
necromancers, and them wha seekis helpes, re-
sponse, or consultation of them." The sheriff had
power to banish all " sorners, over-lyars, masterful
beggars, fuilles bairdes, vagaboundes, and dessemu-
late thieves, and abusers called Egyptians."

All idlemen the sheriff put under caution,
that the inhabitants of the country should not be
harmed by them, and if the party failed to find a
master or work at some craft within forty days,
the sheriff imprisoned him during the king's
pleasure. If idlemen were found going at large,
the sheriff was fined in twenty pounds to the king.
The sheriff had power to grant licences to beg within the parish of birth, but only to the " cruiked,
seik, or weake," under the penalty of fifty shillings
to the king.

The sheriff had also the charge of the rivers
and streams within his sheriffdom, and ordered to
destroy all obstructions to the smolts getting to
the sea; to present the slayers of salmon in forbidden times to the justice in his *aire*, and to execute the acts anent herring and white fish. He
was obliged to hunt the wolf and her whelps three
times in the year, between St. Mark's-day and

Lammas, and was empowered to call upon the country people to rise and hunt with him under the penalty of "ane wedder." He also superintended archery, and saw that bow-marks were put up in each parish.

The sheriff was also conservator of the game within his bounds. He had the charge of the markets, and searched for those persons who bought victual and kept it back during a dearth. It was part of his duty to prevent nolt, sheep, or other cattle being transported out of the country. He was intrusted with the charge of the plantations, woods, forests, orchards, brooms, dovecots, &c., and he also punished those persons who did not plant woods nor make hedges or hainings.

Persons dressed contrary to the law, such as those who wore clothes of gold, silver, velvet, or silk, were to be apprehended by the sheriff and sent to the king for punishment. All those who used excess in banquetings the sheriff punished. He was bound to inquire into the order in which every man's house was kept, the quantity of meat, and dishes used. The sheriff also caused innkeepers to keep by the rates fixed by the provost and bailies of the burgh for a man's dinner and supper, and also the wages of craftsmen. He was the general tax-collector in his district. It was part of his duty to see that weapon-shawings were kept four times in the year, and that each man was armed according to his estate or rent. The execution of the acts for threshing corn was entrusted to the sheriff; he, along with the chamberlain, surveyed the measures used in the sheriffdom. The sheriff was also required to see that no one under a baron or landed man worth a thousand merks of yearly rent kept his horse at hard meat after the 15th of May, or took them in before the 15th of October, under the pain of forfeiting the horse, one-half to the king and the other half to the sheriff. He was also bound to apprehend all cursed and excommunicated persons at the desire of the bishop or his official, and put them in prison till they satisfied God and the kirk. The sheriff had the power of convocation of the king's lieges to pursue fugitives and rebels, and present them to the justice to be *justified.*

In civil matters the sheriff's ancient jurisdiction was very great. He was entitled to judge in all actions between one man and another, bond or free. The brieve of right and free tenements was also used before him in the second instance to review the judgments of the baron courts. He judged in all actions of possession of property with the assistance of a jury, " of the best and worthiest of the countrie least suspect and that best knaws the veritie." The sheriff took cognizance of all complaints by parties of being wrongously ejected from their possessions, restored them to their own

lands, and imprisoned the wrongful occupiers thereof. The sheriff seems to have tried all causes, civil
as well as criminal, by an inquest or jury. In 1271,
we find, the sheriff of Roxburgh and a jury tried
the right of the monastery of Soltra to a thrave of
corn every harvest out of the manor of Crailing,
which the possessor of that land refused to pay.
The jury consisted of twelve men taken equally
from the manors of Eckford, Heton, and Upper
Crailing. The verdict of the jury was that the
brethren of the house of Soltra had very long
been in use to receive the said thrave of corn,
and judgment in accordance with that finding was
pronounced by the sheriff.* It rather appears that
all causes were tried by jury at that early period,
and even down to comparatively recent times,
when a controversy occurred in regard to the
right of lands, the king caused an inquest to be
summoned, who often in his own presence inquired into the dispute, and in terms of the verdict
the king granted a charter defining the rights of the
parties.† The jury generally consisted of twelve
fideles homines, presided over by the constable,
justiciar, or sheriff. A great number of grants may
be traced to these jury findings. On these trials it
is important to notice that individuals of the jury

---

* Law Tracts, 78 ; Chart. Soltra, 17.
† Chronicle of Melrose, p. 90-3. ; Lib. of Mel.

were often challenged, and removed on the ground of interest in the matters at issue. Servants or dependants of the parties were not allowed to form a part of the inquest.* At the present day a strong feeling exists against trial by jury, and many take it upon themselves to allege that such a mode of trial is of recent introduction into the kingdom; but an examination into our early history will show that trial by jury, so far from being an innovation on our olden practice, was coeval with the beginning of the Scoto-Saxon period, and continued in use till the institution of the College of Justice, when the fifteen judges came in place of the jury.

The sheriff had also important duties to perform in connexion with the justiciar on his aires. The brieve of dittay was addressed to the sheriff, and by him executed and reported to the justice clerk who attended on the day named in the writ, and took up the dittay against those charged with the commission of crimes. A roll of the names was then handed by the justice clerk to an officer called the coroner, or crowner, who took means to secure their attendance at the aire to answer to the crimes imputed unto them. The sheriff was obliged to

---

* In an inquest before Robert de Keth, justiciar in the north, for settling a dispute between the Abbot of Lindores and the burgesses of Newburgh, in 1339, one of the jury was objected to, and removed on the ground that he was a servant of the abbot.

attend the justice aires. The sheriff was answerable for all those persons who appeared in presence of the justiciar till justice was done to them. On the last day of the aire the sheriff and crowner underwent a trial as to the manner in which they had performed the duties of their office. If found guilty, they were deprived of their office, and otherwise punished at the king's will.

Closely connected with the sheriff was the CROWNER, or CORONER, whose duty it was to attach and arrest the persons whose names appeared in the Porteous roll, and place them in the king's castle within the shire, and if no castle in the hands of the sheriff. All the inhabitants within a town or village were bound to assist the crowner, and if the person accused was powerful, he was entitled to call upon the sheriff to be surety to enter the person at the justice aire, or to furnish sufficient force to assist in the apprehension of the disobedient person. For each man fined at the aire the crowner had for his fee a *colpandach*,* or thirty pennies. When a person was condemned the crowner got all his *dantoned* horses, that is horses intended for work and not the saddle, and never shod or used to shoes; all the corns lying in *bings and mowes;* all the insight utensils in the house; all the sheep within twenty, and all the

---

* Now called a *quey.*

swine within ten. Part of the duties of this
officer resembled those of the English coroner of
the present day. It was his duty to bury quietly
the body of a person found murdered, and to
inquire into the circumstances by which the party
had met with death.

The crowner for the county of Roxburgh, or the
district of the justice aire of Jedburgh, lived at
the village of Lanton, and certain lands there are
still called the crowner's lands. These lands, in
1627, were held by Lord Cranston.* In 1687
they seem to have been in the possession of
William Douglas of Cavers.† The present possessor of the subjects is named Scott, the father
of whom was commonly called the crowner.
He attended the circuit court of justiciary at
Jedburgh, acted as a guard at the door of the
court, and watched over the safekeeping of the
prisoners. It is thought that crowner, or coroner,
is derived from the duties of the office pertaining
to the crown.

We possess very little information in regard
to the Scots crowner, but there can be very
little doubt his duties and those of the English
coroner were originally similar. The *Rotuli Scotiæ*
contain several notices of the appointment of a
coroner for the county while it was in possession
of the English king.

---

* Retours, No. 131.   † Ib., No. 271.

When the bishops and abbots, through the liberality of the kings and princes, acquired large possessions, and numerous vassals and tenants, they obtained grants of regality from the sovereign, by which they were empowered to hold courts within their own possessions, and exempted from the authority of other jurisdictions. These regalities are said to have commenced during the reign of Alexander I. Each succeeding king confirmed the grants of his predecessors, and enlarged the ecclesiastical exemptions, till the religious houses, with all their exclusive privileges, were swept away by the Reformation.

David II. erected the town of Kelso with its pertinents, the barony of Bolden, and the lands of Redden with their pertinents, into a free regality with the exclusive jurisdictions of justiciaries, sheriffs, judges, and other privileges. Robert III. confirmed to these well-endowed monks all their exclusive powers and privileges. After the Reformation the Earl of Bothwell obtained a grant of the ample possessions of these monks, but which he lost on his forfeiture, in 1594. In 1605 Sir Robert Ker of Cessford succeeded to these great estates, which are now vested in the present Duke of Roxburgh. At the abolition of the heritable jurisdictions, his grace received for the office of heritable bailie of the Abbey of Kelso the sum of £1,300 sterling.

The extensive possessions of the monks of MEL-
ROSE were erected into a free regality by David II.,
with many exclusive privileges. The Reformation
vested these estates in the crown. Queen Mary
granted the lands and titles to James, Earl of Bothwell, and on his forfeiture, James VI. disponed the
abbacy and whole lands, with all the powers and
privileges thereto belonging, to James Douglas,
second son of William Douglas of Lochlevin, as
abbot or commendator. In 1606 the Douglas
resigned the monastery with all its pertinents into
the hands of the king, that he might erect the same
into a temporal lordship for the Earl of Morton. In
1609 the monastery and its property were erected
into a temporal lordship for Viscount Haddington
for services said to have been rendered the king at
the Gowrie conspiracy.

In 1625 the patronage of the church of Melrose
and other rights were bestowed on the Earl of
Buccleuch, in whose family they now remain. In
1747 the Lady Isobel Scott obtained for the heritable office of bailie of the Abbey of Melrose, in so
far as the same extended over the lands belonging
to her, the sum of £1,200 sterling.

The property of the church of Glasgow, situated
in this county, comprehending the baronies of
Ancrum, Lilliesleaf, and Ashkirk, was included in
the regality of Glasgow. The Monastery of Jedburgh, lying within the archdeanery of Teviotdale

and diocese of Glasgow, had no separate jurisdiction, but had a bailiary distinct from the regality of Jedburgh Forest.

The Kers of Fernieherst had long been bailies of the regality, and seem to have acted in the same capacity for the abbey of Jedburgh, notwithstanding many domestic feuds between them and the Douglases as to the exercise of the right of the former bailiewick. In 1587 Ker obtained from James VI. a grant of the bailiary of the lands and baronies of the abbey of Jedburgh. As no profit was derived from the office of bailie of the monastery, the Marquis of Lothian did not put in any claim for compensation.

The lands of Huntlaw and part of the lands of Moll and Hassendean were included in the regality of Paisley.

The great barons were not long in obtaining possession of the same privileges which had been too liberally bestowed on the various monasteries. Robert I. conferred upon his favourite companion in arms, the good Sir James Douglas, extensive possessions, which his services had assisted in gaining from the English. In 1320 the market-town, castle, forest, and mains of Jedburgh were gifted to him, and in 1325 a new grant was made by the king, which included all the lands and possessions previously bestowed upon him, with the addition of the forests of Selkirk, Ettrick, and

Traquair, in free regality, giving possession thereof by placing upon his finger an emerald ring. The regality of Jedburgh is thought to have comprehended the whole parishes of Jedburgh, Crailing, Southdean, Abbotrule, and parts of Oxnem and Ancrum. Being close upon the border, the regality was often in the hands of the English king, and was by him uniformly conferred upon Percy of Northumberland. On the Scottish power prevailing, the Douglas resumed possession. The rival claims of these two houses to the forest and its hunting-ground caused many a contest between the two gallant men for possession of the territory, one of which is described in the ancient ballad of " Chevy Chase." On James, the second Earl of Douglas, dying without issue in 1398, Isobel, his sister, appears to have granted a part of the forest to her second husband, Alexander Stewart, a natural son of the Earl of Buchan, but who died without issue. During the forfeiture of the Douglases, the Countess of Angus and her children were in possession of the lands and lordship. Archibald, Earl of Douglas, resigned the lordship of the forest into the hands of James IV., who granted the same to the earl's son and heir. In 1540 the lands and lordship of Jedburgh Forest were annexed to the crown by act of parliament. Queen Mary in 1547 granted the lordship of the forest to Archibald, Earl of Angus, and which grant was ultimately confirmed by act of parliament. In 1602 King James VI. granted a charter of the regality and lordship to Earl William Douglas. For this regality £900 was paid as compensation.

The regality of Sprouston comprehended an extensive tract of land. The lands belonged to the crown in the time of David I., and about 1193 William the Lion granted them to Sir Eustace de Vescy, who married Margaret, the daughter of that king. These lands seem to have been held by that family till the reign of King Robert I., when they were conferred on his son Robert Bruce as the barony of Sprouston.* David II. granted the barony of Sprouston and Hawick to Thomas Murray.† In 1451 the baronies of Sprouston, Hawick, Bedrule, and Smailholm were erected into a free regality for William, Earl Douglas.‡ In this regality were included the lands of Moll, of Altownburn, and of Blackdean, on the Bowmont water.§

Hawick as a barony appears among the many grants of Robert I., but the period of its erection into a regality is not known. The Lovels seem to have been the first barons of Hawick, which they forfeited by their adherence to the king of Eng-

---

* Robertson's Index, 12.   † Ib. 45.
‡ Reg. Mag. Sig., lib. iv., No. 148.
§ Douglas's Peerage, 591.

land. The barony of Hawick and lands of Branxholm were at one time gifted by the Bruce to Sir Henry Baliol. King David II. granted the same territory to Maurice Murray, Earl of Strathern. About the same period the barony, as we have seen, was in possession of Thomas Murray, who was also Baron of Sprouston. About the beginning of the fifteenth century the barony was in possession of Sir William Douglas. About 1511 the territory was in the crown, and was by James IV. granted to Sir William Douglas of Drumlanrig, for services rendered. The lands are described in the charter as "the lands and barony of Hawick; viz., in property, the town of Hawick, with the mill of the same, the lands of East Manys, West Manys, Crumhauch, and Kirkton Manys, Flekkis and Murinese, Ramsayclewis and Braidle; and in tenandry, the lands of Howpaslet, Chesholm, Quhithope, Dridane, Commonside, Vuirhardwood, Emitscheles, Teneside, Carlinpule, Netherharwood, Weyndislandis, Ester and Wester Hesliehop, Longhauch, Laris, Toftes, Kirkwod Hardwodhill, Qutchester, Fennych, Edgaristoun, Edgaristounscheles, and Quholmes."* All these lands were created and united into one free barony under the name of the barony of Hawick. The lands passed in the beginning of the eighteenth century into

---

* Reg. Mag. Sig., lib. xvii., No. 50.

the family of Buccleuch, in whose hands they now remain. At the abolition of heritable jurisdictions his grace of Buccleuch received £400 as compensation for the loss of his baronial rights.*

The lands of Liddesdale were at an early period erected into a regality. David I. granted the territory of Liddesdale to Ranulph de Sules, a Northampton baron, who had left his own land to follow the fortunes of that prince.† He witnessed several charters of David I., of Malcolm IV., and his brother William.‡ At his death his nephew Ranulph succeeded to the lands, and whose descendants possessed the territory till 1320, when William de Sules conspired against the king, for which he was attainted, and the lands of Liddesdale, with the barony of Nisbet, Longnewton, Maxton, and Caverton, were forfeited.§ This family furnished accomplished statesmen and gallant warriors, and such was their influence as lords of Liddesdale that their armorial bearings were adopted in after times as the feudal arms of their ancient territory.|| King Robert Bruce conferred the lands and lordship on his natural son Robert, who fell on the

---

* List of Compensations.   † Caledonia, vol. ii. p. 116.
‡ Chart. Newbattle.   .
§ Robertson's Index, 12. Lord Hailes' An., ii. 95-6. Border Minstrelsy.
|| Nisbet's Heraldry, Part i. pp. 19—158. Astle's Scots Seals, plate iii. No. 2. Rymer, ii. 577.

field of Duplin.* The territory then passed into the hands of the Douglases, by whom it was held till near the end of the fifteenth century, when the king compelled the Earl of Angus to exchange it for Bothwell.† In 1540 the lands and lordship were annexed to the crown by act of parliament.‡ Queen Mary restored the same to Francis Stewart, who was created Earl of Bothwell and Lord of Liddesdale.§ It was again forfeited by Bothwell. At the abolition of heritable jurisdictions the regality was possessed by his grace of Buccleuch, who then obtained for the loss of jurisdiction £600 sterling.

These jurisdictions circumscribed the power of the sheriff and impaired his usefulness. The mere erection of a territory into a regality conferred jurisdiction on the court to try all crimes and offences excepting the pleas of the crown, murder, robbery, ravishing of women, and fire-raising.|| But such jurisdiction was generally conferred on the court of regality, and in process of time treason came to be the only crime which the lord of

---

* Robertson's Index, 12, No. 54; p. 15, No. 2.

† Godscroft, 237.

‡ Acta Parl. Scot., vol. ii. pp. 361, 405.   § Ib. p. 551.

|| The barons of regality had the power of pit and gallows, i.e. the ordinary instruments of execution in capital crimes, the women in the early times being drowned in a pit, and the men hanged on a gallows. It is said the power was first granted by King Malcolm.

regality was not competent to try. The bailies of
regalities had the power of repledging from the
king's courts all persons charged with offences
competent to the court of regality to try. The
effect of this power was, that when any individual
living within the territory of the lord of regality
committed a crime, and for which he was placed
at the bar of the king's court to answer thereto,
the lord of regality was entitled to appear before
that tribunal and demand the person of the criminal, on caution that the party accused should be
tried for the crime before the court of regality on
a day fixed, and if the lord of regality failed to do
so, he *tined* his jurisdiction for a year and a day.*
If the criminal was not tried in the court of the
lord of regality within the period fixed, the justiciar or the sheriff could then proceed to try him,
and if the party was not made forthcoming the
bond of caution was forfeited. But these proceed-

---

* At the trial of the Turnbulls and Kers before the jus-
tice-depute at Edinburgh for slaughter in the burnwynd of
Jedburgh on the rude day, held on 14th September, 1601,
the Earl of Angus appeared and repledged Jaque Laidla in
Ancrum, as being within the regality of Jedburgh Forest.
He also claimed Ker of Fernieherst, on which a long and
curious discussion occurred as to whether that place was
within the regality of Jedburgh Forest. The regality court
was held at Douglas's house at Lyntalie, which seems to
have been the first residence of the Douglas in this part of
Scotland.—*Pitcairn's Criminal Trials*, vol. ii. p. 371.

ings were often a mere farce, as a powerful lord of regality was seldom without the means of appeasing the king's wrath, and possessed sufficient power to bid defiance to the injured party. The civil jurisdiction of a lord of regality was equal to that of a sheriff. The English courts of counties-palatine seem to be analogous to the regality courts of this country.

Next to the courts of regality were the courts of the Baron. The jurisdiction of these courts was not so extensive as the regality courts. They could not exercise the power of *pit* and *gallows,* unless in the case of a manslayer taken *red-hand,* or a thief with the *fang—i.e.,* in hand, having or bearing on his back the thing stolen. In such cases sentence was required to be pronounced within three suns after the crime, but it was lawful to respite a party so condemned for nine days thereafter. They also had the power of trying destroyers of plantings, stealers of bees, breakers of pigeon-houses, warrens, parks, orchards, and contraveners of the statutes for preserving game, if taken within the territory of the barony in the commission of the act, or red-hand. It is probable that the practice of the baron courts under these acts originated the popular rhyme—

" Oak, ash, and elm tree,
    The laird may hang for a' the three ;
    But for saugh and bitter weed
    The laird may flyte, but make naething be't."

The lords of regality and barony held their courts within the territory over which they possessed jurisdiction. Originally the court assembled in the open air, on the summit of an eminence, which from that circumstance was called the *mute* or *mote-hill*, the *plea-hill*. From this place the laws were published to the people. It was the duty of the sheriff to proclaim the laws which were enacted by the estates of the realm at the cross of the king's burghs, and to furnish copies of these laws to the courts of regality and barony, and see that the people were made aware of the enactments. Of these *mute*-hills, the one for the regality of Hawick affords a good illustration. It stands between the old town of Hawick and the Slitrig, near to the old church. When James IV., by his charter in favour of Douglas of Drumlanrig, created and united certain lands into one barony, to be called the barony of Hawick, he ordained that sasines taken by Sir William and his heirs " at the *moit* of Hawick should stand for the lands of the barony held of the king and his heirs in blench ferme, without any other special sasine being afterwards taken at any other part of the said barony."* Occasionally the courts were held at bridges. When the Abbot of Kelso visited Selkirk Forest, he held his courts at the bridge of Ettrick.†

---

* Reg. Mag. Sig., lib. xvii., No. 50.   † Chart of Kelso.

Each district had its mute-hill, which was generally placed to the westward of the mansion, and
called the chair or seat of justice. These mute-hills
were often retained by the lords of regality, though
the lands were conveyed. We are inclined to think
that the *mounts* to be seen in various parts of this
county, and called by several writers "exploratory
mounts," are simply the *mute-hills* of a previous
age, when justice was administered to the people
in the open air. Notwithstanding what is said by
historians as to Sir Alexander Ramsay having been
pulled from the judgment-seat at the church of
Hawick by Douglas, in 1343, it is thought that
the sheriff was not holding his court within the
church when seized by Douglas, but that the seat
of justice referred to was the top of the *mute-hill*
adjoining the church. This view is strengthened
by the fact that the laity were, by the canons of
the Church of Scotland, prohibited from holding
their courts in the churches—*quoad laici non
teneant placita in ecclesia.**

In addition to the regality and barony courts,
was the court of the Heritor. The right to hold
such courts might be granted by barons, or other
immediate vassals of the crown, to any heritor of
land within the baron's territory. These were
formerly called *soytors,* and it seems that the

---

* Lord Hailes' Canons, 1296, p. 46.

sheriff was enjoined to see that they were possessed of sufficient qualification to act as judges. The office of constable also interfered with the exercise of the power of the sheriff. In the time of David I., Hugh Morville, who possessed considerable property between the rivers Gala and Leader, was the Great Constable of Scotland, and in whose family the office became hereditary. In early times the constable attended upon the king, and possessed a jurisdiction extending to six leagues around the person of his majesty, and which was anciently called the " chalmer of peace." In this district the constable, Richard Morville, is seen acting, in 1184, along with twelve *fideles homines*, in the settlement of a keenly contested controversy which existed between the monks of Melrose and the men of Wedale regarding the right to the pannage and pasturage of the King's Forest, lying between the Gala and Leader. At this time, it appears, King William, his brother David, and a number of prelates and nobles were present. The settlement of this dispute was called the " peace of Wedale." In the Chronicle of Melrose this event is recorded in the following terms :—" Controversia que fuit inter ecclesiam de Melros et homines de Wedale super pasturam foreste regis, Deo opitulante, coram Rege Willelmo et Davide comite fratre suo, et coram episcopis, comitibus, baronibus, et multis

aliis probis hominibus in die sancti Luce evange-
liste (Oct. 18), super Crosseleiye per Ricardum de
Moreuile constabularium regis, et per alios xij
fideles homines qui eo die presente rege super
reliquias ecclesie nostre cum timore et tremore
juraverunt,* et veraciter affirmaverunt quod foresta
regis téndit usque ad viam que vadit ad occiden-
tem partem ecclesie beate Marie de Wedhale, et
est pastura ecclesie de Melros usque ad terminos
de Wedhale et usque ad rivulum qui vocatur Fas-
seburne, ex donatione trium regum scilicet Dauidis,
Malcolmi, Willelmi, et per iiij. sive v. Romanorum
pontificum privilegia firmiter confirmata et irre-
fragabiliter solidata."† But this peace does not

---

* Do we see in this the origin of swearing on the gospels?

† Chronicle of Melrose, p. 93. " A controversy which
existed between the church of Melrose and the people of
Wedale anent the pasture of the King's Forest, with God's
assistance, and in the presence of King William and Earl
David, his brother, and in presence of the bishops, earls,
barons, and many other approved men, on the day of St.
Luke the Evangelist (Oct. 18), at Crosseleye, by Richard
de Morville, the king's constable, and twelve other faithful
men who on that day, in the presence of the king, and with
fear and trembling, swore upon the relics of our church, and
declared that the King's Forest extends as far as the road
which leads to the western part of the church of the blessed
Mary of Wedhale, and the pasture as far as the boundaries
of Wedhale and as far as the rivulet called Fasseburn, belongs
to the church of Melrose, in virtue of a gift made by three
kings (consecutively)—viz., David, Malcolm, and William
—and by four or five special statutes (*privilegia*) of the
Roman pontiffs confirmed and ratified."

seem to have been of long continuance, for in a few years thereafter we find the abbot and several of his brethren excommunicated by the Provincial Council of Perth for having violated the peace of Wedale, by attacking the houses of the Bishop of St. Andrews, killing one ecclesiastic and wounding many others.*

Each of the king's castles had also a constable, who exercised jurisdiction within the castle and the bounds thereof. The castles of Jedburgh and Roxburgh had constables appointed by the kings of Scotland and England according as the balance of power on the borders inclined in favour of either king. Occasionally the constable appears acting as sheriff of the county of Roxburgh. The first constable noticed acting at Roxburgh is Ralph de Campania.† Robert de Cockburne appears as constable about 1242.‡ Sir Alexander of Striuelin was constable between 1243 and the death of Alexander II.§ About 1250 Sir William de Hauden was constable.|| Alexander of Maxton was constable in 1285.¶ Brian Fitzallen was constable of Roxburgh Castle under Edward I., in 1291. The writ is dated at Berwick on August 4.**

---

* Fordun l. x. c. 25.   Chron. Melros.
† Lib. de Melros, pp. 227, 250.   ‡ Lib. de Melros, p. 260.
§ Lib. de Calchow, pp. 194, 401. || Lib. de Melros, p. 306.
¶ Lib. de Calchow, p. 180.
** Rotuli Scotiæ, vol. i. pp. 1, 2, 3, 4.

Three years after the constable was ordered to deliver up the castle to John de Baliol, or his deputes.*

Shortly after Baliol delivered up the castle of Roxburgh to the English king in security during the continuance of the war with France.† In 1336 William de Felton was constable.‡ In 1347 John of Coupland filled the office of constable, and continued to do so for eight years, when he delivered it to Henry de Percy at the command of the English king.§ When Edward was about to proceed to France, in 1359, he appointed Richard Tempest constable as well as sheriff of the county of Roxburgh, at a salary of £300 sterling.|| Allan de Strother was constable about 1367. After this period a number of persons are noticed as having the custody of the castle, but it does not very clearly appear in what capacity.

The notices of the constables of the castle of Jedburgh are few. The castle appears as the residence of our early kings, and where they often held their courts. It was in the hands of the English king after 1174. In 1288 the castle seems to have been put under the charge of John Comyn, the steward of Jedburgh. In 1291 Edward commanded the steward to deliver it up to Laurenz de Seymnor, and shortly after Brian Fitzallen got

---

* Rotuli Scotiæ, vol. i. p. 12.   † Ib. pp. 21, 22.
‡ Ib. p. 400   § Ib. p. 732. || Ib. pp. 842, 843.

possession of it.* John Baliol handed it over to the Bishop of Carlisle and the Abbot of Newabbey, commissioners of the English king.† In 1296 Thomas of Burnham, and Hugh of Eyland, were entrusted with its keeping by the wily Edward.‡ In 1305 the castle as well as county was placed under the government of the lieutenant of the English king. It was recovered in 1318, and two years after was gifted to the good Sir James Douglas by the grateful Bruce.§ It was ceded by Edward Baliol to the English king, who appointed William Presfen to take possession thereof in his name.|| In 1336 he appears acting as constable thereof.¶ Sir William Douglas, at the head of the men of Teviotdale, took the castle about 1342, but it was again in the hands of the English, and the officers thereof appointed by the king of England. After it was ceded by Edward Baliol, Percy of Northumberland was made constable by Edward III.** For a short time about the beginning of the fifteenth century Sir Robert Umfraville had charge of the fortress, after which it returned to Percy. When the family of Percy did not furnish a constable, the lords of Jedburgh

---

* Rotuli Scotiæ, vol. i. pp. 1, 3.
† Ib.   ‡ Ib. pp. 23, 36.
§ Robertson's Index, p. 10, No. 17 ; p. 21, No. 27.
|| Rotuli Scotiæ, vol. i. p. 271.
¶ Ib. p. 401.   ** Ib. p. 793.

Forest did. The castle was demolished in May, 1409.

The constable had also jurisdiction in trespasses committed by any inhabitant of the castle upon a burgess of the king's burgh.* If a person of the castle was injured by a burgess, the men of the castle behoved to seek justice from the burgh court. Disputes were of common occurrence between the men of the castle and the burgesses, owing to the peculiar privileges of the king's servants who occupied the castle. Three times in the year, "at Zule, Pasch, and Whitsunday," the "castellans" were entitled to go to the house of every burgess and demand his " swyne, gryses, geise, or hennes," for the king's use, for payment in silver, and if the burgess was possessed of such stock and would not sell, the castellans could not enter the house to search for them, but if they found them upon the " calsay" it was lawful to take and slay the animals, and the price was fixed by the neighbours of the rebellious burgess. The burgesses were also bound to lend their goods to the servants of the castle to the extent of forty pennies and for forty days, and if the goods were not restored within that time or debt paid the burgess was exempted from lending for the future.

---

* Laws of David I. cap. xlix.

The royal burghs exercised an important jurisdiction in matters civil and criminal. The courts
of the king's burghs were competent to try all
pleas between man and man native and free. In
matters of trade the burghs were supreme. They
granted licences for trading; the rates of wages
were fixed by them and enforced throughout the
county by the sheriff. The provost and bailies
were bound to choose twelve of "the maist sufficient discreet men of the burgh" and swear them to
keep the laws and cause them to be observed
within the burgh. The penalty for disobedience
was severe: "his house sall be cassin down to the
earth, and he sall be banished out of the burgh."
The punishment of a thief was speedy, and of a
kind to make others fear and tremble. If a man
was taken within burgh "with ane breade, the
price of ane half-pennie," he was scourged through
the town. For the theft of a pair of shoes of the
price of four pennies, the thief was put on the
pillory, and thereafter at the head of the town
banished forth of the burgh; from four to eight
pennies, the pillory, and then conveyed to the head
and chief place of the town, "and the taker sall
cause cut anc of his lugges;" for any sum between
eight and sixteen pennies, the pillory, and conveyed to the end of the town, "and his taker sall
cause his other lug to be cutted." And thereafter

if the same person was again taken with eight
pennies, "his taker sall cause him to be hanged."
A thief taken with thirty pennies and a half-penny,
"his taker sall cause him to be hanged." The
bailies had the power of repledging the men of the
burgh from other courts, in the same manner as
lords of regality.

, The "*chalmerlain*" of Scotland held his aire
once every year in the burgh of Jedburgh and
Roxburgh, and inquired into the conduct of the
magistrates and council and traders within the
burgh. Before this court all burgesses were
bound to appear, whether dwelling within the
burgh or not. All complaints were tried by the
chalmerlain with the aid of a jury, "na way suspect,
of the best and maist worthie of the burgh." Judgments pronounced in this court were reviewed by
a court composed of three or four burgesses from
each of the burghs of Edinburgh, Stirling, Roxburgh, and Berwick, and when the two latter
burghs were in the hands of the English, Lanark
and Linlithgow were substituted. The seat of this
court seems to have been at Haddington, and the
chalmerlain president thereof. The "doom" or
judgment pronounced by this court had the
same effect as "gif it were finalie ended and done
in parliament."

Such were the various jurisdictions which afforded justice to the inhabitants of the county

of Roxburgh during early times. If the people did not obtain justice it must have been the fault of the judge, for the laws were admirably calculated to secure it equally—"To all pure men, and rich men and principalie to all religious and kirk men, and also to husbandmen."

CHAPTER II.

OF THE BURGH AND CASTLE OF ROXBURGH.

DURING the British period the houses were formed of wood, and easily destroyed. While the Romans possessed the land they made roads, erected towns, and built houses, but, owing to this district being exposed to the ravages of the Caledonians, scarcely a vestige of that mighty people exists within its bounds. But when the Saxons, Normans, and Flemings arrived and obtained grants of land, a castle or fort first appeared, and then a village and mill beneath its walls. Jedburgh, Edinburgh, and Roxburgh are supposed to have been the first towns. In the early days the kings were anxious to have towns built, and peopled with the new colonists, as a check to the native people; indeed, they built towns, and invited the colonists to enter and occupy. The houses of these towns were mostly formed of wood, as appears from notices in the various chartularies of the religious houses, and Acts of Parliament. The chartulary of Paisley contains several of these notices of the early houses. At an inquisition in 1233 a witness is found swearing that, sixty years before, a person called Bede inhabited near the church the great house built of twigs. In the course of time houses came to be conveyed as stone houses, showing that even at a comparatively recent period the generality of houses were of wood. Originally the towns all belonged to the kings, and to induce traders to settle therein certain rights and privileges were conferred on the inhabitants. These towns were called king's burghs, or royal burghs. In after years, when the abbots built towns near the abbeys for their vassals and retainers, these were called the towns of the abbot, to distinguish them from the burghs of the king. Erelong the barons built towns for their vassals and tenants, in imitation of the kings and abbots, which were called the towns of the baron, and subsequently burghs of barony or regality. But before either the abbots or barons could build towns they required the consent of the king. Burghs of regality and barony had no right of trade till 1693, when they obtained leave to exercise trade on condition of paying a proportion of the public taxes. The trade of the country was at first wholly in the hands of the king's burghs, subject to the control of the king's chamberlain. Although there are good grounds for believing that Jedburgh is the oldest town of the district, or even of this part of the kingdom, the town and castle of Roxburgh are, in a work of this kind, entitled to the first place on account of having conferred a name upon the shire, and continued for many years the capital thereof.   Of the town not a stone remains to mark its site, and were it not for the evidence derived from history, charters, and other documents, it might well be doubted whether on the fields in which cattle now graze, or which are carefully tilled by the husbandman, a powerful city once flourished. A small portion of the ruins of the castle remains to mark the place where in former days kings held their court, and where the nobles of either king-dom performed deeds of valour in the battle-field, or called forth the admiration of the spectator in the tournament.

The situation of the castle is about a mile and a quarter from the town of Kelso, and upon the neck of a peninsula formed by the rivers Tweed and Teviot.   Doubts are entertained by many as to the exact site of the town.   It is imagined by some that the town originally stood to the west of the castle on the banks of the Teviot, and that the straggling houses that remain in the neighbour-hood of the present church formed a part of the once celebrated burgh.   Others again think that the town existed near to the castle, and that the pre-sent village at the church is of more modern date. The first time that an old and new town appears on record is in the charters of David after he became king. When that good prince acquired at the death of his brother all the land to the south of the Forth as his appanage, the castles of Jedburgh and Roxburgh were used by him as royal residences. A new burgh town then for the first time makes its appearance, and it is likely that David was its founder. As early as 1115 the church of Old Roxburgh appears as the original parish church, and is so called to distinguish it from the more recently erected churches in the town and castle.* About 1190 Helias appears as the parson of Old Rokesburc.† Morton, in his monastic annals, states that the church of Old Roxburgh is the same with the church of the Holy Sepulchre situated within the town.‡ But I do not see how that could be, and am disposed to place the church of Old Roxburgh to the west of the castle; indeed, there are more grounds for believing that the present parish church occupies its site than to identify it with the Holy Sepulchre. From 1128 down to a comparatively recent period an old and new town seem to have existed, and at the present day the name of Old Roxburgh is still retained. In the charter removing the monks placed at Selkirk to the milder banks of the Tweed, King David speaks of a toft lying " *in novo burgo.*" It is probable that the

---

* Register of Glasgow, p. 14. † Lib. de Kelso, p. 136.
‡ Annals, p. 111.

town lay both on the east and west of the castle, and it would appear, from the hospital or *maison-dieu* of Roxburgh lying on the east bank of the Teviot, further up the river than the fortress, that a portion of the burgh also stood in that lovely locality. Casting the eye over the ground at this place, it is hardly possible to resist the conclusion that considerable buildings at one time stood on that side of the river Teviot. Neither is there, I repeat, anything to exclude the presumption that the present parish church stands on the foundation of the church of which Helias was pastor. The present church of Roxburgh was built about the middle of the last century, but on the foundations of a church which had been almost wholly beneath the ground. An examination of the fields around the church leads to the conclusion that extensive buildings at one time existed there. The present incumbent, while making a drain from his manse, came upon a pavement at a considerable depth, and which he thought might form a part of a road from the west, but I am rather inclined to think it to have been one of the streets of the town. Another reason why I think that the old parochial church of Roxburgh is not likely to have stood near the castle is, that the Tweed was the march between the property of the two religious houses of Glasgow and St. Andrews, and it is not likely that the principal church would have been placed at the limit of the parish. The situation of the present church would be more convenient for the parochial district. But, be this as it may, there can be little doubt that the town of Roxburgh, which fills such a space in history, and felt so much of the miseries of border warfare, was close to the castle. So late as 1516 proclamations were made at its cross.*

The locality of the town and castle is at the present day very beautiful. In whatever direction the eye is turned, a rich prospect presents itself. Standing on the ruins of the castle and looking westward, the eye surveys the windings of the Teviot as it descends from the lovely vale which bears its name. In the distance are the Cheviot mountains, forming the border line. On the southeast the eye wanders over the dark woods which clothe the right banks of the Teviot and Tweed, catching a glimpse here and there of several mansions, each set as it were in a frame of foliage. From this place Kelso is seen to great advantage, and I cannot help thinking that the best view of this lovely town is obtained from the east end of the ruins of the castle. On the north the scenery is equally fine.

The domain of Floors Castle, the modern palace of the dukes of Roxburgh, stretches from Kelso

---

* Lord High Treasurer's Deed, April 23, 1516.

along the margin of the Tweed for nearly two miles, the ground gradually rising from the river to the front of the palace. From an opening in the woods caused by the buildings of the palace, a fine view is obtained of Hume Castle, Millerstain, and Stitchel. The north bank of the Tweed is richly wooded. Looking westward the triple-headed Eildon comes within the range of vision. Taken as a whole, the picture is magnificent. I know of no place in the district which can be compared with the scenery around Roxburgh Castle. The vale of Jed contains a succession of beautiful pictures, but, lovely though they be, not one is entitled singly to compete with the scenery at the meeting of the rivers Tweed and Teviot. There is, however, this remark to be made in favour of the scenery in the neighbourhood of Jedburgh, that at each bend of the river a new scene is presented to the view, while at Kelso the eye takes in the whole picture at a glance.

The castle has been built upon the termination of a ridge between the rivers Tweed and Teviot. Its height is about fifty feet. The site of the castle measures nearly four hundred yards long, and about one hundred yards broad, excepting at the east end, where it is considerably narrower. On the north and east it seems to have been surrounded by a deep ditch. On the south side the waters of the Teviot lave

RUINS OF ROXBURGH CASTLE.

the base of the ridge. Along the south top are
remains of the wall, some portions about fifteen
feet high and nearly twelve feet thick. On the
west a part of its gateway still exists. The walls
must have been of great strength; some appear to
have been built of square blocks of stone on the
outside, and filled up with · smaller stones and
mortar in the middle. The springings of several of
the arches are still to be seen. At each corner
there have been immense towers with walls of
great thickness. On the north summit of the
ridge there are also the remains of buildings. On
the west part of the castlestead two large mounds
run across from north to south, and enclosing a
space of · about ninety yards square, which is
thought to be the work of Somerset when he tried
to fortify the place on his return from the battle of
Musselburgh. The space within the walls is covered
with oak, ash, plane, and other trees, many of which
measure ten feet in circumference. At the west end
there are thorn trees of nearly a foot in diameter.
At the west end of the castle the ridge appears to
have been divided by a cut extending entirely across
and separating the castlestead from the high
grounds further to the west. On the opposite side
of this ditch are parallel mounds running north
and south. Pennant says that when he visited the
place in 1769 the remains of a weir or dam dyke
were visible across the Teviot, and by which it was

said the ditch of the castle was filled with water.* Hutchison, who examined the locality seven years later, states—"This mount is defended at the foot on the north and west sides by a deep moat and outward rampier of earth; a fine plain intervening between these outworks and the Tweed. The dimensions within the walls, where the interior fortress stood, we could not obtain for the trees and thickets. The western part is guarded by an outwork and mound of earth which is severed from the chief part of the castle by a moat, but included in the outward works, the fosse and rampier before described. The fosse or moat was supplied with water by a dam which crossed the river Teviot in an oblique direction, the remains of which still appear. The south and east sides are defended by an inaccessible precipice, at whose foot the river runs with a rapid current."† No part of the weir or dyke across the Teviot seen by Pennant and Hutchison now exists.

There are no means of ascertaining at this day, with any degree of certainty, the extent of the town of Roxburgh, or the number of its inhabitants, but it may with safety be inferred to have been large and populous.

From a passage in the Chronicle of Melrose, it

---

* Pennant's Tour, vol. iii. p. 273.
† Hutchison, vol. i. pp. 271-2.

appears that when Roxburgh was reduced to ashes
in 1216, it was surrounded with villages and
suburbs.*　At that period the appearance of the
town must have been imposing.　On the opposite
side of the river Tweed stood the monkish village
of Kelso, connected with Roxburgh by a bridge—
the scene of many a conflict—and would look as if
forming a part of the royal burgh.　Close to the
town, on the east side of the Teviot, lay the village
of Maxwellheugh with its church and mill, and
would also bear the appearance of a suburb of Roxburgh.　A little further to the east the village of
Sprouston lies within sight of the castle towers, and
on the west the Highton, while lower down both
banks of the Teviot would be studded with buildings.　In the middle of this scene, and encircled by
the waters of Tweed and Teviot, rose the " Towering Fortress"—the curb and guardian of the border
land—and around it the town, with its many
churches, schools, hospitals, and mills.　At a very
early period the town seems to have been fortified
by a wall and ditch.　Earl Henry granted to the
abbey of Dryburgh a toft "extra murum de
Rokesburg," which was confirmed by David I.
and Malcolm IV.†　In a charter of Herbert, the
Bishop of Glasgow, granted during the reign of
David I., certain lands are described as lying

---

* Chron. Melrose, p. 122.　† Lib. Dryburgh.

" extra fossatum burgi de Rokesburg inter Tuedam et Tevieth versus abbatam " of Kelso.*

The town was governed by a provost, bailies, and
a council of burgesses; occasionally the names of
the members of the corporation are to be seen in
the chartularies and other writs. In 1235 Master
Adam of Baggot, Peter of the Halch, and Gervase
Maunsel, three of the burgesses of the town, were
witnesses to a charter by William, Bishop of Glasgow.† Two years after, the same Baggot is seen
acting as sheriff of the county, and Sir Peter of
the Haugh as the provost.‡ In 1291 the burgesses
of the town swore fealty to Edward I.§ Next year
the burgesses, at the command of the same king,
paid the wages of Robert Heron, parson of Ford,
who officiated for some time as chamberlain of
Scotland. In 1293 Heron's wages, £13 10s., were
paid to him out of the dues collected in the town,
and also £6 11s. 8d. to Brian Fitzallan.‖ In
1296 the whole of the burgesses took the oath of
allegiance to the English king.¶ The names of the
town-council entered in the roll are—Walter, the
goldsmith of Roxburgh, burgess and alderman;
Richard de Furblur, or Furbur, Richard Vigrus,
Michael le Sealeer, William of Bosewile, Adam
of Mindrom, Adam Knowt, Geffrey of Berewick,

---

* Lib. of Kelso.   † Ib. p. 321.   ‡ Ib. p. 285.
§ Rotuli Scotiæ, vol. i. p. 2.   ‖ Ib. p. 16.
¶ Ragman's Rolls, p. 122.

Adam of Eurewyk, Adam Corbend, Austin Le Mercer, and John Knowt of Rokesburgh.* In 1309 a brief was directed by the English king to Sir John de Segrave, warden of Scotland; William de Bevercot, chancellor; John de Weston, chamberlain; and Robert de Malo Lacu, constable of the castle of Rokesburgh, to examine into a complaint of several burgesses of the town that they were kept out of certain lands and tenements in the burgh, contrary to the ordinance of peace by the king's father to those Scotsmen who had taken the oath of allegiance to him; but the execution of the writ was delayed on information that the complaining burgesses were not well disposed to England, and that there might be danger to the castle were the lands and tenements restored.† About the same time the burgesses got leave to raise a yearly murage from articles brought into the town for sale, for the purpose of enclosing the town.‡ In 1329 Hutred the baker was provost or alderman; Alan of Mindrum, and John of Linton, bailies; Robert of Keth, Andrew Homyl, John of Sprouston, and John the clerk, burgesses.§ Next year Hutred was still provost, and Alan of Mindrum one of the bailies; Robert of Keth was the other bailie; Richard of Kellor, John Sawsilver, Andrew

---

* Ragman's Rolls, p. 122.   † Rotuli Scotiæ, vol. i. p. 64.
    ‡ Ib.   § Lib. de Kelso, pp. 369, 372.

Homyl, and John of Sprouston, burgesses.   About eight years afterwards Alan of Mindrum was provost; Bridinus (called Candelaue) and Thomas Vigurus, bailies; William Macone, William of Boseville, Roger the son of the deceased Hutred the baker, Waldeue Darling, Thomas of Rydell, Henry the hangman, Thomas Small, Adam the son of Hugh, and John the clerk, burgesses.* Near to the same year William Boseville was provost, Andrew Homyl bailie, and Alan of Mindrum a burgess.† In 1345 Thomas Vigrous was alderman; Hugh of the bishoprick and Robert Couke, bailies; William of Boseville and Alan of Mindrum, burgesses. In 1368 Edward III. ordered his chamberlain of Berwick and his sheriff of Roxburgh and Berwick to protect the community in the exercise of all their rights and privileges which had been violated.‡

In 1369 an Act of Parliament was passed by which it was enacted, that so long as Roxburgh and Berwick remained in the hands of the English king Lanark and Linlithgow should be substituted for them in the court of four burghs, and that when these two burghs should be recovered by the King of Scotland, they should be immediately restored to their ancient privileges.§

---

* Lib. of Dryburgh, pp. 262, 263.
† Rotuli Scotiæ, vol. i. p. 547. .   ‡ Ib. vol. i. p. 922.
§ Acta Parl. Scot. vol. i. p. 149,

The burgesses of 1370 received from the English king forty marks for the repair of the bridge over the Tweed near the town of Roxburgh.* In 1379 the community of the town was taken under the protection of Richard II.† In 1401 Gerard Heron and William Asplion were collectors of customs on wool, leather, and hides, under Henry IV.‡ About the same time John of Wark was comptroller of customs, and Hugh Burgh, collector of customs on wool, leather, and hides, and of taxes on wine.§ In 1363 David II. granted to Henry of Ashkirk the custody of all the measures of the burgh.||

The corporation had a common seal; it was appended to the submission of the town to Edward I. in 1296. On the seal were impressed the arms of Scotland with a bird on either side. The legend was " *Sigillum communi burgensii de Rokesburg.*"* The seal was appended to several charters granting property or other privileges to the chantry in the church of St. James; the founder Roger of Auldton having granted the final *jus devolutum* of the patronage thereof to the community of Roxburgh. There was also another seal kept at Roxburgh, " *quod dicitur cochet.*" In 1319

---

* Rotuli Scotiæ, vol. i. p. 937. † Ib. vol. ii. p. 16.
‡ Ib. vol. ii. p. 156. § Ib. pp. 157-9.
|| Reg. Mag. Sig., p. 30. ¶ Astle's Seals, plate ii. p. 13.

Edward issued a precept commanding this seal to be sent from Rokesburgh to the chancery of England.*   During the reigns of David I., William the Lion, King Alexander II., Alexander III., King Robert II., and James II., Roxburgh was a place of coinage.   These coins generally bore on the reverse side the name of the coiner and the place, *i.e.*, " *Raul de Rocesbu*," " *Raul on Rocab*," and " *Raul on Rocebu*."   The coinage by James II. while besieging the town bore on the reverse and on the interior circle the inscription " Villa Roxburgh."†

The notices of the streets of the town are few, and only to be met with in the grants or transferences of property recorded in the chartularies of the various abbeys.   One of the streets was called King Street, and must have run east and west, as certain subjects in it are described as lying on the north and south sides of it, and adjoining tenements to the east and west of those conveyed.   In 1246 Geoffrey of Melrose purchased

---

* Originally the *cochet* was a parchment *sealed* and delivered to the merchant by the officers of customs as a warrant that his merchandise had paid customs and been regularly entered.   It was afterwards enacted by James VI., parl. 15, cap. cclv., that the parchment should contain the quantity and quality of the goods, and the names of the, owners.

† Cardonel Numism. Scotiæ, plate i. Nos. 6, 7, 8.   Lindsay's Coinage of Scotland.

from John the son of Aylbrith of Rokisbure several burgages in the town, in the street called King Street, for the relief of the poor arriving at the gate of the Monastery of Melrose. These burgages had been "fermed," or rented, by John the son of Richmund, and John the son of Peter.* Hutred the baker, who was for a time provost of the burgh, possessed property in this street, and probably lived there. From the chartulary of Dryburgh it appears that a trial by jury took place in 1329 between the canons of Dryburgh and Hutred in regard to the yearly rent of a burgage lying on the north side of that street opposite to the church of the Holy Sepulchre, bounded on the east by a tenement called Blackhall, and on the west by the tenement of Peter of Old Roxburgh. The verdict of the jury was against Hutred.† Thomas Vigurus had also a tenement in this street which he sold to Sir William Feltoun, the sheriff of the county, for a sum of money which the sheriff had advanced to him in a time of need.‡ Roger the son of Hutred the baker seems to have lived on the one side of Vigurus, and Hugh, the chapman, on the other. A person of the name of John Flecher occupied the next house on the east to Roger the baker. Emma Kennilis' wife possessed the tenement on

---

* Lib. of Melrose, p. 215.   † Lib. of Dryburgh, p. 256.
‡ Ib. pp. 260-1.

the west side. · Hugh of Auldhaugh was proprietor of the Blackhall tenement on the north side of this street. After his death Alice his daughter and heiress, "in her virginity and full and lawful power," quit-claimed in 1329 to Roger of Auldtoun, and Margaret his wife, all right which she had in that tenement.*

In the same year Roger founded a chantry of one priest in the church of St. James, and conveyed *inter alia* his three burgages in King Street, one of which lay on the south side of the street, for the maintenance of the chantry and officiating priest. Henry of Heton had also land in this street. Robert Sellar possessed land adjoining to one of the tenements which formerly belonged to Roger of Auldtoun. The chapel of St. John also had property in the same street.† The church of the Holy Sepulchre, which originally belonged to the Knights of the Hospital of St. John of Jerusalem, was situated on the south side of this street.

Another street was called Market Street. This street must have either been a square or run north and south, as the tenements which bound the one conveyed are said to be on the north and south sides thereof. William the *skinner* had

---

* Lib. of Kelso, p. 372.
† Ib. pp. 368-9 ; Register of Glasgow, p. 244.

property in this street, and which was granted by Margaret the wife of Roger of Auldtoun to the chantry which he had founded. William Boseville adjoined on the north side. A tenement belonging to the Abbot of Melrose lay on the south side of that which belonged to the wife of the pious Roger. There must have been booths in this street, for another tenement belonging to Margaret is described as lying behind the booths, next to the tenement of Richard of Killor on the south, and that of John Knoice on the north. The warrandice of this grant is peculiar, the grantor binding herself and her heirs, in case they should contravene the grant by litigation, to pay on every day of the litigation so caused one hundred shillings sterling to the fabric of the church of Glasgow, one hundred to that of Kelso, one hundred to the fabric of the church of St. James of Roxburgh, and one hundred towards the expenses of the priest of the chantry and those aiding and advising him and defending the said cause before they should be heard before any judge spiritual or secular in any case touching her charter.*

There was also a street called the Senedgate or Sneydgate. The locality of this gate is not known. Edolph the miller held property in it. Half of the property of the miller in this street was

---

* Lib. of Kelso, pp. 379, 380.

granted in 1290 by Robert Boneirc, burgess of
Roxburgh, to the canons of Dryburgh for payment of fivepence yearly to the nuns of Rides-
dale.* The nuns had a house in the territory of
Heton. The Westgate also appears, but without
any further notices. It is likely that it lay to the
west of the castle.

Within the bounds of the town were several
churches; two of these churches were within the
walls. The church of the Holy Sepulchre stood
on the south side of King Street, and is noticed
as early as the days of Malcolm IV.† The castle
had a church dedicated to St. John the Evangelist, which existed previous to 1127. It was
served by two perpetual chaplains.‡ Malcolm IV.
granted this church, with a ploughgate of land,
the parochia, and tithes, and offerings, and all
other rights and dignities, as held by Adam the
chaplain in the time of Bishop John, David the
King, and Earl Henry.§ Between 1164 and 1216
the grant was confirmed to the bishops Ingleram,
Joceline, and Walter, by Popes Alexander III.,
Lucius III., Urban III., and Honorius III. William the Lion confirmed Malcolm's grant. The
chaplains of the castle were called the king's

---

* Lib. of Dryburgh, pp. 254-5.
† Charter of Malcolm IV. in Spottiswood's Religious
Houses.
‡ Reg. Glasgow, pp. 9, 10, 146.   § Ib. p. 14.

clerks. In 1347 and 1349 Edward III. granted the chapel to Richard of Hoghton and Edward of Kellesye. The church of St. James stood beyond the castle walls. It was dedicated to the saint in April, 1134—the day on which St. Paul's Church, London, was burned.* Many important public transactions took place in this church, which will be found afterwards fully noticed. It was along with the other churches of the burgh granted by David to the monks of Kelso. In 1388 Richard II. granted to his beloved chaplain Bertin Harre the fruits of the vicarage, because, as he said, the diocesan of St. James was a schismatic and a rebel, and obstinately adhering to his adversary of Scotland, " and to that child of perdition the antipope Clement."† Before 1426 the church had become unfit for use, and remained in the same state for about ten years. Roger of Auldtoun, as it has been seen, founded a chantry in this church, and at his earnest entreaty was granted a burying-place in the choir thereof for himself and wife Margaret.‡

The churches of the burgh were with all their pertinents granted by David I. to the monks of Kelso. In the arrangement made between the

---

* Chron. Mailros, p. 69 : " Et combusta est ecclesia Sancti Pauli Londini."

† Rotuli Scotiæ, vol. ii. p. 93.

‡ Reg. of Glasgow, pp. 245-6.

bishops of St. Andrews and Glasgow and the monks of Kelso, before Cardinal John Stephanus, the pope's legate at Perth, regarding the churches belonging to them in these dioceses, the churches of Rokesburg were excepted as being "free of all synodals, aids, entertainments, and corrodies," but it was provided that there should be perpetual vicars, who, before induction, should be presented to the bishop.* This arrangement was confirmed by Pope Innocent IV.

The Grey Friars had previous to 1235 a convent in the town of Roxburgh, lying beyond the walls. The Chronicle of Melrose says that the friars first came into this country in 1231.† Their church was dedicated to St. Peter. A burying-ground for the brethren of the order was dedicated in May, 1235, by William, Bishop of Glasgow.‡ The right of the brethren to have a burying-ground at that place seems to have been disputed by the monks of Kelso, and it was only granted by the bishop after hearing the Abbot of Kelso and the warden of the order. The order claimed the privilege of having a burying-ground wherever they had a fixed residence, and the abbot held their claim to be well-founded. In 1295 Adam

---

* Lib. of Kelso, pp. 355-6.

† Chron. Mail. p. 142—"Hic primo ingrediuntur fratres minores Scotiam."

‡ Lib. of Kelso, p. 321.

Blunt was warden of the order; it was his companion who presented to the King of England John Baliol's letter renouncing his allegiance to that monarch. About 1297 the friars appear to have been pensioners of the town, and had right to a part of the fishings in the Tweed. The order appear to have had possession of the old *ferries* of the burgh.* In 1564 Henry Cant was warden of the order at Roxburgh, and who, with consent of the brethren and other wardens of the order in Scotland, conveyed all the possessions, rights, and privileges in the place to Sir Walter Ker of Cessford for money advanced to him in time of great trouble, and for payment yearly of twenty-four marks, two shillings Scots.† In 1560 this grant was confirmed by James VI. In 1614 the Lord of Roxburgh was served heir to his father in the possessions conveyed by Cant, and James VI. granted a charter *de novo* of these subjects. They form a part of the dukedom of Roxburgh. The site of the convent is now occupied by a farm-house which still retains the name of Friars. Several years ago the occupant of the farm came upon the burying-ground of the order, which had formed matter of dispute between them and the monks of Kelso. A few of the coffins were in a good state of preservation, and ornamented with

* Reg. Mag. Sig., lib. xxxii., No. 13. † Ib.

rude plates of iron. At the entrance of the chapel of St. Peter a skeleton was found, and near to it a large key. The workmen in the course of their operations laid open several vaults and subterranean passages built with freestone, in one of which they found a malt-steep, and beside it a bottle and glass with the name of John Hayman upon it, both clumsily made.*

The Hospital of Roxburgh stood on the right or east bank of the Teviot. It existed previous to 1140. David I. granted to it a ploughgate of land in Rauenden.† Nicol, the chaplain, swore fealty to Edward I. in 1296.‡ John of Oxford was warden of the hospital in 1319. Robert Archibald was appointed chaplain for life by Robert II. in 1390.§ Robert III. confirmed the appointment. It was with the castle and messuage of Roxburgh granted by James IV. to Walter Kerr of Cessford. The grant was renewed in favour of Andrew Kerr of the same place. It was included in the grant by James V. to Walter Ker of Cessfurd.|| Queen Mary granted the same property to Walter Ker and his wife Isobel. James VI. granted the guardianship of the hospital to Robert Ker younger of Cessfurd. In 1623

---

* Mason's Records of Kelso, p. 152.
† Lib. de Kelso, p. 279.   ‡ Ragman's Rolls, p. 159.
§ Robertson's Index, p. 126, No. 12.
|| Reg. Mag. Sig., lib. xxviii., No. 426.

Andrew Ker of Whitmuirhall possessed the hospital lands. In 1616 it was attached to the earldom of Roxburgh.

The town of Roxburgh was at a very early period remarkable for its schools. In 1241 Master Thomas, the rector of the schools of Rokesburc, was, with the constable of the castle, a witness to a charter of William the son of Patrick Earl of Dunbar.* The schools of the town were included in the grant of David I. to the monks of Kelso in 1152. The grant of David was confirmed by Bishops Herbert, Joccline, and Walter, and by Pope Innocent IV. William the Lion also confirmed the grant.

A mill belonged to the burgh previous to 1120. David, while Prince, granted to the monks of Selkirk the seventh part of the mill of Rokesburg. On the monks being transferred to Kelso, David I. granted them twenty chalders, half meal, half wheat, in the mills of the burgh. These grants were confirmed by Malcolm IV. and William the Lion between 1159 and 1174.† From the grants it would rather appear that there was more than one mill, but there are few notices on the subject. It is probable that the present mill of Roxburgh occupies the position of the mill of the burgh.

---

* Lib. of Kelso, p. 194.   Caledonia, vol. ii. p. 107.
† Lib. of Kelso, p. 5.

In the beginning of the seventeenth century, the mills formed a part of the barony of Roxburgh, strengthening the conjecture that the present mill is on the site of the old. It is thought that the mill near the mouth of the Teviot known as Maxwellheugh mill is on the same place as the mill which served the *vil* of Macchus in the early days. Kelso mill seems to have existed from the beginning of the twelfth century, and then, as now, easily stopped by floods or frost.* The burgh was possessed of valuable fishings in the waters of Tweed and Teviot. Before David ascended the throne he granted to his favourite monks of Selkirk a seventh part of these fishings.† As king, he renewed the grant to them as monks of Kelso. David afterwards granted to the monks of Melrose the fishings of old Roxburgh in the Tweed as far as the Brokestream. These fishings are now possessed by the Duke of Roxburgh.

Roxburgh was famed for its markets and fairs, which were attended by the traders of both Scotland and England. The great yearly fair of St. James existed during the days of David I. The burgh, with Jedburgh, had the exclusive privilege of fairs and markets in the dis-

---

* Reg Mag Sig.

† Lib. of Kelso, p. 4. The monks got a grant of Edenham mill to grind their corn when their mill at Kelso was so stopped.

trict. Down to 1693, as has been already adverted to, the trade of the country was entirely in the hands of the burghs royal. But the monks of Kelso obtained a grant whereby they and their men living in Kelso had liberty to buy in Kelso, fuel, timber, and provisions, on every day of the week except the statute day of the king's market at Roxburgh—that dealers passing through Kelso might sell to them—that the men of the monks had liberty to expose for sale in their windows bread, ale, and flesh; fish imported in their wains and with their own horses might be sold at the windows; but wains passing through the town could not unload or sell there, but must proceed to the king's market; and that on the day of the king's statute market, they were prohibited from buying anything in their town, but at the market of Rokesburgh, and along with his burgesses.* The fair of St. James was held on the festival of St. James the apostle, the patron saint of the burgh, and lasted for many days. The fair of St. Lawrence was held sixteen days after that of St. James. Since the fall of this once populous and flourishing burgh, the magistrates of Jedburgh have exercised jurisdiction over the fair; they punish breaches of the peace and other irregularities, and decide differences which happen to arise between traders,

---

* Lib. of Kelso, pp. 15, 305.

in a summary manner without any writing. The
bailie of the Duke of Roxburgh claims right to
exercise jurisdiction during the time of the fair,
and to draw a portion of the customs; but I have
failed to discover the origin of such a right. It is
however easy to account for the origin of the
jurisdiction of the magistrates of Jedburgh. From
the earliest times Jedburgh and Roxburgh were
the only burghs royal in the district. While Roxburgh existed the magistrates and council levied
all the customs due within the bounds of the
royalty, and accounted for the same to the chamberlain of the king. When the town was destroyed
these customs, with the exception of those levied at
the fair of St. James, also ceased to exist. The
fair, being one of the great border trysts, was not
greatly influenced by the rise or decline of the
burgh, but continued as the place for the traders
of either kingdom meeting to dispose of their
merchandise and exchange of commodities. At
this time, as noticed above, the sole commerce of
the country was in the hands of the royal burghs,
and when Roxburgh ceased to be a burgh of that
kind, any customs which remained after the down-
fall of the burgh belonged to the king, and could
only be levied by the magistrates and council of
the only other burgh the king possessed in the
district. Hence it is obvious how the burgh of
Jedburgh derived right to the customs due at St.

James, the only customs which could exist independent of the town. The magistrates of Jedburgh merely collected the customs for the crown. For a long time after the magistrates of Jedburgh entered into the exercise of the right, the inhabitants of Kelso were sorely displeased thereat, and often attempted to remove the fair to their own side of the river; but in those days the burgesses of Jedburgh did not easily give up their rights and privileges. In the matter of the customs of St. James, they could not yield to the Kelso people; being bound as the servants of the king to collect the dues and account for them in exchequer. These duties could not be levied elsewhere than on the ground of the fair. The records of Jedburgh contain many curious and instructive notices in regard to the fair of St. James, and the rivalry of the inhabitants of Kelso.

The fair of St. James was the scene of many a fierce encounter between the inhabitants of the two kingdoms, and it seems also to have been the spot where the followers of rival chiefs met and settled their differences. It is said that the fair day was a term long observed in the settlement of money transactions, but it appears to have been a place for squaring accounts of all sorts. It has not yet lost its character.

Roxburgh was often used as a royal residence; it was also the scene of many festivities, and in

other times it felt all the miseries of border warfare.   It was the favourite abode of David, both
before and after he ascended the throne of the
kingdom.   From this place he dated many of his
charters and writs.   His successors Malcolm IV.,
William the Lion, and the two Alexanders, II. and
III., delighted to dwell at this place, and a number
of their charters are dated in the castle thereof.
In 1125 John, the legate of Honorius II., held a
council at this town.*   In 1134 Malcolm the son
of Macbeth was imprisoned in one of the towers of
the castle.†   In 1137, Thurston, the archbishop of
York, was at Roxburgh suing for peace.‡   In 1151,
Wimond, an English monk, who disturbed the salutary rule of David, was mutilated and imprisoned
in one of the towers of the castle.   In 1156,
Donald, the son of Malcolm, was imprisoned in
the same dungeon.   As the safeguard of the
border it was surrendered to Henry II. in 1174,
by William the Lion, as a part of his ransom.§
In 1189 the castle was restored by the generous
Richard.   In 1193 the marriage of Eustace de
Vesci to Margaret, the daughter of King Wil-
liam, was celebrated here.|| In 1197 Harold
the earl of Caithness was confined in the castle
till his son Torfin should yield himself as an

* Chron. of Mail. p. 68.   † Ib. p. 69.   ‡ Ib. p. 70.
§ Lord Lyttleton's Henry II., p. 22. Major, 135.
|| Chron. Mail. p. 100.

hostage.* He died in prison in 1206.† In 1207 the greater part of the town was by accident burned to ashes.‡ In 1209 a large army assembled here to oppose King John, who then lay at Norham, but a truce was concluded. In the same year Herbert Poore, bishop of Salisbury, and Gilbert Glanville of Rochester, took refuge, one in Roxburgh castle, and the other in Kelso. William generously supplied them with wheat, malt, and oats.§ In 1216, in consequence of a number of the English barons swearing allegiance to the king of Scotland, King John followed them and destroyed by fire and sword their houses, towns, and estates. Roxburgh with its villages and suburbs was burnt and destroyed to prevent John taking advantage of the post.‖ In 1227 Alexander II. made a number of knights in the castle, and amongst others John Earl of Huntindon, son of the Earl David. In 1231 the same king held his courts here.¶ In 1239 in the month of May, Alexander II. was married here to Mary the daughter of Ingleram de Coucey, a French nobleman. Two years after (4th September, 1241) a son was born to them in the castle.** In 1244 the

---

* Chron. Mail. p. 103.　　† Ib. p. 106.

‡ Ib. "Combusta et magna, pars Rokesburch accidentaliter."　　§ Chron. Mail. p. 109.　　‖ Ib. p. 122.

¶ Chron. Mail. p. 140; Acts of Parl. vol. i. p. 77.

** Chron. Mail. p. 154. In a note the editor remarks,

whole town was reduced to ashes.* In 1255 Alexander III. and his queen, Margaret, the daughter of Henry II., arrived here. They were received with great joy and made a grand procession to the church of Kelso.† In the same year Henry the father of the queen, at the invitation of the young king of Scotland and his councillors, arrived at Roxburgh, and was by the king conducted with a pompous procession to the church of Kelso, where he was royally entertained.‡ The English king after-

---

"Wynton places this event in 1242, vol. i. p. 374. However for the credit of our chronicle it is fortunate that we can prove that the birth of Alexander happened in 1241; for the feast of the translation of St. Cuthbert, on the 4th of September, fell upon a Wednesday in 1241, but not in 1242. Alexander II. was born on 24th of August, 1198, consequently had commenced his forty-fourth year eleven days before the birth of his son, and the twenty-seventh of his reign would finish on 3rd December 1241. I have entered thus minutely into an examination of the accuracy of the dates since it is a point on which hangs the value of every chronicle."

   * Fordun, lib. ix. c. 61.

   † Chron. Mail. p. 181. The royal couple had been prohibited consummation of their marriage by the guardians of Scotland on account of their age. The young queen complained to her father that she was kept a prisoner in Edinburgh castle and not permitted to see her husband. Richard Earl of Gloucester, assisted by Patrick Earl of Dunbar and others, surprised the castle of Edinburgh and seized the persons of the king and queen, and conveyed them to Roxburgh, where the queen's distresses were relieved. The royal spouse was only fourteen years of age.   ‡ Ib. p. 181.

wards returned to Wark Castle. King Alexander remained here sixteen days, and during that time his nobles, prelates, and barons entered into certain resolutions as to the care and government of the kingdom, which were reduced into a deed and delivered in name of their king to Henry at Sprouston. On receiving this deed Henry caused his letters patent containing Alexander's deed and his declaration to be delivered to his son-in-law. In 1258 Alexander assembled an army here to subdue his rebellious subjects.* In 1266 the English princes Edward and Edmund visited the king and queen of Scotland at Roxburgh, and were received with great pomp. Here also the marriage contract of the princess Margaret with Eric, king of Norway, was settled on the feast of St. James.† In 1283 the nuptials of Alexander, prince of Scotland, with Margaret the daughter of the Earl of Flanders, were here solemnized. Edward of England twice celebrated his birthday here.‡ In 1291 the castle, which had previously been in possession of William de Soulis, was entrusted to the care of Brian Fitzallan.§ In the same year a safe-conduct was granted by Edward I. to Richard de Furbur, cutler merchant of the town.‖ Next year Baliol obtained possession of the castle from the English

---

* Chron. Mail. p. 188.   † Rymer, vol. i. p. 595.

‡ Walsingham, pp. 134, 140.

§ Rotuli Scotiæ, vol. i. p. 13.   ‖ Ib. vol. i. p. 2.

king, to whom he delivered it and the town in
1295.* It was again restored and again yielded
by the Steward of Scotland to the English king, to
whom he had sworn fealty.† On 30th August
1296 the whole commune of Roxburgh swore
allegiance to the ambitious Edward.‡ In the same
year Edward kept the feast of Pentecost here.
When this politic king tried to settle Scotland,
after a bloody struggle the castle of Roxburgh was
deemed of such importance as to be put under the
special charge of Walter Tonk, his own lieutenant,
and soon after it was in the charge of Robert Has-
tang the younger.§ Robert Wishart the bishop of
Glasgow was a hostage in the castle, and against
whom it was alleged that he had got himself
covertly introduced with a view of betraying the
garrison.|| Wishart was one of the securities of
Bruce. To save Wishart Sir William Wallace
attacked Roxburgh in 1297, but was obliged to
retire on the advance of the English army.¶ In
1305 John de Bretagne had charge of the castle.
In 1311 the English king was at Roxburgh. When
the same king ordered a levy of troops for England
and Scotland, part of the troops were appointed to
appear at Roxburgh within three weeks after the

---

* Rotuli Scotiæ, vol. i. p. 21, 22; Rymer, vol. i. p. 829.
† Pryne, vol. iv. p. 649.   ‡ Ragman's Rolls, p. 122.
§ Rotuli Scotiæ, vol. i. pp. 23, 30. || Rymer, p. 995.
¶ Redpath, p. 209; Haig's History of Kelso, p. 226.

feast of St. John, and at latest by the feast of St. Peter.* In March 1313 the castle was surprised and taken by Sir James Douglas, assisted by Simon of Ledhouse. Bruce ordered the fortifications of the castle to be immediately destroyed, and entrusted the execution of the works to his brother Edward. This prince granted to Nicol Fowler the ward of the castle, and to Bernard Hauden a certain duty for keeping it, on which he set little value; experience had taught him that wasting the country and retiring behind the Firths, were the most efficient mode of defence. In 1319 Edward II. was at Roxburgh. In 1323 Adam Ruff was constable of the castle. By the treaty of Northampton in 1328 Roxburgh was relinquished to Robert Bruce. It did not, however, remain long in the hands of its ancient owners. In 1335 Henry of Douglas was imprisoned in the castle. In 1336 Edward Baliol swore fealty to Edward III., and two years afterwards he delivered to the same king, as part of £2000 worth of lands and rents on the borders, the town, castle, and county of Roxburgh, with almost all the southern shires of Scotland.† The same year Edward ordered the fortifications of the town and castle to be repaired. He also ordered the castle to be victualled with 100 quarters of

---

* Rotuli Scotiæ, vol. i. pp. 97, 101-105.

† Rymer, vol. ii. p. 388 ; Redpath's Border History, p 312.

wheat, 150 quarters of malt, 200 quarters of oats, four casks of wine, and six quarters of coarse salt.* Next year men called hobblers were employed in the defence of the castle at sixpence per day.† In 1346 Henry de Percy and Ralph de Neville were appointed overseers for repairing, furnishing, and defending the castle.‡ In 1341, while Edward kept his Christmas at Melrose, the Earl Derby, his lieutenant, celebrated the same festival at Roxburgh. During the truce which then existed, Derby was visited by Sir William Douglas and other Scottish knights. The spirit of chivalry which predominated at that age, insured them a welcome reception, and they were entertained with the martial sport of jousting with Derby and the knights of his train. Next year, about the time of David's return from France, Sir Alexander Ramsay took the castle by escalade and put the garrison to the sword. It seems that the castle had been in bad repair at the time, for we find in the same year the king ordering his chamberlain to pay to Ramsay £26 13s. 4d. for fortifying the castle, on the ground that the fortifications were incomplete.§ The garrison, at the time the castle was taken by Ramsay, only mustered forty men-at-arms, and the captain had been slain. Fordun states that

* Rotuli Scotiæ, vol. i. p. 534. † Ib. p. 559. ‡ Ib. p. 576.
§ Compota Camerar, vol. i. p. 279.

a person named Hodd of Ednam is said to have instigated Ramsay to scale the walls of the castle. On the capture of David II., in 1346, the English again obtained possession of this important fort, and retained it for many years. In 1356 Baliol resigned the kingdom into the hands of the king of England. Three years after, Richard Tempest, the sheriff and constable, was ordered by Edward III. to keep the castle safe from hostile invasion, and to get its defences repaired, at the sight of notable persons to be deputed by Ralph de Neville, and whose wages were to be paid out of the issues of the castle and county. The garrison was greatly augmented. Next year when Edward returned from France, understanding that defects still existed in its bridges and ditches, he commanded John of Coupland and Robert of Tughale to inspect and report thereon.* Two years after it was again ordered to be repaired. On a treaty of peace being concluded between Edward III. and David II., it was agreed that the former should deliver up the castle, town, and surrounding territory.† But it does not appear that the agreement was ever implemented on the part of the English king. In 1378 Richard II. appointed commissioners for overseeing and repairing the castle. Next year

---

* Rotuli Scotiæ, vol. i. pp. 842-3.
† Rymer, vol. iii. p. 715; Acta Parl., vol. i. p. 135.

Henry Percy got the same directions.* Persons engaged in the work had letters of protection from that king.† In 1381 Matthew of Redman was appointed warden of the castle, and obtained the herbage and profits of the castle ward and the town tolls of Rokesburg. Next year Thomas Blenkinsop had the castle in charge. In 1385 commissioners were appointed to purchase in York, Northumberland, Cumberland, and Westmoreland, provisions for furnishing the castle of Roxburgh.‡ Next year the same orders were given to Henry de Percy, and also to purchase stones, lime, and timber for fortifying the castle.§ Thomas of Swynburn was entrusted with the charge of the town and castle, and instructed to go out with Ralph de Neville and the other wardens of the Marches, when required, taking care to leave always a sufficient force of men-at-arms and bowmen for its safe keeping in his absence.|| In 1389 it was in the keeping of Thomas Earl-Mareschal. In 1392 Sir Gerrard Heron and John of Mitford were appointed overseers of its walls, bridges, and gates. In 1396 Richard II. required a report of the wastes, breaches, dilapidations, and defects of the castle from the time of his ascending the throne. The same year Sir John Stanley was ap-

---

* Acta Parl., vol. i. p. 16. † Ib., pp. 16, 37, 43.
‡ Rotuli Scotiæ, vol. ii. p. 79. § Ib. || Ib., vol. ii. p. 89.

pointed to the charge of the town and castle for ten years, with power to appoint a substitute in his absence when the king required his services elsewhere, with power also to both him and his lieutenant to seize and take carriages for the conveyance of provisions and other things necessary for the castle. In 1398 the town of Roxburgh was plundered and burnt, and the bridge over the Tweed broken down by a son of the Earl of Douglas, Sir William Stewart, and others, on which occasion hay and fuel were destroyed to the amount of £2000.* The castle was again victualled in 1400, at the command of King Henry IV., to Richard le Gray and Stephen le Scrope. Two years afterwards Ralph Neville, and the Earl of Westmoreland and lieutenant, had charge of the town and castle. In 1405 commissioners were appointed by Henry to treat for peace with Scotland, also to ascertain the bounds of the lands and possessions assigned by the treaty to his castle of Roxburgh on the Marches.† In 1410 letters of protection were granted to all persons employed in the defence of the castle.‡ In 1411 Sir Robert Umfraville had it in keeping. In 1414 king Henry V. commanded the castle to be properly victualled. Two years after the same command

---

* Rymer, vol. iii. p. 53. † Rotuli Scotiæ, vol ii. p. 174.
‡ Ib. vol. ii. pp. 194-8.

was issued. In 1419 the English king appointed Richard Fakenham his own mason for competently repairing and, where necessary, rebuilding the castle with all celerity, with power to him to employ as many masons and workmen as he thought necessary for repairing or building.* In 1422 the town and castle were besieged by the Earl of Douglas. Three years after letters of protection were granted to Edgar Heton abiding in the castle. Next year John Shipton was appointed by the English king overseer of works, and in 1434 John Learmonth was clerk thereof. In 1436, on James I. laying siege to the castle, King Henry commanded the Earl of Northumberland, Ralph Earl of Westmoreland, Sir Thomas of Clifford, Sir Thomas Dacre, Sir John of Greystock, George of Latymer, and Sir William Fitzhugh to assemble all and each the knights, squires, valets, and other fencible men of the counties of York, Nottingham, Derby, Northumberland, Cumberland, and Westmoreland, the county of Lancaster and the bishopric of Durham, to be ready according to their rank to march for its relief.† In 1460 James II. took the town of Roxburgh, and with a numerous army laid siege to the castle, which since the battle of Durham had remained in the hands of the English.‡

---

* Rotuli Scotiæ, vol. ii. p. 224.   † Ib. vol. ii. p. 295.
‡ Redpath's History, p. 422; Pinkerton's History, vol. i. p. 243.

The bursting of a piece of ordnance deprived the
king of life, but the arrival of the widowed queen
at the camp so encouraged the army that the
siege was renewed with vigour, and in a few days
the castle was taken.*   The castle was afterwards
levelled to the rock, but it seems to have been
partly rebuilt within twenty years. In 1488 James
IV. granted *inter alia* the castle and the place of
the castle called castlestead, with pertinents, to
Walter Ker of Cessfurd, his familiar esquire.†   In
1509 it was granted to Andrew Ker of Cessfurd
and his wife. In 1542 the same was granted by
James V. to Walter Ker of Cessfurd.‡   In September 1545 the Earl of Hertford, while lying with
his army at Kelso, paid the castle a visit and wrote
his king that Rockesburghe was " surely the veraye
seate and place which shall and maye scourge and
keep in obedience both the marches and Tevoy-

---

* It would rather appear that the queen was not at the
siege before the death of the king, (Holingshed, vol. ii. p.
101.)   Pennant says that when he visited the spot in 1769
a holly tree marked the place where the king was killed;
vol. iii. p. 274. The new Statistical Account states that a yew
tree enclosed by a wall marks the spot. There are not sufficient data to fix the locality of the accident, much less the
kind of the tree that grew upon it.

The English possessed the castle and town for more than a
hundred years.

† Reg. Mag. Sig. lib. xii. No. 16.·

‡ Reg. Mag. Sig. lib. xxviii. No. 428.

dale." In 1547 Hertford—then Protector Somerset—on his return from the disastrous battle of Musselburgh, passed the river Tweed and encamped on the plain between the ruins of the castle and the confluence of the rivers. The protector, impressed with the strong position of the castle, determined to make it tenable. He made a ditch of twenty feet broad with depth accordingly, and a wall of like breadth, depth, and height, was made across within the castle from the one side wall to the other, aud forty feet from the west end; and a like trench and wall cast traverse within about a cart's cast from the east end, and hereto that the castle walls of each side where need was mended with turf, and made with loopholes for shooting directly forward and flanking at hand.* So anxious was Somerset to have the castle made defensible, that he and the principal men of his army worked at it with their own hands two hours every day, which so encouraged the army that the castle was made capable of being defended in the course of six days. On the protector leaving the place he appointed Sir Ralph Bulmer governor, with a garrison of three hundred soldiers and two hundred pioneers. In a treaty made between the kings of France and England, one of the articles bound

---

* Patten's account of the expedition. The works of Somerset can be distinctly traced at the present day.

the latter to give up the forts of Lauder and Douglas, and if these were not in his hands to raze the
towns and castles of Roxburgh and Eyemouth.*
In 1553 the castle and castlestead were resigned
by Sir Walter Ker of Cessfurd into the hands of
Queen Mary for the purpose of a new grant in
favour of his son Andrew Ker.† In 1574 James
VI. granted the castlestead to Robert Ker, son of
William Ker of Cessfurd.‡ The same king granted
it to Robert, Lord Roxburgh, and Jean Drummond, sister of the earl of Perth.§ It now forms
a part of the estate of the Duke of Roxburgh.

The religious houses of Selkirk, Kelso, Dryburgh, Jedburgh, Melrose, Haddington, St. Andrews, Dunfermline, and Haliston, obtained grants
of property in the burgh, from David I., Malcolm
IV., William the Lion, and Alexander, and many
other pious persons.

The notice of this once flourishing burgh cannot
be more appropriately closed than by the lines of
a poet of Teviotdale :—

Roxburgh ! how fallen since first in gothic pride
Thy frowning battlements the war defied,
Called the bold chief to grace thy blazon'd halls,
And bade the rivers gird thy solid walls !
Fallen are thy towers, and, where the palace stood,
In gloomy grandeur waves yon hanging wood ;

* Rymer, vol. xv. pp. 214-15 ; Redpath, p. 570.
† Reg. Mag. Sig., lib. 31, No. 328.
‡ Ib., lib. 34, No. 67.   § Ib., lib. 47, No. 214, Retours.

Crushed are thy halls, save where the peasant sees
One moss-clad ruin rise between the trees ;
The still green trees whose mournful branches wave
In solemn cadence o'er the hapless brave.
Proud castle ! fancy still beholds thee stand,
The curb, the guardian of this border land,
As when the signal flame, that blazed afar,
And bloody flag, proclaimed impending war,
While in the lion's place the leopard frown'd,
And marshall'd armies hemm'd thy bulwarks round.*

---

* Leyden's Scenes of Infancy, part iii., p. 135-6.

Note.—While treating of the Grey Friars at page 76, *supra*, I omitted to notice that when Hutchison visited Roxburgh in 1776, he saw " the confused foundations of buildings and one gateway of excellent workmanship," which denoted the place where the house stood.   Hutchison, vol. i., p. 277.

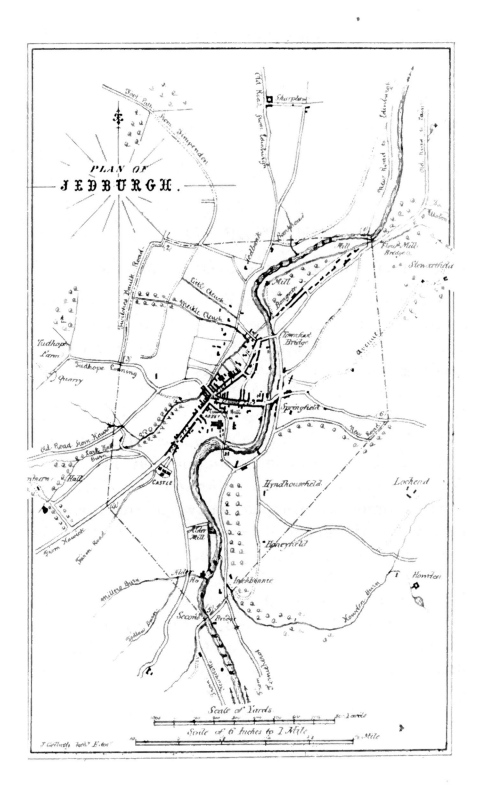

PLAN OF
JEDBURGH.

Scale of Yards

Scale of 6 inches to 1 Mile

CHAPTER III.

OF THE BURGH AND CASTLE OF JEDBURGH.

THE next objects of inquiry are the burgh and castle of Jedburgh. The editor of the "Origin of Parishes" has collected about 82 different modes of spelling the name.* It appears first as *Geddewrd*, and also, with an *"e"* added, *Geddewrde*. *Jedworth* is seen about 1147. Fordun calls the town "Jedwood." *Jedburgh* does not appear till about the 15th and 16th centuries. Chalmers, in his "Caledonia," derives the name from *Jed* the river, and *worth* a hamlet. But the early spelling throws a doubt over the generally received opinion that the name describes a hamlet on the Jed.

The town of Jedburgh, the capital of Teviotdale, is situated in a warm sheltered vale, around which the waters of the Jed make a beautiful curve. It stands exactly in the centre of the British Islands, distant from Edinburgh forty-nine miles, Kelso

---

* Origines Parochiales, vol i. pp. 366-7.

H

eleven, and Hawick ten. The situation of the
town is picturesque. The approaches to it lead
through the finest scenes, especially that from the
south, which for several miles accompanies the
course of the sylvan Jed :—

> " Round every hazel copse and smiling mead,
> Where lines of fir the glowing landscapes screen,
> And crown the heights with tufts of deeper green."

Little if at all inferior is the approach from the
north. On the right, sloping plantations overhang
the road, and on the left the waters of the Jed
sweetly murmur round the alder bushes with which
its banks are covered.

The town is built upon a spur of the Dunion
ridge, and in such a manner as to have been in
former times under the protection of its powerful
castle ; which self-preservation made the sturdy
borderers level with the ground in the beginning
of the 15th century. In ancient times it was
dangerous to reside at any distance from a fortified
place; and accordingly it is found that in whatever
place a castle was erected it soon gave birth to a
town, church, and mill, as it was only in such situa-
tions that the people could follow their lawful
occupations, or hope to retain their property for
any length of time. Even with all the aid afforded
by these powerful castles, the inhabitants often
experienced barbarous treatment from the depre-

dating bands of the sister kingdom. The town is in the form of a cross—Castlegate and High-street being the long body thereof, and Canongate and Burnwynd the transept. The market square is where the Canongate and Burnwynd meet. It is an oblong square of considerable size. On the south side thereof stands the Town Hall, built in 1812, of polished freestone, without any claim to architectural taste. It was erected at the sole expense of the heritors of the county, the burgh merely contributing the old hall or stance, in consideration of which the heritors granted the community rights to an apartment in the upper ·flat for an office to the clerk of the burgesses and record-room ; two apartments on the ground-floor for the public weights; the privilege of the Hall for the magistrates holding their courts and other public meetings of the burgesses. Adjoining the Town Hall stands a building which was once the prison of the county. It was built in the year 1756, but part of the steeple is of a later date. At that period the finances of the burgh were so low that the burgesses were only enabled to build the steeple on a level with the roof of the prison to hang the watch bell. After the lapse of several years it was raised twelve feet higher, where it remained till an election opportunely occurred, when the *generosity* of the candidate, Sir Hew Dalrymple, enabled the town-council to complete the work which they had begun. The spire is 120 feet high, and was finished in 1791.

There are in the town two fine streets extending from north-east to south-west, nearly half a mile, and rising in a gradual ascent on the slope of the Dunion hill, to where the new prison stands on the site of the old castle. One of these streets is called the High-street, and is the principal street of the town. It is well-built, and contains two banks, two chapels belonging to the United Presbyterian body, two well-frequented hotels, dispensary, brewery, and many excellent shops with plate-glass fronts, not surpassed by the shops of any town in the south of Scotland. The other is Castlegate, running from the market-place to the Castle-hill. It contains, besides the Town Hall, an infant school and a number of shops. The buildings of this street are chiefly occupied as private dwellings. No. 7 of this street is the house in which the unfortunate Charles Stuart resided on his way to England in 1745. It was then the property of Ainslie of Blackhill. The arms of the owner were till lately to be seen over the principal door of the house, but were removed by the last owner of the subjects. On the east side of this street, at the entrance of the Abbey Close, formerly stood a tower popularly called Dabie's Tower, and therefore supposed to have been named after the saintly David, who often resided here. But I am now satisfied that it was the Tower of the Abbey, and that Dabie's Tower is a corruption of the Abbey Tower, or Abbot's Tower. It was situated at the entrance to the Abbey, and within the territory of the house. A modern mansion occupies its site, the property of the Marquis of Lothian. The monks of Kelso had two tenements on the north side of this street, which they let to John of Rutherfurd of Hundalee and his wife Elizabeth, for payment of half a mark for each land to the monks, the burgh ferme to the king, and board and lodging to the monks when necessary.* I have not been able to identify these two tenements, but in the lease of the chartulary of the Abbey of Kelso it appears that the subjects were contiguous to each other, bounded on the east by the tenement of a person named Robert Lorymer, and by the land of Patrick Vauch on the west. The same monks, during the beginning of the fourth century, drew an annual rent of eightpence for land in the same street, which at one time belonged to a person named Fossard.† The monks of Melrose had also property in this street, which they let out in 1426 to John Moscrip, a burgess of the town, and his wife Christian, for their life-rent, and one heir after their death, for the payment of five shillings, the burgh ferme, and all other dues, the monks re-

---

* Lib. de Kelso, p. 425.   † Ib. p. 459.

serving right to resume the possession in the event of three terms falling in arrear. Moscrip and his wife were also bound to find the monks lodging, chamber, and stabling, in the tenement, when they visited Jedburgh. The subjects also lay on the north side of the street, and were bounded on the west by the tenement of William Burrel deceased, and on the east by the property of the deceased Grey of Denome.* In the middle of the fifth century John Dunn, burgess, had a large house lying on the north side of this street, which he sold to his next neighbour, James Smith, with the buildings and walls constructed therein, to be held of the king for ever, for the payment of four shillings Scots, and the usual burgh ferme.† In 1494 a tenement in this street formed the subject of a litigation before the lords of the privy council, between John Douglas and his wife, and Thomas Adamson and Catherine his spouse. Catherine established a life-rent in the subject, and obtained judgment in her favour. It would rather appear that at an early period there had been few or no houses on the south side of this street or gate. The buildings seem chiefly to have lain between the gate and the burn on the north, and ascended the hill considerably higher than they do at present. The entrance to Glenburnhall was at one

---

* Lib. de Mailros, pp. 533-4.   † Ib. pp. 568-9.

CANONGATE BRIDGE.

time a wynd or street of the town, running from
the castle to the rivulet. No doubt the burgesses
of old would be anxious to possess property beneath the castle walls. In this street the lawn
market was held, to the west of the entrance to the
Abbey Close. The cattle or nolt market was held
at the head of the street. The corn market was
held in the square of the burgh. The High-street
proper extended from the square eastward to two
wynds, one called the Smiths' wynd on the east,
and the other on the north called the Jewellers'
wynd. From that place to the Townfoot, or Plais-
ance, it took the name of the Blackquarter.

The Canongate, a well-built street, runs from the
Market-square to the river Jed, in an easterly direction. This street was once the principal approach to the town from the east and south,
but after the formation of the present road by
Bongate it lost its pre-eminence. The whole of
the south side of this street from the market-place
to the river is out of the royalty. It is entirely
built, as its name would imply, on the property of
the abbey. The Abbey Place, lying behind the
Canongate, is likewise out of the royalty. Down
to the latter part of last century the proprietors of
the south side of this street were exempt from all
the burghal taxes; but at that time the burgesses
had several meetings with them, and it was ultimately arranged that the owners of the south side

were to contribute towards the town burdens, and, in consideration thereof, were admitted into all the privileges of the burgh. This was certainly a novel method of extending a royalty. The arrangement seems, however, to have been faithfully kept, although it must be obvious that the magistrates and council could not make royalty that territory which was not declared to be so by the charter of the crown.*   It was in this street that the bard of Scotland, Robert Burns, lodged while making a tour of the border in 1787. The house is now marked No. 27 and is next to the Dean's Close on the west. While here the poet says he " was waited on by the magistrates, and presented with the freedom of the burgh,"† but I have failed to discover any traces of such an event in the burgh. The burgess book is very correctly kept, and had Burns been presented with the freedom of the burgh there is every reason to believe that his name would have appeared in the roll of burgesses.   I have also carefully examined the minutes of the town-council, without finding any entry relating to Burns. Before any person could be admitted a burgess, authority must be given by the council of the burgh, and the party obtaining the freedom requires to subscribe the book. At the time Burns visited Jedburgh the freedom of

---

* Burgh Records.   † Memoranda of Tours.

the burgh was deemed of more consequence than it is now, and the forms of admission were strictly observed. Notwithstanding the poet's statement, it is thought that the freedom of the burgh was not presented to him, and if anything of the kind occurred it must have been a sham ceremony, performed during the drinking of the *riddle of claret*, said to have been bestowed on the bard in the inn on the occasion.* Besides, none of the persons with whom Burns from his *memoranda* seems to have come in contact while in Jedburgh had anything to do with the management of the town's affairs. They were managers under the authority of the Court of Session some years before the time of the bard's visit. The house in this street through which Crown-lane runs was formerly the Old Black Bull Inn. It was in this house that Elliot of Stobbs, the grandfather of the present Sir William Elliot of Stobbs, killed the laird of Stewartfield. The two gentlemen had been attending a county meeting, and after it was over they retired to the Black Bull Inn, where they indulged in drinking and gambling. While so engaged they quarrelled about some trifling matter, when the laird of Stewartfield threw part of the contents of his glass in the face of Stobbs, who immediately drew a cane sword and stabbed his

---

* Burns' Prose Works, Edin., p. 127.

friend with it below the table. This tragic occurrence is often told as having taken place in the
mansion of Stewartfield, but there can be little
doubt that the scene of the murder was the Old
Black Bull. The cane sword is in the possession
of the Marquis of Lothian. The house which
forms the corner of Queen-street, or Backgate, belonged to Rutherfurd of Ladfield, who was out
in 1715, and who concealed himself in one of the
presses of the house for nearly three weeks. It is
probable that the searchers were not over-zealous;
as the cause Rutherfurd espoused had many adherents in the neighbourhood. Further down
on the same side of the street stands the old
schoolmaster's house, the birth-place of Sir David
Brewster, whose father was the teacher of the
burgh schools. The corner house on the same side
of the street was the abode of the town piper, an
important appendage to royal burghs in the by-
gone days. The last hangman or lockman which
the burgh possessed had his abode in a close on
the south side of the same street. In 1666 the
treasurer informed the council that he had paid
the hangman, and the officers were ordered to
banish him and his family out of the town. About
a fortnight after, this functionary claimed a certificate of character, which the magistrates granted,
declaring that he had been guilty of no miscar-

riage or iniquity.* The labour of this functionary seems to have been hard, as the magistrates were under the necessity of offering a reward for one who had run away, contrary to his agreement.†

In a line with the Canongate is the Burnwynd, worthy of notice in so far as it appears to have been an entrance of consequence during the border feuds. At the head of the wynd stood the north port of the burgh till 1856, when it was forced to bend before the modern notions of improvement. It was the last remnant in the burgh which connected the warlike past with the present peaceful period.

The Friarsgate runs from the Burnwynd port to the east end of the town, parallel with the High-street. In this gate stood a convent of friars, founded by the magistrates and inhabitants in 1513; but as these religious orders were suppressed at the Reformation, the building was converted to a different purpose, and now no other memorial of the old-fashioned piety which planted them there remains than a dwelling-house called Friars, on the site of the ancient convent. It is said that Adam Bell, the author of a work called the "Wheel of Time," lived and died in this convent. It is

---

* Burgh Records, vol. i.
† Harris's Historical Gleanings.

thought the property of the house extended between the Friarsgate and the High-street, and that
the burying-ground of the order was where the
British Linen Company's Bank now stands. The
situation is very pleasant, and well adapted for the
performance of religious duties. Between the
property of the friars and the river Jed stood the
Maison-Dieu of the burgh. The site of this house
is thought to have been in the garden on the west
side of the road running from Friarsgate to the
Townfoot. In 1296 the master of this house
took the oath to Edward I. of England.* Henry
Percy obtained the advowson of this hospital for
Henry IV. in 1404.† In 1491 the right of patronage was granted to Walter Kerr of Cessford, ren-
dering for the same, if demanded, a rose. The
land belonging to the house is still called the
Maison-Dieu acres. The grant of the king to
Kerr produced in later times many a dispute between him and the magistrates of Jedburgh, they
both claiming a right to the rents of the house
and lands after the house ceased to be an hospital.
The road up the hill from the Friarsgate still retains the name of the *Sick Man's Path.*

The next street of any consequence is one which
runs in a parallel direction with the High-street
on the south. In this street the unfortunate and

---

* Ragman's Rolls, p. 25.   † Rotuli Scotiæ, vol. ii. p. 172.

ill-used Mary resided while administering justice
to her rude border subjects. The house in which
she is said to have lodged is on the east side of
the gate, in a garden with railings in front. It
appears to have been at one time of greater extent,
with a large paved court at the west end. The
principal entrances have been by large arched
doorways. In the front of the house are the
united arms of the Homes and Kerrs. The garden
extends from the house to the river, and it would
seem as if the approach to the house had been
from the bridge at the Canongate foot and through
the garden.

The street called Abbey Place consists of a row
of neat houses, containing several shops, and the
united schools of the burgh and parish. This street
was purchased from the Marquis of Lothian at the
same time with Bongate and Richmond. The
ground on which the street of houses is built belonged at one time to the convent. Opposite this
street, and running parallel with it, is a place
called the Rampart, about twelve yards broad, and
seven or eight feet high, which at one time formed
the fashionable promenade of the burgh, but has
for several years been nearly deserted. The Abbey
Close runs from the Castlegate to the western
gable of the abbey. It also was the property of
the monks. The magistrates purchased it from
the Marquis of Lothian. It was in olden times

the principal approach to the abbey. Here all unfree traders were wont to resort for disposing of their wares, as it was not subject to the burgh laws. On Tuesdays and Saturdays this place was much frequented by fleshers from the neighbouring towns, who supplied the inhabitants at a cheaper rate than the butchers of the burgh.

Opposite to the Canongate foot, on the east side of the river, is the little suburb of Richmond, not included in the royalty, and also acquired from the Marquis of Lothian in 1669. The origin of the name is doubtful. It is thought that it signifies the great mount or mound, which, with *row* added, makes the modern name of Richmond-row, or the *row* of houses at the great mound. The great mound is supposed to be the high mound lying between Richmond and Bongate. This place is called in some maps *Stone* hill, and it is more than probable that the large stone long seen at the corner of the garden, at the end of the Townfoot-bridge, formed a part of an ancient building on this mount, but of which there are now no traces. It is however certain that near this place a number of coins of the Heptarchy have been turned up by spade and plough. There was formerly a noted hostelry in this little village called the Horseshoe-inn, and kept by a blacksmith and his wife of the name of Fair. The hostess, it is said, was of gentle lineage, and drew many customers to this suburban hostelry. Her descendants filled the office of provost of the burgh, and one of them was the first banker in the town. The property is at present possessed by a blacksmith, and the sign of the horseshoe and hammer is still to be seen.

A little further down, and on the bend of the river, the village of Bongate is pleasantly situated. It too was the property of the monks in the early days. The burgh purchased it from Lord Jedburgh. There is nothing in the annals of these two small suburbs different from the burgh. They appear to have arisen at the same period, and grown up together in the midst of perilous times. All these places which we have described as lying out of the royalty of Jedburgh were, previous to the Reformation, the property of the monks, and formed part of their barony of Ulston. The streets are well paved. The town was first lighted with gas in December, 1834. After the passing of the police improvement bill it was adopted by the inhabitants, and, in virtue of the powers therein given, the magistrates and council thoroughly drained the town, laying tubular pipes along all the streets, with branches to each tenement. The doing so cost about £1,400, but the benefits conferred on the burgh were cheaply purchased. Previous to that period the condition of the town was a great reproach, now it is as well drained as any town in the kingdom.

The town, although in the vicinity of excellent springs, is ill supplied with water. Before 1720 the inhabitants had no water excepting what was carried from a distance, but at that time water was brought from a well in Tudhope-path to a pant erected for its reception at the cross. To defray the expense of bringing in this water the inhabitants contributed by voluntary subscription, and what was wanting was made up by the magistrates and council from the common good of the burgh. By an act passed in 1721 the burgh of Jedburgh was granted an impost of two pennies on the pint of ale for *inter alia* supplying the town with fresh water. In 1799 the Pipewell brae spring was introduced into the Canongate, but, this supply of water being insufficient, an additional supply was collected in the glebe, and conveyed by means of a siphon into a reservoir at the abbey mill, and driven by machinery to the head of the Abbey Close, whence it is distributed to the lower quarters of the town. These operations cost the burgh above £400, and yet the supply is not equal to the demand. The town is situated in a vale, bounded by hills full of the finest springs, one of which is sufficient to supply double the number of inhabitants.

In the burgh there are seven places of worship —the parish church, two belonging to the United Presbyterians, the Free Church, a Congregational chapel, a Scotch Episcopal chapel erected in 1843, and, on the opposite side of the river, a Roman Catholic chapel, erected in 1855. The sect called the Relief had its origin in Jedburgh. In 1755 the town-council and the majority of the inhabitants of Jedburgh applied for a presentation to Mr. Boston, minister of the neighbouring parish of Oxnam, and, being disappointed in that application, they built a place of worship by contribution, and invited Mr. Boston to be their pastor, several of the most substantial members of the congregation guaranteeing payment of £120 a-year as stipend. He accepted the call, and prevailed upon Mr. Gillespie, who had been deposed for disobedience to the orders of the general assembly, to join him under the above denomination of Relief Presbytery, professing to differ from the Established church on no other point than the right of patrons to appoint ministers contrary to the inclinations of the people. This sect quickly spread over Scotland, and is now united with the burghers and anti-burghers.

There are several schools in the burgh. Previous to 1804 the burgh kept an English schoolmaster, at a salary of £20 sterling. In the selection of a schoolmaster the town-council appear

I

always to have acted with great caution, and for the interests of the inhabitants. At that period the English school was united with the grammar school, and the rector paid by the burgh and by the heritors of the parish. The election was by fourteen delegates, seven chosen by the council and seven by the heritors. Like other parish schoolmasters, he holds his office for life. The school is situated in the Abbey-place, and numerously attended by children of residents in the town and neighbourhood, and by pupils from a distance, who live in the house of the rector. The salary of the rector is now £29 odds, and since 1843 wholly paid by the heritors of the parish. The magistrates regulate the fees and the hours of teaching.

There is also a long-established private academy, called "the Nest," occupying a healthy situation on the margin of the river, and commanding a beautiful view of the vale of Jed. The house stands on what was formerly abbey property, and, in 1610, was granted by James VI. to Alexander Earl of Home. In that charter it is called "The Wrain's Nest."

THE LIBRARIES OF THE BURGH.—The first notice of a library existing in Jedburgh is in the early part of last century. In 1714 Thomas Rutherfurd, of Rutherfurd, presented the burgh of Jedburgh with a sum of money and a quantity of books to form a library, and for that purpose built a room, at his own expense, over the English school in the Laighkirkyard, above the door of which his family arms were engraved. It is probable that on this foundation the company's library arose about eighty years ago. This institution was superintended during its early years by Mr. James Brewster, parish schoolmaster, the father of Sir David Brewster of world-wide reputation. The library went on thrivingly till about 1835, when it began to show symptoms of decay, chiefly owing to the want of popular influence in its councils. The directors, instead of being elected annually, remained constantly in office, and vetoed all works proposed at general meetings, unless those appearing in their own vocabulary. The result might have been anticipated. In 1856 the whole library of books, consisting of about 1,500 volumes of standard works and valuable works of reference, which had taken nearly a century to collect, were sold by auction at not one-fifth part of their value.

The religious library was next founded by men of honest and good repute, with the view, it is said, of discountenancing the vain and frivolous tastes which then existed, and promoting reading of a thoughtful and religious character. For a time the affairs of the library went on smoothly, till an edition of Dr. Young's writings, containing the dramatic works of the Bard of Night, got upon the shelves. The orthodox party resented the intrusion of the book, and, after discussions long and keen, a compromise was effected. The religious library then took the name of the Jedburgh library, and, while admitting miscellaneous works, its old character predominated. It is said that Shakspeare was not so fortunate as Dr. Young in getting admission to its shelves, and that a majority of members year after year refused to hear the Bard of Avon knocking at the door. After an existence of fifty years, the company was dissolved, and the books sold in August, 1843.

Waugh's library was managed by men of a different character. While the managers of the Jedburgh library rejected every book not strictly orthodox, Waugh's library received all with open arms. This library existed for nearly sixty years. The books were divided among the members about 1837. Blackfriars church, formerly the burgher congregational meeting-house, established a library about twenty years ago, and now numbers a great many volumes. It is accessible only to members of the congregation, and the only means by which the public can get into it is by taking a seat in the church. As may be imagined, the works are generally theological, and have to undergo a *test* before getting admission to the shelves of the library. An itinerating library, on the principle developed by Samuel Brown, of Haddington, was tried here, but did not succeed. A library in connection with the Mechanics' Institute was founded in 1841, and contains an excellent variety of works of science, history, poetry, and general polite literature. It has been the means of doing great good in the burgh and neighbourhood.

FRIENDLY SOCIETIES.—There are several of these yearly societies in the town, having the same rules and regulations. The objects of these societies are to assist the poor man in cases of distress and death, and be the means of keeping a spare pittance together till it accumulates to a sum sufficient to pay the landlord's rent, or purchase clothes for the family at the New Year. The business of the society is managed by a committee, treasurer, and clerk. Every member, besides paying any sum not less than 6d. nor more than 2s., pays the further sum of 2d. weekly as sick-money, which entitles him to receive, in cases of affliction, the sum of 6s. per week for the first six weeks, 4s. per week for the six following weeks, and 3s. per week for the successive weeks of illness, till the end of the year. When a member dies, a sum of £4 sterling is given by the society as funeral-money, and £1 at the death of a member's wife. Members needing money may borrow from the society any sum not exceeding 2s. short of what his weekly payment will amount to at the end of the year, according to priority of application, upon finding caution to the satisfaction of two members of the committee; but members cannot be caution for one another. A member not paying all arrears at the end of the forty-ninth week forfeits his right to any division of the sick-money and interest. It is believed that societies of this kind exist in every town and village in the district, conferring incalculable benefits on the poor labourer and tradesman. By putting into the society sixpence every Saturday night as he receives his wages, the poor man is not only enabled to live without terror of the term-day, but to look forward with pleasure to the day when his young family and himself will appear in suitable attire from the savings of a twelvemonth. The small sum of sixpence is not felt when taken weekly, and is safe when placed in the treasurer's hands. The saving of the money is, however, the least benefit conferred upon a poor family. To eke out the wages of a labouring man to meet the demands of a numerous family requires the utmost skill of a careful wife, and the manner in which almost every one of them does so is greatly to their credit. But if this be the case when the family is in perfect health, what must their situation be when sickness pays a visit to their dwelling?—if the family have no other resource than the labours of the parent, starvation in a few days stares them in the face. But by being members of a society, and paying into its funds sixpence weekly, they become entitled to a sum sufficient to procure them food. Societies of this nature cannot be too widely imitated.

TRADE.—Like most other burghs, Jedburgh possessed exclusive privileges, and no person could carry on a trade within the town and suburbs, by buying and selling, unless he became a burgess. At present the burgesses number about 140. There were formerly eight incorporated trades, who enjoyed the exclusive privilege of working to the inhabitants within the burgh—viz., the hammermen, weavers, shoemakers, masons, tailors, wrights, fleshers, and glovers.* Each one of these crafts had an act by the magistrates and council, containing their powers and privileges. This act was called a "seal of cause," and in virtue of which each trade regulated its own body, and also prevented unfreemen from working within the royalty. Each trade had its deacon, who judged all disputes that occurred between the brethren of the craft, and in the recovering of debts to the amount of £5 Scots (8s. 4d.). In former days the trades

---

* The masons do not appear as a part of the corporation till near the end of the seventeenth century.

were tenacious of their rights, and many a squabble took place between them and the magistrates and council. Of the whole trades, the shoemakers seem to havè been the most unruly, and on several occasions the magistrates were under the necessity of employing the soldiers quartered in the burgh to compel the sons of Crispin to yield due obedience to their lawful superiors.*

In 1736 Robert Dick, a dyester, was summoned before the deacon of the weavers, fined, and imprisoned, for taking an apprentice without duly acknowledging the trade, and paying into the box the usual dues. · Dick appealed to the convener of trades against the judgment, but the appeal was dismissed. An appeal was then lodged with the magistrates and council, when the convener and deacons declined the authority of the magistrates, and claimed exclusive jurisdiction in matters of trade. On the magistrates granting an order of liberation, the deacons assembled the whole brethren of the different trades in the Laighkirkyard, and threatened to break the prison doors. The magistrates and their friends refused to comply, and the trades broke to pieces the door of the gaol. The riot act was then read, but the trades regarded it as little as the verbal orders of the magistrates. While things remained in this situ-

---

* Burgh Records, vol. iii. p. 9, *et seq.*

ation, the magistrates acted in a manner becoming the descendants of those who had led the burgesses in many a border fray. They seized the person who had broken open the door, on which a regular battle ensued between the trades and the magistrates, and was only put an end to on the appearance of a company of · dragoons. In 1743 the deacons were fined ten pounds ·Scots ·each for irregular procedure, in having fined fifteen of the weaver trade in four pounds ·Scots each, and ordained them to lie in prison till paid.* In 1790 the magistrates committed Thomas Henderson, James Stevenson, and Thomas Turnbull, as acting for the convenery, to prison, till the books of the trades were delivered up.† The disputes with the magistrates, although serious, were few in number to the *rows* which they had among themselves, especially the shoemakers, while travelling to distant markets to dispose of their shoes. The various incorporated trades were, in the days of exclusive privileges, numerous. The flesher trade alone in 1673 consisted of thirty-seven members. At present there are only five persons of the trade. The meat is sold in the fleshers' houses, and not, as formerly, in the public market. In the beginning of the last century the flesher trade had a common good, which they let yearly at fifteen

---

* Burgh Records, vol. iii. p. 183. † Ib. vol. iv.

pounds sterling. By one of their regulations, no unfreeman could have either nolt or sheep killed within the burgh, or within the fleshmarket, by any of the three tradesmen of the trade, under the payment of forty shillings; and the freeman that killed the same was bound to pay other forty shillings to the trade, for the use of the poor of the trade. None of the trade were allowed to kill any nolt, sheep, or lambs, on Wednesdays or Thursdays, unless on the 20th October or 25th December, under the fine of five pounds Scots. Each quarter of the year the flesher trade distributed certain sums of money among the poor of the trade, as their needs required.

The trades of the burgh were always ready to go out to war, and in many a border fray did good service. Under the banners of Sir William Ruthven, the burgesses fought with Wallace, and they bled with Bruce.* On the field of Bannockburn they took a flag from the English, which the weaver trade preserve to this day with as much care as ever pilgrim did a holy relic. After the Douglas settled in the forest, the burgesses followed the banner of the bloody heart through

---

* " Fra Tawydaill cum gud men mony ane;
Out of Jedwart, with Ruthvane at yar tyd,
Togyddyr socht fra mony diuerss syd."
Blair's History of Wallace.

many a deadly conflict; and when the slughorn of
that gallant house was heard, the staffis of Jeddart bristled in the front rank.* Under the
Rutherfurd ·the burghers stemmed the tide of
battle at the Redswyre.† When Surrey assaulted
the town with the whole English army, the defence
was so well sustained by the burghers, that the
brave general declared he had never met their
equal, and that " could 40,000 such men be assembled, it would be a dreadful enterprise to with-
stand them." The battle continued during the
night, and though the town—which was without
walls—was set on fire in many places, those who
manned the towers and abbey continued the contest for a whole day. Surrey alleged—so fearful
was the strife—that the devil had been seen visibly
six times during the contest. At the pass of Kil-
liecrankie, the burghers possessed themselves of
another flag. The inhabitants of Jedburgh were
trained to war, and hardly a skirmish took place
that the staffis did not share in it. Even at this

---

* This weapon was a stout staff, with a steel head four
feet long. Its use was prohibited by parliament in 1516.
The staffe was manufactured in the town. It is sometimes
called an axe.

       † " Bauld Rutherfurd he was fow stout,
          Wi' a' his nine sons him round about;
          He led the town o' Jedburgh out—
          All bravely fought that day."
                       Old Ballad.

day it is alleged that the inhabitants of the district are too ready with their hands.*

MANUFACTURES.—There are three woollen manufactures carried on within the parliamentary bounds of the burgh. The first notice that is observed of a woollen manufactory in Jedburgh is about 1728. At that time the secretary to the trustees for improving the fisheries, and who were entrusted with the grant of £700 for encouraging the manufacture of coarse wool in Scotland, intimated that the trustees had fixed upon Jedburgh as one of the places where one of the fourteen sorters was to be placed. The magistrates and council readily embraced the offer, and proceeded to get ready a house and yard for the use of the sorter. But these staplers and combers dispersed through the country rather discouraging than otherwise the manufacture, the convention of burghs, in 1731, recommended to the magistrates of the towns where coarse wool was produced, to meet with the gentlemen of the shire, for the more effectual promoting of the manufacture of wool, concluding, as their opinion, that there was a great prospect of encouragement by spinning of

---

* The slughorn of the burgh was *"Jethert's here!"*
" Then raise the slogan with ane shout—
Fy Tinedaill to it!   Jedbrugh's here!"
Battle of Redswyre.

the wool, and exporting of it in yarn, and for that purpose the spinners should be brought from about Stirling, where it was best understood. The council, however, paid little attention to this branch of trade, till several of the burghers, seeing that other places in Scotland had not only accepted of the grant, but were carrying on the manufactures with spirit on the funds properly belonging to them, applied to the magistrates to grant them a charter for creating a joint-stock company to carry on the trade, which they agreed to. Open proclamation was made by the magistrates to the inhabitants, that certain proposals had been made to them for carrying on a manufactory, and inviting all those inclined to join as partners to attend at the council-house in the following week, to concoct such measures as might be necessary for that purpose. On the day fixed, George Merton, Archibald Douglas, William and John Ainslie, Archibald Crombie, and George Kemp, writers; Robert Richardson, late provost; and Andrew and William Waugh, late conveners of the trades, appeared and intimated that they were ready to join as partners in carrying on the manufactory, on condition that the magistrates in their patent transferred their rights to certain premiums to the company, who would thereupon be empowered to transact with the trustees, and enter into proper contracts with them for the application of the premiums. On considering these proposals, the magistrates granted a charter empowering the company—1st, To import and export the several subjects of their manufactures without trouble or molestation; 2nd, forasmuch as, by His Majesty's letters patent, it is appointed that £700 sterling should be annually employed in carrying on woollen manufactures within the several shires which produced tarred wool, whereof the shire of Roxburgh was one, and that the trustees named in said patent had condescended on Jedburgh as one of the stations, the council enacted and agreed that the company should have full liberty and allowance to apply to the trustees who had the distribution of the said £700, to the end that they might receive such share thereof as might be by them allotted for carrying on the woollen manufactory at Jedburgh; 3rd, power to make byelaws consistent with the public law of the realm and acts of council.

Such, then, was the commencement of manufactures in the burgh of Jedburgh, and it is believed in the district. Owing, it is said, to ignorance of the trade and bad management, the company did not succeed; but the failure of the first attempt did not deter others from entering into the speculation. In 1738 John Mitchel, skinner, Robert Wood, and Robert Dick, weavers and clothiers of the burgh, entered into an agreement for carrying on the manufacture of wool; and, to encourage them to proceed vigorously, they received from the Lord Justice Clerk and Captain Faa the sum of £60, and the council provided them with workhouses and a grassyard adjoining the water, the company being obliged to employ the poor of the burgh in so far as they were capable of working. For this trade the council afterwards purchased the house and yard of Sir John Scot of Ancrum in the Backgate, at the price of £200 sterling.

In 1745 Robert Boswell, merchant and tobacconist in Jedburgh, entered into a contract with the magistrates, whereby he agreed to take the waulk-mill, on a lease of twenty-one years, at a rent of £7, with power to build a snuff-mill at his own expense at the southend of the waulk-mill; and, to encourage him, the magistrates enacted that no dyer should have the privilege of drying their dyed or waulked cloth upon the Canongate bridge, but such as was waulked or scoured in Boswell's mill, under a penalty of half-a-crown. The manufactures in the burgh, however, made very little progress till 1786, when the waulk and snuff-mill passed into the hands of the Messrs. Hilsons, who still possess it, and carry on an extensive trade. In the course of time the corn and lint mill, called the town's mill, was converted into a woollen-mill, and at the present time is in full employment. In 1806 a manufactory was established at Allars, but did little work till it was purchased by a manufacturer from Hawick, who rebuilt the premises, in which he placed improved machinery. At the present time a considerable quantity of material is manufactured at this mill.

THE MILLS OF THE BURGH.—At a very early period a mill is noticed serving the inhabitants of the town. It may be inferred that the mill was coeval with the town, but the first time it appears on record is in the charter of David I. to the canons, granting to them the multure of the mill at which all the men of Jedworth grinded their corn.* Earl Henry repeats the grant in the same words. After William the Lion ascended the throne he confirmed the grant.† There is, however, great difficulty in identifying the mill referred to in these early grants. It is thought that it stood at Allars, near to where the present woollen-mills are situated. There can be no doubt that a corn-mill had been at that place. The late Wm. Veitch, millwright, Jedburgh, informed me that while making a deep cut to carry water from the woollen-mills he came upon the axletree of a mill-wheel of

* Monast. Scotiæ, 29 ; Caledonia, vol. ii. p. 111 : " Multurem molindeni de omnibus hominibus Gedworth ubi castellum est."

† This Charter is engraved, and the original, it is said, is at Dalkeith.

black oak, and from its position and other indi-
cations at the place he was satisfied that a mill had
at an early period existed there. Then there is
something in the rivulet which flows from the
high ground into the river at this place being called
the Molindinear, or miller's burn. It must be kept
in view that the mills at present existing, *i.e.* the
abbey-mill, the two woollen-mills, and the east-mill,
are not within the royalty, and did not become the
property of the burgh till 1669, when they were
purchased from the Marquis of Lothian. At the
Reformation these mills belonged to the Abbey of
Jedburgh, and were all corn-mills. They appear
in the charter of erection of the property of the
monks into a lordship for Alexander Earl of Home
in 1610, and are described as the three corn-mills
of Jedburgh, commonly called the abbey-mill,
town-mill, and east-mill.* A waulk, or fulling-mill,
is also included in the same grant. In the charter of King Charles II. to the burgh of Jedburgh,
in 1671, the descriptive words of the grant to
Earl Home are repeated. It seems plain that at
the dissolution of the monastery the monksmono-
polized all the mills of the locality. It is equally
certain that Home came in place of the monks,

---

* " Tota et integra tria molindena granaria de Jedburgh
non cupatum lie abbay myln, lie town mill, lie east miln ac
moleudenum, fullonum cum multuris sequles, &c." Charter,
dated 1610.

K

and that the family of Lothian, by an excambian with Home, obtained possession of the mills. When the mills were purchased by the magistrates of Jedburgh the community entered into a contract of thirlage, by which they bound themselves to grind their corn at the same mills which their forefathers had selected. But the tacksmen of the burgh proved less liberal than the benevolent monks. While the magistrates enforced their rights with the utmost severity, the inhabitants evaded the thirlage when they could. At last the manner in which the dues were exacted became so burdensome, that the inhabitants refused to grind at the mills, and the magistrates carried the question before the supreme court in 1842, but being unable to connect the present mills with the church or king, as has been done above, the inhabitants were relieved from the thirlage claimed. The principal source of the income of the burgh being thus taken away, the mills were sold to assist in paying the debts contracted by the council.

THE MARKETS OF THE BURGH.—There are several markets and fairs held in the town. A weekly market is held every Tuesday, and during the winter a cattle-market is held on the third Thursday of each month. The Rude-day fair for horses and nolt is held on the 25th September, or the following Tuesday if it should fall on Saturday or

Monday.* In 1556 Queen Mary granted a charter to the burgh, which *inter alia* empowered the " provost, bailies, councillors, and community to have and hold within the said burgh perpetually in all time coming a market cross and weekly market days on Monday and Friday, and free market days annually on the day of the exaltation of the Holy Cross (September 14th) in autumn and during eight days of the same, with a common market annually on the festal day of Pentecost." It was formerly held in the streets of the town, but in 1855 it was removed to a slope of the Dunion, to afford room for the multitude of bestial exposed for sale. This fair in former times was the scene of strife, and many a time and oft have the slogans of the border clans re-echoed through the streets. The most unruly of these clans were the Turnbulls, and so powerful were they, that they defied all local authority till James

---

* The fairs were in the early days held on the Sabbath at the kirk door and yards thereof, but fairs came to be prohibited on that day, and, by act of Parliament Charles II., the royal burghs were prohibited from keeping any market or fair on Monday and Saturday. Fleshers were allowed to keep market on these days. Fairs so held must have had their origin in the feasts which were kept at the Pagan temples, and continued by the Christians, as directed by St. Gregory in the end of the sixth century. When the people met to feast they seem to have taken the opportunity to transact business.

IV. marched an army to the Rule, and seized the heads of the clan. The fair of Our Lady is held on the second Tuesday of August, at which cattle are exposed and shearers hired. The proper day for holding it is on the fifteenth of August, as authorized by the charter of Mary. There is also a fair held on the first Tuesday after Whitsun Tuesday, at which horses and nolt are exhibited.* There was formerly a weekly market held within the

---

* In 1641 an act was passed in favour of the burgh. It proceeded on the narrative " that the brughe of Jedbrughe hes only the priviledge of ane fair in the yeir, and that it is verie necessar, and will contribute and conduce muche to the weill and proffeitt of the country, and of his Magesties subjectis in these pairtis about, if the said brughe had the priviledge of uther twa faires yeirlie for the saill of thair guidis and cattle in the borderis, and these pairtis of the country, next adjacent to the said brughe. Thairfoir our said Souerane Lord and Estaits of Parliament geivis grantis and dispones to the proveist, and bailies, counsall, and communitie of the said brughe of Jedbrughe, and thair successors, proveist, baillies, counsall and communitie thairof, all and haill the priviledge and libertie of uther twa faires yeirlie to be halden at the said brughe of Jedbrughe within the boundis of any pairt of the landis and liberties thairof, wher they sall think maist expedient, the ane thairof to be halden upon the fyfteine day of August, call it the first Lady day, and the uther to be halden upon the fourt day of November, call it St. Leonard's day ;" with customs great and small, and other duties pertaining to a free fair. Sir William Douglas, sheriff of Teviotdale, consented to the act being passed, without any reservation of his privileges in the new fairs.

burgh for horses, nolt, and sheep. This market was generally held at the Townfoot, but was removed to the Abbey Close, where it was held for several years, while the Townfoot quarter was nearly in ruins. In 1750 proprietors of houses situated in that quarter represented to the magistrates that they had not only repaired but rebuilt a great number of the houses that were lying in ruins—that manufactures of both "tanning and weaving, which had arrived at great perfection, were carried on there"—and that they, the inhabitants of the Townfoot, had always cheerfully paid the town's burdens, while the inhabitants of the Abbey Close had refused to pay any public burdens; on which the magistrates called a public meeting of the inhabitants, who came to the conclusion that it would be for the advantage of the town were the market restored to the Townfoot. The meeting also fixed the limits of the market, *i.e.* from Smiths' wynd and Friars' wynd on the west, eastward down the street to the port on the north, and the *Barrass** on the east and west on both sides of the street. The market for corn, which was sold in bulk, began at 12 o'clock, by the ringing of a bell. The cheese and butter market commenced at 9 o'clock in summer and 11 in winter. The salt, herring, and fish market began at 11, as well as the market for

* Forts, or places of defence.

meal and oats.   Unfreemen were allowed to enter
the town with their goods during market days, and
sell the same in the Lawnmarket between the
hours of 12 and 2.

THE GARDENS OF THE TOWN.—David I., restorer
of the magnificent abbey, introduced horticulture
at his castle of Jedburgh, where he had a garden.
There are yet many orchards in and about the
town, indeed almost every spot capable of being
planted seems to have been occupied in this way.
The principal orchard belonged to the monastery;
but there were, and still are, various other gardens
or orchards on the same range of ground, extending
down the river to the foot of the town.   Gardens
have also extended a great way on the north and west
of the town, many of the trees still remaining.   So
famed were the gardens of the town for their produce, that "Jethart pears," *par excellence,* were
frequently cried, at no very remote period, in the
streets of London; and it was not uncommon to
hear in the streets of Newcastle-on-Tyne the cry
"fine *Jethart Burgundy* pears."   The crier, it is
thought, meant *Bergamont* pears, a variety said to
have been introduced by the Romans, and, though
become somewhat liable to canker, still one of
the finest pears in the land.   The remains of the
old pear-trees are fast disappearing.   Within the
last thirty years there remained some very aged

specimens of the Lammas, Bonchrétien, and a few still continue to bear well. The Bonchrétien, Longueville, and autumn Bergamont, are the finest of the old trees. The ancient variety of the Longueville, cultivated in the orchards of the town, is now unknown in France and Belgium. There are still two or three trees of the Longueville remaining in the gardens of the town, one of which, thought to be the oldest, is still to be seen in the friars' garden. About fifty years ago the tree was very large, but then beginning to fall into decay from extreme age. Nearly thirty years since, the top of the tree was removed as dangerous, when the old stock sent out a number of young branches, which bear excellent fruit to this day, many of the pears weighing fifteen ounces. It is now in the last stage of decay. The high winds of 1856 overthrew three of the warden's pear-trees, believed to be about 700 years old, leaving only one of the kind standing in the garden of the convent. The warden's and worrycarl pears seem to have been extensively cultivated by the monks. It is probable that they were used by them in making a beverage like perry, and as vegetables and articles of food at a period when the means of life were scanty. The worrycarl especially is unfit for eating when taken from the tree, but when kept for months and boiled makes an excellent dish. There were also lately several fine old specimens of the Grey Auchen, a pear in high repute as table fruit. A few of the new continental varieties of pears succeed well on standards, such as Marie Louise, Napoleon, &c., which are successfully cultivated in the Anna nursery, producing fine fruit. There is also a plum-tree peculiar to Jedburgh, of great excellence, little inferior to the greengage, and very productive. It has been, it is said, recently introduced into the experimental gardens of Edinburgh and London. The orchards contained many sorts of apple-trees, now little known, having been superseded by new varieties. There are at present no old trees of this kind, as even the robust seldom attain more than 150 or 200 years.

THE GOVERNMENT OF THE BURGH. — Although there is no doubt that Jedburgh was a royal burgh previous to the days of David, there are no notices of the persons composing the corporation till 1296, when the community took the oath of fealty to Edward I. On that occasion the members of the corporation consisted of John Dameson the alderman, and Symon de Ramington, Hewe de Lindsay, Robert le Marshal, Robert Freemanstone, Rauf le Spicer, Stephane le Mareschal, Thomas le Tayllur, Symon le Tayllur, Richard le Clark, Ewy le clerk de Jedworth, Hugh de Walten, the burgesses.*

---

* Prynne, p. 655.

In 1401 Henry IV. appointed Hugh Burgh comptroller of the customs of the town, and about the same time Gerard Heron and William Asplion collected the customs on wool, leather, and hides.* In 1425 Archibald Murray and John Oliuere were baillies of the burgh.† Nine years after John Cant was one of the baillies. In 1454 Philip Pyle was one of the baillies‡; he seems also to have acted as town-clerk. Robert I. granted a charter to the town.§ There are traces in the Town-Council Records of a charter having been granted by one of the Jameses. It was in existence in the seventeenth century.‖ In 1556 Mary gave a charter to the town.¶ From the terms of

* Rotuli Scotiæ, vol. ii. pp. 156-7-9.
† Compota Camerar. vol. iii. p. 155.
‡ Lib. de Mail. pp. 568-9. § Robertson's Index, No. 12.
‖ Burgh Records, vol. i.
¶ MARY, BY THE GRACE OF GOD, QUEEN OF THE SCOTS, greets all the loyal subjects of her realm, both clerical and lay : Know that whereas our burgh of Jedburgh was, by our noble progenitors of blessed memory, to whose souls may God be gracious, erected into a free royal burgh and endowed with sundry privileges, liberties, and advantages, and as such was held and reputed from time immemorial until lately, when our foresaid burgh was, by the inroads and invasions of our old enemies the English, burned, torn down, and laid waste, whereby the evidences and infeftments of the same were destroyed and taken away, so that the provost, baillies, councillors, and community of the same require to suffer heavy loss in their privileges and liberties belonging to said burgh, unless provision be made

this charter it will be seen that the burgh of Jedburgh is raised to an equality with any burgh in
the kingdom. All the charters and grants were

---

against the same; and we, considering that the same burgh is
situated near the borders of our kingdom, and that the
same is a place of refuge to residenters and inhabitants of
the county as well in time of peace as in war, and will afford
aid (*predictis munitis*) in resisting rebels, and that no other
royal burgh exists within the county of Roxburgh, nor any
other place within the same county, so convenient and suitable to protect and receive the liege men of our kingdom for
the resistance of our said English enemies and rebels: And
we wishing that our foresaid burgh may suffer no loss in its
ancient privileges, but rather that it may possess the same
privileges it formerly had, and wishing to afford the inhabitants of the same an opportunity of establishing municipal laws
and secure abodes within the same for the suppression of said
enemies, thieves, and traitors, and of receiving with hospitality the lieges of our kingdom when they come to the same
burgh: Wherefore we, in the exercise of our regal authority
and kingly power, infeft anew and create our foresaid burgh
of Jedburgh into a free royal burgh, perpetually; and further,
we give to the provost, baillies, councillors, and commonality
of the same, all the common property which formerly they
had, and likewise we give to the burgesses and inhabitants
of the same burgh present and future full authority, free
power, and special licence to buy and sell within the said
burgh perpetually in all time coming, wine, wax, woollen
and linen cloth broad and narrow, and every other kind of
merchandise and goods, and to have and hold within the
said burgh millers, bakers, fishers, hangmen, and slaughter-
ers of flesh and fish, and every other artificer appertaining
to the privileges and liberties of a free burgh: We have
granted likewise that there will be free burgesses within the
said burgh, and that the same in all time coming, with the

ratified by parliament in 1597. The act of ratification proceeds on the same narrative as the
charter of Mary, but is more explicit in regard to

---

advice of councillors and office-bearers of said burgh, shall
have the power of electing provosts, baillies, councillors,
and other necessary office-bearers, for the ruling and govern-
ing of the same, with power to the foresaid provost, baillies,
councillors, and community to have and hold within the
said burgh perpetually in all time coming a market-cross,
and weekly market days on Monday and Friday, and free
(*nundinæ*) market days annually in the day of exaltation of
the holy cross in autumn and during eight days of the same,
with a common market day annually in the festal day of
Pentecoste and with tolls, customs, privileges, liberties, and
advantages, free market days, appertaining or seeming justly
to appertain to a free royal burgh in whatever way in the
future, and as freely as our burgh of Edinburgh, or any
other royal burgh, is infeft within the kingdom by us or our
predecessors.

And likewise we give, in virtue of the tenor of our present
charter, power to the foresaid provost, baillies, and office-
bearers of our said burgh, to seize and arrest every person
committing or resetting theft within the said burgh, and to
bring the same to the notice of the assize or assizes, and
to drown, hang, and justify them, and upon them to execute
justice even to death for the like crimes according to the
laws of our kingdom, and for that purpose to summon assizes,
and to build and keep up (*pentibula*) prisons: Our foresaid
burgh of Jedburgh, with the common property of the same,
is to be held and had of us and our successors in free
burghal royalty perpetually, with all and every privilege,
liberty, and concession foresaid, and with all and every
other liberty, advantage, easement, and just pertinents
whatsoever, appertaining, or seeming justly to appertain, to
a free royal burgh, and as freely as our burgh of Edin-

the previous erections, including commonities and common lands, which erections are confirmed, with all privileges, immunities, " freedomes, commonities, and common landis belonging" thereto, with whatever infeftment made thereof before, and wills the same rest and remain with the inhabitants of the said burgh present and to come, and their posterities, as valid and sufficient titles whereby they may possess their said burgh.* Very little

---

burgh, or any other royal burgh of ours, is infeft within our kingdom by us or our predecessors.

In consideration whereof the said provost, baillies, councillors, and community shall render annually to us and our successors the service of the burgh, used and wont, and by making annually with our exchequer a reckoning in respect to the burghal dues, as was wont to be done in all times past.

In testimony whereof we have ordered our great seal to be put to this our present charter. Witnesses, the Most Reverend Father in Christ John Archbishop of St. Andrews, and our chosen relations George Earl of Huntly, Lord Gordon, and Badenoch Chancellor, and Gilbert Earl of Cassilis, Lord Kennedy, Treasurer; our Venerable Father in Christ Donald, Abbot of our Monastery of Cupar, keeper of our Secret Seal; our chosen familiar friends Masters James McGill, of Rankeiller, nether Register of our Rolls, and Clerk of Council; John Ballendine, of Auchinaule, our Justiciary Clerk; and Alexander Livingston, of Donipace, Director of Chancery, at Edinburgh, the twenty-fourth day of the month of November, in the year of our Lord one thousand five hundred and fifty-six, and the fifteenth of our reign.

* Acta Parl. vol. iv. p. 153, No. 62.

information exists as to the sett of the burgh previous to the granting of this charter, or till 1708, when the convention of burghs appointed each royal burgh to return its sett and ancient constitution to the clerk of the burgh, to be recorded in a particular register, under the penalty of £200 Scots. The council of Jedburgh reported that by the ancient constitution of the burgh the council consisted of twenty-five persons, *i.e.* a provost, four baillies, a dean of guild and treasurer, four deacons of trades, including the convener of trades, and fourteen common councillors. The council, with the exception of the deacons of trades, consisted of inhabitants or merchants ; no tradesmen being allowed to enter, the council being represented by their deacons. The election usually took place on the 27th, 28th, or 29th days of September of each year. On the 23rd the provost convened the council for receiving the treasurer's accounts of the preceding year, and electing and leeting of the new council and deacons of crafts for the year to come, and which with the old council, then being eleven, chosen out of the two-and-twenty for the new council, and eight deacons of crafts, making up, with the old council, the number of forty-four persons, who elected the provost, four baillies, dean of guild, and treasurer for the ensuing year. These being so chosen and elected, the eight deacons were removed from the council table, and the old and new council elected four of these to be again on the council. Thereafter the old and new council were all removed, except the magistrates, dean of guild, and treasurer, who put out four of the old council and took in four of the new council in their room. The trades then met and made choice of one of these four to be their convener.* The clerk to the council seems to have been occasionally elected for life, at other times he was elected annually, and frequently the office was disposed of by public roup. Owing to the destruction of the burgh records during the wars with England, there are few notices of the corporation affairs till 1618. At that period it appears that the annual election took place under the auspices of a royal warrant. Andrew Kerr, the Master of Jedburgh, is then seen attending in the council chamber with the king's warrant, and in virtue thereof giving out the provost's leet, and it is said by the clerk of the day that the procedure was according to the usual custom.† The warrant seems to have been engrossed in the council books before proceeding with the election. After Charles I. ascended the throne Lord Jedburgh appeared before the council in 1629 with a commission from the king, and in consequence thereof gave out the leets for provost.‡ In 1630 the pro-

---

* Burgh Records, vol. iii. pp. 29, 30.   † Ib. vol. i. p. 1.

‡ Ib. vol. i. p. 57.

cedure at the election was directed by David Aikenhead, the agent of the royal burghs. At this election the council for the first time voted the leets of the magistracy.* The election of the magistrates and council is now regulated by recent statutes.† The council consists of fifteen persons, including a provost, two baillies, dean of guild, and treasurer.‡ The town-clerk is appointed for life.

The territory over which the magistrates were entitled to exercise jurisdiction cannot be exactly defined, owing to the only charter extant not fixing the bounds of the royalty. It is certain that they could not exercise any authority over the lands which belonged to the monastery, and these included the gardens on the south side of Castlegate, the Abbey Close, Kirkyards, all the south side of the Canongate, Richmond, and Bongate. These subjects were only acquired by the council from the family of Lothian in 1669. The charter of Charles II. in favour of the burgh is dated in 1671, and grants to our beloved John Rutherfurd, present provost, John Haswell, William Scougal, William Ainslie, and Thomas Rutherfurd, bailies ; John Oliphant, dean of guild, and Thomas Porteous, treasurer of our burgh of Jedburgh, for themselves, as the pre-

---

* Burgh Records, vol. i. p. 64. † Acts of Parliament.

‡ It is worthy of notice that the present sett of the burgh is nearly the same as fixed in the eleventh century for all royal burghs.

sent magistrates, and respective office-bearers of our borough aforesaid, and community of the same; and to their successors of provost, bailies, dean of guild, and treasurer, council and community, in all time coming, of our said burgh of Jedburgh, for the common use and utility thereof, and to their successors and assignees whatsoever, heritably and irredeemably, without any reversion or regress, all and every the mills with the lands and others particularly undermentioned, viz.: all and hail the three corn-mills of Jedburgh, commonly called the abbey mill, the town mill, and the east mill, with the waulk mill of Jedburgh, and all and every multures, sequels, mill lands, houses, biggings, yards, and hail respective parts and pendicles thereof, together likewise with the rectorage, tiends of the said lands, mills, and others aforesaid, all presently possessed by James and George Millars, James Riddell, and James Rutherfurd, and, in like manner, all and every the lands, tenements of lands, houses, biggings, yards, orchards, parts, pendicles, and pertinents commonly called the Richmond, as well the property as the superiority of the same lying on the south side of the water of Jed, between or among the mill lands, the foresaid abbey mill possessed by the said James on the west; the lands, houses, and yards, belonging to Sir Francis Scott of Mangerton towards the east, and the public highway on the south, and the foresaid water of Jed on the north parts ; and likewise all and hail the houses and lands of Bongait with the parts, pendicles, and pertinents whatsomever of the same, as well the property as the superiority thereof, bounded by the said water of Jed on the west, the foot of the tower burn on the east, the acre of land belonging to John Scougal and James Robson towards the north, and the acres of land belonging to William Scougal and James Kirkton on the south parts ; and sicklike all and hail the lands and piece of ground of abbey close, with the hail houses, biggings, yards, parts, pendicles, and pertinents whatsoever of the same; together also with the over and nether kirkyards of Jedburgh, and the hail houses, biggings, and yards therein, or in any other part thereof, as well the property as superiority of the same (excepting always therefrom the abbey kirk of Jedburgh with these three houses commonly called Dabies Tower, Wrain's nest, and old Hall, with the cloister on the south-side of the said church of Jedburgh, extending between the minister's manse and the house of George Turner allenarly) ; and in like manner all and hail the yards commonly called the convent-yards of Jedburgh, presently possessed by William Rutherfurd, with the old tower or tower-house in the Dean's Close, and its pertinents, possessed by James Ker, surgeon, and all and hail the houses, biggings, barns, kilns, yards, orchards, and others

whatsomever lying between the west and south
sides of the Canongate and the foresaid water of
Jed; sicklike all and hail the yards called the
friars yards, presently possessed by George Moscripe, late bailie of our said burgh; together with
all right of superiority, jurisdiction, bailliary, feu
duties, profits and emoluments and casualties,
whatsomever any manner of way pertaining and
belonging to the mills, lands, and others particularly above described, excepting and reserving
always therefrom that tenement of land called the
Tower, situate near the cross of our said burgh of
Jedburgh, presently belonging to our beloved cousin
Lord Jedburgh;* and it is declared that sasine taken
at one of the three corn-mills, and upon any part
of the grounds above specified, or any part or
portion of the same, shall be held sufficient for all
and every of the mills, lands, houses, yards, etc.,
notwithstanding any law or custom to the contrary. The said subjects to be held by the provost
and magistrates, council and community, for the
common use and utility of the burgh, " in fee and
heritage for ever," paying yearly furth thereof
the sum of five marks of good and lawful money
at the feast of pentecoste." Under this charter the
jurisdiction of the magistrates over the acquired

---

* This tower stood at the entrance of the Kirkwynd,
and guarded the approach to the abbey from the market-
place.

territory seems ample. The police improvement act extends their jurisdiction over the whole parliamentary bounds.

The powers and privileges of the burgh of Jedburgh have always been as extensive as those of any other burgh in the kingdom.* The magistrates possessed the jurisdiction of sheriffs within the royalty, and by special statute a power was given them to value and sell ruinous houses where the proprietors refused to rebuild or repair them. They also acted occasionally as commissioners of justiciary. In the year 1646 they held a justice court for the trial of Donald M. Vandiller, Hutchinson, Macdonald, and Fogo Hart, who were charged with having been out with the rebels at Kilsyth and Philliphaugh. The prisoners pleaded not guilty, and a jury of burghers was impanelled, who returned a verdict of guilty, and the magistrates sentenced them to be taken to the river Jed, and held below the water till they were " drowned dead."† By the charter of Mary the magistrates were empowered to "drown, hang, and justify," every person committing theft or resetters of stolen goods, and also to execute justice to the death on other offenders, according to the laws of the kingdom. In the Burgh Records (unprinted) there are many instances of persons being banished by

---

* Charter of Mary, Acta Parl. 1597.   † Burgh Records.

the magistrates under the "penalty of death without an assize" in the event of their returning from banishment. It was also a common practice for persons who had offended to enact themselves in the court books to leave the burgh, never to return under the pain of "hanging without an assize." The place of execution of those unfortunate persons sentenced to be hanged or burned was on the top of a hill to the south of the town, called Doomshill, near to where the Free Church manse is situated. It is now properly called *Duns*-hill, the *m* having been changed to an *n*. In 1625 the place is described as consisting of four acres of land, "commonly called *Dums*-hill." At that period Thomas Alison, burgess of Jedburgh, owned the lands. The pool in which criminals were drowned in the river Jed is not known with certainty. Some imagine that it was a deep pool called the black cauldron, a little above the abbey, while others fix upon a part of the river near the Canongate foot.

The burgh has been more than once without magistrates and council. On 15th September 1737, the council having met, it was overtured by the Marquis of Lothian that a new council should be immediately chosen; to which Bailie Waugh answered that no council could be convened in less than 48 hours' notice; besides, it was not the practice to choose a new council sooner than the day immediately before the election of the magistrates and treasurer. These objections being overruled, Bailie Waugh protested and left the room, followed by seven councillors who adhered to him.

The remaining council, however, proceeded and appointed that day eight days for the trades to give in their leet. Deacon Billerwell protested against giving in his leet till the day fixed for that purpose, and also that there was not a quorum of council who had ordered the leet. The deacon's protest was carried by a majority, when the provost and his supporters left. The council again met on the 21st, when Billerwell's right to sit was objected to, on the ground that another deacon of his trade was chosen. The clerk being required to put the vote, Lord Lothian protested, and asked the clerk, was he resolved to obey his order or not ? The clerk meekly said he would mark whatever the majority ordered him ; on which the provost ordered the books to be laid on the table, and a new election proceeded with. Against this procedure Andrew Chalmers protested. It was then moved that the council be adjourned, but the provost refused to put the vote. On the 23rd the dissenting members met and attempted to get into the council-house to proceed with the election, but the provost's party was in possession and refused admittance. His Lordship issued a proclamation, requiring the inhabitants to meet in

the kirkyard to suppress the mob, as the majority
of council and their supporters were called. The
riot act was read by the newly-elected clerk.
The majority then returned to Bailie Riddell's
house, voted the proceedings of the minority null,
and appointed the next day for the deacons giving
in their leets. By the appointed time the council
met and elected the new council. To prevent
Deacon Billerwell voting, he was shut up in the
Tolbooth by the provost's orders. Two days after
the majority of the council, being still refused
admittance to the council-house, elected the magistrates in the market-place. Both parties raised
mutual actions against each other, before the
Court of Session, to have the opposite election
declared illegal. The House of Lords, on appeal,
voided both elections, by which the town was left
without magistrates. On this judgment being
known in the burgh, the inhabitants bearing a
share in the burdens of the burgh presented a
petition to his Majesty, stating that there was a
total obstruction of justice in the burgh, and
praying that his Majesty would be graciously
pleased to empower them to proceed to a new
election of magistrates. On considering the petition, with a report thereon by the Lord Advocate,
his Majesty, by the advice of his Privy Council,
on 31st July, 1730, ordered a poll election to take
place by all the burgesses and inhabitants residing

within and bearing a share of the common burdens of the burgh; and Archibald Douglas of
Cavers, the Lord Cranstoune, Robert Elliot of
Midlemmill, Robert Scot, Archibald M'Auly, Lord
Provost of Edinburgh, James Carmichael, James
Fall, William Kirk, Patrick and Alexander M'William, or any of them, were required to convene
and assemble the burgesses and inhabitants, and
direct the said election according to the rules
observed in such cases. By virtue of this warrant,
the commissioners met and superintended the
election, which was afterwards confirmed by his
Majesty.

The next time the burgh was bereaved of its
magistrates was in 1767. At this period Colonel
Warrender and the Hon. Captain Maitland stood
for the representation of the burghs, and, in order
to get the good will of the council, both offered
freely for the seat. The Colonel, who had neither
interest nor connections in the burgh, finding that
he had to contend against a family who had the
greatest influence in the burghs of Lauder and Jedburgh, offered £1,000 to the town and £100 to
the trades. An offer of this kind could not fail to
have staggered the good faith of the burgesses,
even supposing their finances to have been in a
good state, but, when these were at a low ebb, it
not only made a deep impression, but many of the
fastest friends of the Lauderdale family veered

round and declared in favour of the gallant Colonel. But the Captain and his friends were not idle, and endeavoured to fight the Colonel with his own weapons. They accordingly entered into a regular bargain with the Town Council, whereby Captain Maitland agreed to give them a bill for £1,500, on condition that he should receive their support at the election. This, being £400 higher than the offer made by Colonel Warrender, was accepted by the Council, with the exception of Robert Oliver, innkeeper, who refused to sign; but it turned out that this refusal to sign the corrupt bargain did not arise from pure motives, but from the fact that £1,700 of the Colonel's money was deposited in bags under his charge, and that of Robert Boswell. Although this transaction was confined to the election of a member of Parliament, an action of reduction of the annual election of magistrates was raised by Colonel Warrender's party, in consequence of which the burgh was under the care of managers appointed by the Court of Session for six years. The defenders to the action stated, " that in Jedburgh it was never deemed wrong to accept of a present from the candidate for the representation; on the contrary, it was meritorious to get something done for the good of the town upon an occasion of this kind."*

* Session Papers.

When the burghs of Scotland were taxed in 1556, Jedburgh ranked as to wealth with Kirkcudbright, Wigtown, Whitern, Dunfermline, and Elgin. In 1695 Jedburgh stood seventeenth in wealth of the sixty-five burghs of the kingdom, and paid £100 out of the £10,000 of assessment. In 1788 the revenue of the corporation, as reported to parliament, was £309 13s. 7d. sterling. With the exception of a small sum drawn from customs, the burgh has now no revenue whatever.

ARMS OF THE BURGH.—The armorial bearings of the burgh are different now from what they were at a previous period. In the year 1296, when the community of Jedburgh swore fealty to Edward I., the seal attached to the declaration had for the device—*azure an unicorn tripping, argent, ringed, maned, and horned.* It is said that these arms were to be seen upon the cross during the end of last century, and it is thought that the unicorn was discovered lately in a cell of the old prison.* There can be little doubt that the above armorial bearings are the earliest yet discovered of the burgh, and there can be as little doubt that the seal was carried off by Edward along with the seal of Roxburgh and many others. I have been able to trace other two seals—one a small seal, the de-

---

* *Ut supra*, vol. i. p. 327.

vice, a unicorn on a shield, and the legend, " *S. comunitate de Jedburgh;*" the other a large seal, having the Virgin and Child in the centre, with the legend in the outer circle, " *Sigillum comune burgi de Jedburgh.*" Both these seals, it is thought, belong to a period later than the middle of the seventeenth century, as the name of the town begins about that time to be spelt Jedburgh, as on the seals ; at least I have not been able to discover the name of the town written in that form at an earlier period. The present seal of the burgh owes its origin to a less remote period. The device is a border warrior, armed *cap-à-pie,* with a sword and jeddart staffi, mounted on a charger, also in part covered with armour, and which he is pushing on at full gallop. The legend, " *Strenue et prospere,*" often read " strength and prosperity," but which may be perhaps more properly rendered " fortune attends the brave." The adoption of such a legend and device is obvious, from the fact that Jedburgh is situated close upon the borders of what was once a hostile kingdom, from whence issued many a gallant band of warriors on the Scottish frontier in revenge of a kingly insult, or for the ignoble purpose of seizing the flocks and herds of Scotland, in repelling of whom the men of Jedburgh did good service. The device shows the warrior of Teviotdale hastening

to the rescue, and the legend that the brave are
seldom unfortunate.

ANNALS OF THE BURGH AND CASTLE.—In the beginning of the ninth century, the town and territory
of Geddewrd was the property of Egfird, Bishop of
Lindisfairn, by whom it was gifted to the see of
which he was bishop. It is impossible to fix the
exact period, but as the bishop died in 838, it is
probable that the benefaction was made shortly
after he succeeded to the bishopric in 830. Although the exact period the town was erected into
a burgh is not known, it is certain that about 1097
the town, under shelter of the castle, had risen to
be a burgh and royal domain. David, previous to
and after his becoming king, resided here, and
Earl Henry his son dated a charter at Jedburgh.*
Malcolm IV. delighted to dwell here, and where
he finished his youthful career in 1165.† William the Lion also made it his residence, and
where he granted many charters between 1165
and 1214.‡ King Alexander II. also lived here,
from whence he dated many grants, and where he

---

* Coldingham Charters in Raines Durham, No. 108.
† Chron. Mail., p. 80.
‡ Register of Glasgow, p. 63 ; Lib. de Chalchou, pp. 306,
12, 14, 16 ; Lib. de Mel., p. 58 ; Acta Parl., vol. i. p. 76.

died, in September, 1217.*   Alexander III. met
the English deputies here, and concluded peace;
his army at the time lying in the forest.†   Here a
son was born to him, named Alexander.   On the
14th of October, 1285, the same king was married
to Jolinda, daughter of the Count Dreux.‡   Before
1329 King Robert Bruce granted a charter in
favour of James de Cunningham of the territory of
Hassendean, on the Teviot, which was dated at
Jedburgh.§   The town was also the residence of
Queen Mary, who held her courts here in 1566,
and where she resided from the 8th of October to
the 9th of November of that year.   It was also
the place where the armies of Scotland assembled,
and it was from the earliest times the seat of the
courts of the king for the administration of justice
to the inhabitants of an extensive district.

It does not appear that the burgh was at any
time fortified by walls or ditches, although it was
deemed of great strength.   Though without regular walls, the burgh was strong from its natural
position, and the manner the houses were built,
there being no entrance except by the four ports
of the town, which were continually guarded by
watchful sentinels.   The town was also defended

---

* Chron. Mail., p. 32.   † Ib. p. 184.
‡ Fordun, book x. c. 40, *ut supra*, vol. i.
§ Reg. Mag. Sig., p. 5, No. 13.

by six strong towers, placed so as to protect the four quarters of it; and the monastery possessed a tower in the market-place, which guarded the entrance to their house by the Kirkwynd. The castle commanded the entrance at the town-head, and so long as it remained in the hands of its rightful owners, rendered an attack from that quarter not to be dreaded. Behind the castle lay the impervious forest, and the steep banks of the Jed formed its defence on the south-east. From all this it is obvious that the taking of Jedburgh could be no easy task, peopled as it was with men trained to war, with the *staffs* within their grasp, ready to start at the slightest summons of their leader to join in the thickest of the fight. During the fifth century the military strength of the burgh consisted of 410 men inured to battle. The trades alone mustered one hundred well armed men, under the command of their own officers, *" to go out with the magistrates for the good of the burgh."* It is not therefore to be wondered at that the slogan of *"Jethart's here!"* produced a sensation in contending armies.*

In 1174 the castle was delivered by William of Scotland at the pleasure of the two Henrys and their sons, for ensuring the observance of a treaty

---

* It is reported on good authority that the same cry was heard on the heights of the Alma in the front of the battle.

made at Falaise.   In the following year it was restored.* In 1221 the town and its pertinents, with other lands that were to yield £1,000, were settled on Johanna, the sister of Henry III. of England, when she married Alexander II. of Scotland.   In 1258 conferences were held here between Alexander and the English commissioners, which lasted three weeks, when the Scottish army was assembled in the forest.   The English commissioners, awed by the martial position of the Scots, concluded peace, which was afterwards ratified. In the great tower of Jedburgh Castle, Alexander III., lying sick, admitted into his presence various nobles, who witnessed William Cumming resign certain lands to the Bishop of Glasgow in 1263.   In 1287 the winter storms were so severe that a great number of houses in the town were destroyed.   The wardens of the kingdom issued a mandate, under the common seal of the kingdom, for repairing the walls of the houses.   A Master Imbert was deputed to inspect the town, give in an estimate thereof, which he did, under the seal of the abbot of Jedburgh.   The repairs, including carriage and all other expenses, were estimated at £67 0s. 7½d.†   In 1288 the wardens of the kingdom ordered the castle to be victualled, which was

---

* Redpath, p. 100.
† Compota Camerar, vol. i., pp. 68-9.

done with sixty-six acres of meadow hay, twelve chalders of wheat, eight casks of wine, twelve chalders of salt, at a cost of £54 11s. 11d.* On Edward I. of England being appointed referee in the disputes which followed the death of Alexander, and having obtained seizin of the kingdom, in order that he might give effect to his judgment, committed the castle of Jedburgh to the keeping of Laurence de Seymnor, and in the same year it passed into the hands of Brian Fitzallan, to be held during the king's pleasure.† In 1295 the town and castle were delivered in charge to the Bishop of Carlisle and the Abbot of New Abbey, by John Baliol, for security, while Edward was absent in France.‡ Next year it was delivered to Thomas of Burnham, and in the following year it was committed to Hugh of Bysland, servants of the English king.§ The same year the community of Jedburgh swore fealty to the English king. About this time Bishop Beck of Durham was at Jedburgh, where a cousin of his was slain, in consequence of which Edward I. demanded that the castle should be delivered up to him. About 1297 Sir William Ruthven was governor of Jedburgh. He and Sir Christopher Seton had taken it from

---

* Compota Camerar, vol. i., pp. 68-9.
† Rotuli Scotiæ, vol. i., pp. 2-3.
‡ Ib., vol. i., pp. 21-22 ; Rymer, vol. ii., pp. 692-3.
§ Rotuli Scotiæ, vol. i., p. 23-36 ; Rymer, vol. ii., p. 717.

the English, and the custody of Roxburgh and Jedburgh was conferred on them. In 1304 Edward was at Jedburgh, in his progress through Scotland.* Next year the castle was committed to the custody of the English king.† In 1309 Edward II. ordered Henry de Beaumont to fortify the castle.‡ The trades of Jedburgh were present at the battle of Bannockburn, and took from the English a flag, which is still carefully preserved, and unfurled on great occasions, or when they walk in procession. In 1318 the castle was recovered from the English. In 1320, the town, castle, and forest of Jedburgh, formed part of the grant by King Robert to the good Sir James Douglas.§ In 1334 Edward Baliol ceded the town and forest of Jedburgh and Bonjedworth to the English king, who appointed William de Pressfen to take sasine thereof in his name. During these eventful times the forest of Jedburgh was deemed the most secure retreat for individuals or for armies. About 1342 the town and castle were recovered by the gallantry of William Douglas, aided by the people's zeal, but were again lost on the captivity of David II. While the castle remained in the

---

* Rotuli Scotiæ, vol. i., p. 154.

† Ryley's Placita, p. 505; Rotuli Scotiæ, vol. i., p. 154.

‡ Rotuli Scotiæ, vol. i., p. 80.

§ Robertson's Index, p. 10, No. xvii.; and p. 21, No. xxvii.

hands of the English it proved a serious annoyance to the neighbouring country. When the town, castle, and surrounding country fell into the hands of Edward III., in 1356, he conferred the same on Henry de Percy, in exchange for Annandale.* In 1367 this king granted to the son of the said Henry the same territory, and also appointed him overseer of all the castles and strengths on the border, including Berwick-on-Tweed.† In 1373 letters of protection were granted to all persons who assisted in repairing the castle of Jedburgh and *fortifications of the town and castle.* The letters are dated in the months of January, February, March, May, July, August, October, and November of that year.‡ Next year letters of protection were granted to a number of persons for the like purpose. By a treaty of peace, made by the wardens of the marches, the inhabitants of the town and castle were allowed to enter England for the purposes of traffic.§ In 1393 Robert III. granted to George

---

* Rotuli Scotiæ, vol. i. p. 793. "Castrum et constabulariam ville de Jeddeworth et villas de Jeddeworth, Bonjeddeworth et Hassenden ac forestam de Jedeworth," &c. The places here meant are the present Jedburgh, what is now called Old Jedworth, Bonjedworth, and Hassenden.

† Ib. vol. i. p. 911.

‡ Rotuli Scotiæ, vol. i. pp. 961, 973.

§ Rymer, vol. viii. p. 527.

M

Earl of Angus the sheriffship of Roxburghshire, with the town, castle, and forest of Jedburgh.* In 1403 the whole of Teviotdale was bestowed on Henry Percy, the Earl of Northumberland, who lost it by his rebellion during the same year, but it was restored to him in the course of the following year.† Next year Henry IV. claimed the town, castle, and territory as his own property.‡ In 1409 the commons of Teviotdale, harassed by the garrison of Jedburgh, rose *en masse,* took the castle, and with great labour razed it to the ground. For this service it was proposed in a convention at Perth to raise money by a tax on each house that raised *reek;* but the governor of the kingdom opposed it on the ground that no tax should be levied under his government, lest the poor should curse him as the introducer of such an abuse, and ordered payment to the men of Teviotdale out of the royal customs.§ Thus fell Jedburgh Castle, successively the seat of kings, the scene of pleasure, and the theatre of deadly strife. It is to be regretted that the destruction of this powerful castle was rendered necessary. What a beautiful accompaniment it would have been, had it existed to this day, to

---

* Robertson's Index, No. 7, p. 139.
† Rotuli Scotiæ, vol. ii. p. 172.   ‡ Ib. vol. ii. p. 174.
§ Fordun, lib. xv. c. 21.

the ruined abbey in the vale below! The last portion of the walls was removed in 1820, and a prison now occupies its site. In 1410 Sir Robert Umfraville made an incursion into Scotland, burnt Jedburgh, and laid waste the adjacent country. It was again burnt by him in 1416. In 1434 an act was passed, ordaining all royal burghs to have hostelries with rooms and stables, and that men should find there bread and ale for themselves, and food for their horses.* In 1436 it was enacted that these houses be shut at nine o'clock, and if any person be found therein drinking after that hour he was to be put in prison. In 1461 the Abbot of Jedburgh and the Commissioner for the Burgh sat in the Parliament held at Edinburgh in the month of May. In 1464 the town was burnt by the Earl of Warwick. In 1469 the Commissioner for the Burgh was present at the Parliament held at Edinburgh in November. The disorders on the marches having risen to a great height by the feuds of rival clans, a justiciary court was fixed to be held by Andrew Lord Gray at Jedburgh, on the 17th November, 1510; but as the ordinary powers of the law proved insufficient to apprehend the offenders, James IV., determined to afford protection to his subjects, marched during the

---

* Acta Parl. vol. ii. p. 6.

night of the 8th with a powerful force to the Rule water, seized about 200 of the clan Turnbull, and other broken men, and carried them to the court at Jedburgh, with halters round their necks. Several of the ringleaders were hanged, others imprisoned, and the rest dismissed upon giving hostages for their future good behaviour. Bishop Lesley's account of this remarkable occurrence is :—" That the kingraid furth of Edinburgh the 8th of November, on the nycht, weill accumpanet, to the watter of Roulle ; quhair he tuik divers broken men and brocht them to Jedwart: of quhom sum was justified. And the principallis of the trubillis cum in lyning claithes, with nakit sordis in thair hands and wyddis about thair nechis, and pat thame in the kingis will : quhe wes send to divers castells in ward with sindry otheris of that country men also, quhair the bourdouris wes in greiter quietnes thairefter." * In 1513 a convent of Carmelite friars was founded here. After the death of James IV. and his principal nobles on the fatal field of Flodden the excesses on the borders became greater than ever. A chronicler of the events of that day quaintly informs us that " the oppression done to the poor commons in that wicked and most miserable time, when justice

---

* Lesley, p. 81 ; Hollingshed, vol ii p. 132 ; Balfour's Annals, vol. i. p. 234.

seemed to sleep, and rapine with all the other sorts and rabble of injurious violence invaded her empty seat, trampling over all as a conqueror." To put down the banditti on the borders the Duke of Albany gathered a great army, and came to Jedburgh in the autumn of 1514, but the feeble arm of the regent was unable to repress the violence of the border clans. John Home, Abbot of Jedburgh, was banished beyond the Tay. The Lord Home, his brother William, and Ker of Fernieherst, were arrested. The two former were tried and executed, but Ker was spared. About 1520 a dispute arose between the Earl of Angus and Andrew Ker of Fernieherst in regard to the holding of courts at Jedburgh. The lands belonged to Angus, but the Kers of Fernieherst claimed jurisdiction over the forest as bailies of the Earl of Arran and hereditary bailies of the abbey. Sir James Hamilton, an illegitimate son of Arran, aided Ker with 400 men of the Merse; but Cessfurd, the Warden of the Marches, took part with Angus, and with a large force intercepted Hamilton at Kelso on his way to Jedburgh. The followers of Hamilton, seeing the power of the warden, fled and left him in danger, and it was with great difficulty he escaped to Home Castle. Next morning the parties made a temporary settlement of the dispute by agreeing to hold their courts in the forest three miles distant

from each other.*   It seems that Fernieherst
finally yielded his claim in favour of the Douglas.
It is said that this dispute was the origin of the
noted skirmish in the streets of Edinburgh called
" Clean the Causey."   In 1523 the Earl of Surrey,
in retaliation of several inroads made by the Scots
borderers into England, collected an army of
nearly 10,000 men, chiefly consisting of cavalry,
and marched upon Jedburgh.   The vanguard of
the army was commanded by Lord Westmoreland,
in which were all the men of the bishopric, and
along with him Sir William Bulmer, Sir William
Evers, who acted as marshals, with Lord Dacre
and his company; with Surrey remained· the
men taken from various garrisons of the north,
and the men of Northumberland.   To such a
force, so well commanded and appointed, the
Scots could only oppose about 1500 men, but they
were composed of the *" staffis"* and the pick of
the border soldiery.   The town was defended
with great obstinacy; Surrey led the attack
upon the abbey, which was fiercely defended.
As the English gained upon the Scots the latter
manned the towers of the town and continued
the defence of each with great bravery.   Seeing
that the town could not be taken as long as any
portion of it afforded the means of defence to

* Hollingshed, vol. ii. p. 160.

the inhabitants, Surrey ordered Sir William Bulmer and Thomas Tempest to burn it to the ground; yet in this extremity those in the towers and abbey continued the defence amidst the burning ruins until the town was completely destroyed. Next day Lord Dacre was despatched by Surrey to take Fernieherst, which he accomplished with great loss. In the evening Dacre, contrary to Surrey's command, encamped with his cavalry beyond the limits of the camp, which the latter had chosen. While Dacre was at supper with Surrey, about eight o'clock, the horses of his company broke loose and suddenly ran out of the fold in which they were placed in such numbers as to cause great alarm in the other fold. The camp watch being set, the horses ran along the camp, where they were received with showers of arrows and volleys of musketry, the English imagining them to be Scots rushing on to assault their camp. The horses, maddened by such a reception, ran like wild deer into the fold, above 1500, in various companies; in one place fifty fell down a great rock* and were killed, and above 200 ran into the still burning town, and were seized upon by the women and carried away.

---

* The rock here alluded to is supposed to be a part of the scaur at Inchbonnie.

Surrey himself estimated the loss of his horses at about 800.   In a letter written by the general from Berwick to the king in regard to the expedition, he says :—" I dare not write the wonders that my Lord Dacre and all his company doo saye they sawye that nyght six tyms of sperits and fereful sights.   And unyversally all their company saye playnly the devil was that nyght among theym six tyms.   I assure your grace I fownd the Scottis at this tyme the boldest men and the hottest that ever I sawye any nation, and all the journey upon all parts of the armye kepte us with soo contynuall skyrmishe that I never sawe the like."   In the same letter he states " that the toune was much better than I weened it had been, for there was two tymys moo houses than in Berwicke and well buylded, with many honest and fair houses therein sufficient to have lodged a 1000 horsemen in garysson, and six good towers therein, which toune and toweris be clenely destroyed, brent, and throwne downe, so surely brente that no garyssons nor nane other shal be lodged there until the tyme it be new buylded." *

In 1526 James V., accompanied by Angus, Home, Lennox, Cessfurd, and Ferniehcrst, made

---

* Cott. MSS.; Minstrelsy, Appendix, No. L.

a progress to Jedburgh on the 24th July, for the purpose of quelling some flagrant disorders on the marches, but after remaining three days returned without any obedience being paid them. The king was also in Jedburgh after the battle of Melrose and remained four days. In 1542 William Alison, provost of Jedburgh, sat in Parliament as Commissioner of the Burgh. He was also present in several succeeding parliaments.* Next year the king was at Jedburgh with an army of 6,000 men, to put down the disturbances in the district caused by the feuds of the Scots, Elliotts, Armstrongs, and other border chieftains. Soon after his arrival a general submission was made to him by all the leaders on the borders. Examples were made of twelve of the principal offenders, and the rest spared on giving security for their future good behaviour by oath and hostage. These hostages were executed within a few months, as their friends would not abstain from robbery.† In June, 1544, Jedburgh was taken and burned by Sir Ralph Evers. In February, 1545, Evers and Laiton, having obtained a grant from King Henry of all their past and future conquests in Scotland, arrived in Jedburgh with an army of 5,000 men, where they

---

* Acta Parl. vol. ii. p. 410.
† Hollingshed, vol. ii. p. 174.

stopped a night. In September of the same year, Hereford, commander of the English army in the north, entered Scotland with 12,000 men, and burnt the two towers of Bonjedworth and the town of Jedburgh, with its abbey and the friars. The town was also occupied by part of Protector Somerset's * army after the battle of Pinkie, in 1547. When he returned to England he left a company of soldiers to defend the place, who occupied it till 1549. At that time Monsieur d'Esse was ordered by the queen-dowager to go to Jedburgh, to prevent the English garrison from fortifying the place. On his approach the English left the town. The French general remained for a considerable time at Jedburgh, whence he made several successful incursions into the English border, and reduced Fernieherst and other places in the neighbourhood. The English, grieved at the success of the French, collected an army of 8,000, which they intended to employ in driving him out of Jedburgh ; but he, receiving intelligence of their design, and not having more than 1500 men and 500 horse fit for action, retired into the interior parts of the country, where his enemies could not follow him.† The English army, under the command of the Earl of Rutland, arriving at Jedburgh soon after the French had retired

* Formerly Earl of Hereford.
† Hollingshed, vol. ii. p. 254.

over Ancrum bridge, found the town desolate and the houses uncovered. The goods belonging to the citizens were carried to the forts of Hundalee, Bonjedworth, and other places. After taking these two forts and Hunthill, the English, wanting provisions, retired.

A peace in 1551 put an end to this most destructive war, and the governor and queen-mother turned their attention to the administration of justice on the borders. While the governor was at Jedburgh in 1552 he removed certain magistrates who had negligently governed their district. While the court remained at Jedburgh David Panter, a person of great learning and experience, arrived at the town from France, where he had been for seven years as ambassador *leger*, and having declared in the assembly of the nobility the manner in which he had accomplished the office intrusted to him, he was greatly commended for the wisdom, diligence, and truth displayed by him in the office. He was, in presence of the whole assembly, with great solemnity consecrated Bishop of Ross. At the same time the governor, with the view of stimulating the border chiefs to virtuous actions, conferred the honour of knighthood on Cessfurd, Ferniehorst, Littledon, Coldingknows, Greenhead, Buccleuch, and other valiant men.* Buccleuch enjoyed his honours

---

* Lesley, book x. p. 516; Hollingshed, vol. ii. p. 266.

for a short time; he was murdered in the streets of Edinburgh by his hereditary enemies the Kers, during the following year.

In 1560 Andrew, the Commendator of Jedburgh and Restenot, sat in Parliament. The Provost of Jedburgh represented the burgh.*

In September 1561 Mary arrived in Scotland, and found Knox thundering his anathemas against Popery, and the banditti on the borders so numerous and daring as to set at defiance all lawful authority. By the advice of her council Mary appointed her brother, Lord James, lieutenant and justiciar, empowering him to hold courts at Jedburgh for the trial of offenders, and to employ such forcible methods as should appear necessary for seizing the accused parties, and destroying their houses and places of defence. To enable him more effectually to carry out the purposes of his mission, the nobles, freeholders, and fighting men of the shires of Berwick, Roxburgh, Selkirk, and Peebles, the three Lothians, Stirlingshire, Clackmannan, and Kinross, and the shire of Fife, were summoned to meet him at Lauder on the 13th November, 1561, with sufficient armour and provisions to serve for twenty days, and to pass with him to this town, where the justice court was fixed to be held on the 15th. Attended by the judges,

* Acta Parl. vol. ii. p. 525.

the Lord James held the ayre, and the sword of justice was not wielded in vain. The result is learned from a letter written by Randolph to Secretary Cecil in the beginning of December following :—" Of the Lord James's doings at Jedburgh, and of the meeting at Kelso with the Lord Gray and Sir John Foster, I doubt not but your honour hath been advertized. He burnt many houses; he hanged twenty-two or twenty-three, and he brought to this town forty or fifty, of which there are twenty-three in the Castle of Edinburgh; the chiefest of all the clans on the borders are come in to take what order it pleaseth the Queen to appoint."*

But these rigorous measures did not produce the expected quiet. The borderers were erelong at their accustomed occupations. While at Alloa, in the month of August, 1566, Mary resolved to hold a justice ayre and assemble a parliament at Jedburgh in October following. Accordingly, on the 6th of October, Bothwell, who was at the time lieutenant on the borders, left Edinburgh to bring in the thieves of Liddesdale to the court at Jedburgh.† The Queen, officers of state, and whole court departed for Edinburgh on the 8th of said month, and proceeded to Jedburgh, where

---

* Keith, pp. 203-8.   † Diurnal of Occurents.

she held a privy council on the 10th.   After
holding a criminal court for a week, and transact-
ing other public business, she set out on the 17th,
with an escort, it is said, of twelve horsemen, for
her castle on the Hermitage, to inquire into an
outrage which she was informed on her way out
to Jedburgh had been committed on her lieutenant, while he was endeavouring to apprehend
offenders charged to appear at the justice ayre,
by John Elliot, of Park, celebrated even among
the noted thieves of Liddel.†   The Queen travelled by the way of Hawick, along the high
ground which slopes into the river Teviot, and
from thence between the Slitrig and the Allan by
Pencrestpen, Priesthaugh, and the Maiden Paps,
which form the table-land between Teviotdale and
Liddesdale.   She then descended the west end of
the Greatmoorhill by Braidlecburn to the castle.
When within a short distance of the castle her
palfrey stuck in the moss, and the spot where this
occurred is still popularly called the " Queen's
Mire."   By following this road Mary kept the
whole way upon the territory of chieftains friendly
to her person.   For miles the road ran through
the barony of Cavers, possessed by her own Sheriff
of Teviotdale, and the barony of Hawick, in the

---

* Privy Council Register; Keith, pp. 351-3.
† Birrel's Diary, p. 5; Keith, p. 351; Diurnal of Occurents.

possession at that period of Dru mnrig, would take her to within a few miles of the Hermitage. Close on the west of her route lay the barony of Branxholm, in the hands of Buccleuch, ever ready to support her interests by the sword. Had the Queen taken the road by the *Knott* in the *Gate*, she would in the course of her journey down the Liddell and up the Hermitage have passed in the near vicinity of twelve bastile-houses of clans hostile not only to her rule but to any authority whatever, and who were actually at that time in open rebellion.* While this road was safe I am doubtful whether she could have taken a shorter or better. At that season of the year, and at that period, it would have been almost impossible for any one except a moss-trooper to have travelled in a direct line across the mountains from Jedburgh to Hermitage. Even at this day it requires daylight and an intimate acquaintance with the district to travel that swampy region. The Queen performed this journey in one day, a distance going and coming of fully forty-four miles. Many writers in alluding to this subject express great surprise that a female could accomplish such a journey in one day through such a district, forgetting that the women of that day were accustomed to the saddle, and thought nothing

---

* Map of the district, 1590.

of a ride of forty miles, and that Mary herself had once galloped from Perth to Queensferry when Murray lay on one side of the road and Argyle on the other to intercept her. At the present day it is quite common for persons considerably advanced in years to come on foot to Jedburgh from places situated beyond the Castle of Hermitage and return on the same day. Forty miles is not yet deemed a long day's walk on the borders.

Next day (the 17th) the Queen was seized with a fever, which for ten days kept her in a very doubtful state, but her youth and good constitution, aided by the skill of a physician of the name of Naw, saved her. On her falling sick intelligence was sent to Darnley, her husband, who was then residing with his father at Glasgow, but he came not to see her till the 28th of October, and remained only one night at Jedburgh.

The business of the circuit being finished, and the Queen able to travel, she left Jedburgh on the 9th of November for Kelso, followed by her court and about 1,000 horsemen.*

---

* While it is not my intention here to enter upon a vindication of the character of Mary, I cannot help noticing that the visit to Hermitage is laid hold of by her traducers as an important element in proof of her guilty connection with Bothwell; but an examination of the dates of her

While Mary resided here she occupied, as has been already stated, a house in the Backgate.* The room in which tradition says she slept is on the third floor, with a window looking into the garden. A quantity of old tapestry, which it is said covered the walls of the room, is still exhibited. On the same authority, the bedstead on which her Majesty slept, it is said, was presented to Sir Walter Scott in 1824 by Mr. Winterop, an auctioneer in Jedburgh.

Next year Murray was again at Jedburgh, with the view of apprehending the thieves whom he expected to be present at the Rood-day fair; but they, having got notice of his approach, kept out of his way. On 30th December, 1562, a commission was given to John Knox to come to Jedburgh and take trial of a slander against Paul Methven, minister of the burgh, and to report to the consistory of the kirk at Edinburgh, which he did, and Mr. Methven was deposed and excommunicated. In 1564, on his petition, the

---

arrival at Jedburgh, her stay there, and the circumstances under which she visited Bothwell, removes any impression that her journey to that wild region was in the least degree inconsistent with her dignity as queen or her honour as a wife. It is, however, to be regretted, for the sake of Mary, that the weapon of the thief did not prove fatal to the lieutenant.

* *Ut supra*, p. 109.

N

Assembly admitted him to repentance, but refused to expunge the process against him from the record and to admit him to the ministry. In June 1566 the Assembly ordained him to appear personally before the Assembly, "and having entered, he prostrated himself before the brethren, weeping and howling."* A committee was ordained to take order in the premises, and whatever they appointed Paul Methven was to obey. The committee ordained him to appear at the kirk-door when the second bell rang, clad in sack-cloth, bareheaded and barefooted, and there remain till he was taken in to the sermon, and placed publicly above the people in time of every sermon during two days; and again, on the next Sunday to compear in like manner at the end of the sermon, and declare signs of inward repentance to the people, and humbly require the kirk's forgiveness, which being done he was to be clad in his own apparel, and received into the society of the kirk as a "livelie" member thereof.†

In April 1570 the Earl of Sussex, and Sir John Foster, warden of the middle marches, with their forces, arrived at Jedburgh, where they were hospitably received by the magistrates and inhabitants, in consequence of which the town was

* Acts of Assembly.   † Ibid.

spared; and the like favour was shown to the
Laird of Cessfurd, warden of the Scottish middle
marches, and to his friends and dependants; for
Cessfurd, coming to Jedburgh, made his submission to the Earl of Sussex, and, having satisfied
the general that he had not molested the peace
with England by entertaining any of the English
rebels or being concerned in the late incursions,
was taken under the protection of the English,
and had all his possessions and those of his
kindred preserved unhurt. Next year a Parliament was held at Stirling, at which the young
king was exhibited to the council. At this time
(1571) the kingdom was divided,—one party
standing for the young king, and the other espousing the cause of the queen. The town of
Jedburgh, from the beginning of the strifes, had
always been in favour of the king. A pursuivant
was sent from the newly-elected authority in
Edinburgh to proclaim their letters in Jedburgh.
On his arrival he mounted the cross, which in
ancient times stood in the middle of the market-
place, and proceeded to read the letters to the
multitude congregated on the street. The people,
although not acknowledging the authority who
sent the herald, heard him patiently till he came
to a part of the letters which bore that *the lords
assembled in Edinburgh had found all things done
and proceeded against the Queen null, and that*

all men should obey her only. But no sooner had he uttered these words than the storm of popular feeling arose, and the provost of the burgh, who was on the spot, after abusing the queen in a very rude and indelicate manner, caused the herald to come down from the cross, and after he was on the street made him eat the letters which he had partly read ; and, in order that the herald might be fully satisfied and paid his wages, the provost unloosed his breeches by force and applied a strap of a bridle with a not very lenient hand to his posteriors, threatening him if ever he returned he should lose his life. The Lords Fernieherst and Buccleuch, hearing of such an affront being put upon their authority, collected 3,000 men, consisting of their friends and dependants and of a number of banditti on the marches, English as well as Scots, and marched to reduce Jedburgh. The Regent Murray, hearing of this expedition, immediately despatched to the aid of the burgh the Lord Ruthven with a small body of horsemen and musketeers, which were joined by a few more from the neighbouring county of Berwick. Buccleuch and Fernieherst, informed of Ruthven's being advanced to Dryburgh, moved very early in the morning towards Jedburgh to prevent his entering it. At the same time the Regent charged the Laird of Cessfurd to hasten to the aid of the burgh with a chosen body of troops.

The burghers, although not nearly equal in number to the army of Fernieherst, were not daunted, but with the Laird of Cessfurd and their valiant provost at their head boldly marched out of the town and offered battle on Bongatehaugh. Meanwhile Ruthven, aware of the danger in which the town of Jedburgh was placed, marched with great expedition, and, just as the little band were about to engage in deadly conflict, appeared on the bank in the rear of Fernieherst and Buccleuch, and the latter, placed between two fires, retired into the neighbouring fortresses, and the banditti dispersed to their usual haunts.

In October 1575 the Earls of Angus and Mar, and the Master of Glammis, the Earl of Bothwell, the Laird of Cessfurd, Lord Home, and Sir George Hume of Wedderburn, and others of that kindred, came to Jedburgh with their followers, and there published a manifesto, wherein they charged Arran and his friend, the colonel of the king's guard, with grievous abuses of their power and trust, such as the persecution of the king's faithful nobles, the oppressors of the Church, and showing favour to papists, false and iniquitous conduct towards England, and corresponding with the sworn enemies of the land. They declared their purpose of delivering their sovereign out of the hands of such hated and dangerous counsellors, and summoned in the King's name all

his subjects to promote and assist in the enterprise. In 1576 Andrew, the commendator of
Jedburgh, was charged with intercommuning with
traitors and rebels in his own lodging in the
burgh of Jedburgh in the month of March, and
at the Dunion Hill in the month of January.*
In 1583 John Rutherfurd, sen., Hunthill, and
Thomas Rutherfurd, his son, were summoned at
the cross of Jedburgh for treason.† In April
1588 James, in order to oblige his borderers to
do justice to their neighbours in England, made
an expedition to Jedburgh, carrying with him a
sufficient body of forces to compel the Laird of
Hunthill's sons, the Laird of Greenhead's sons,
and the Laird of Overton's sons, to enter themselves prisoners into England, as they were not
able to make reparation for the injuries they had
done. In September 1592 a proclamation was
issued by the King, calling upon all the freeholders and fighting men to meet at Peebles
within fifteen days, to accompany him in proper
person to take the field against Bothwell and his
retainers in Teviotdale. On the 23rd of said
month Andrew Kerr of Fernieherst, John and
William Rutherfurd of Hunthill, William Ruther-

---

* This is the first time that I have noticed the hill called
by the name of *Dunion*.

† Acta Parl. vol. iv. pp. 3-4.

furd, provost of Jedburgh, and William Kirktoun, bailie there, were ordained to be denounced rebels for not appearing to answer to a charge of treasonable reset and intercommuning with Bothwell. Next year the king, accompanied by Home and Cessfurd, made another expedition to Jedburgh to bring to order Fernieherst, Hunthill, and others of the retainers of Bothwell, when he exacted fines, and ordained several of the border barons to find security to behave for the future as good and dutiful subjects. In the same year the Bishop of Jedburgh attended the Parliament held at Holyrood House. Thomas Henderson represented the burgh.*

In the year 1601 a very serious affray occurred within the burgh of Jedburgh. Thomas Turnbull of Minto, David Davidson of Kaims; George, Ralph, James, and William Davidson, his sons; George Laidlaw of Rawflat; Hector Turnbull of the Firth; James Turnbull, called *Baniest James ;* Mark Turnbull in Beulie; Andrew Turnbull, his brother; and Walter Turnbull, Davidson's *Wattie,* accompanied by their retainers and dependants to the number of about thirty, all armed, entered the burgh by the Burn-wynd Port on the Rood Fair day, in contravention of the usual proclamation, made by Sir Andrew Kerr of Fernieherst and

---

* Acta Parl. vol. iv. p. 50.

the bailies, that none should repair to the fair or market but in a quiet, sober manner, keeping the king's and the provost's peace. Immediately on their arrival at the market-place they appeared before the lodgings of Thomas Kerr, brother to the provost, situated opposite to the cross, and, while he was within the same with his wife and family, challenged him to come out of the house and decide the quarrel which existed between them at the time. The burghers, seeing a crowd of armed men in the street behaving in such a manner, flew to their arms, and a bloody contest ensued, during which many fell on both sides. While the battle raged in the Burn-wynd Thomas Kerr and his servant Glaidner rushed out of the house and joined in the fray in defence of the peace of the town ; but no sooner did Kerr appear than he became the chief object of attack. The people who were present at the fair armed themselves with what weapons chance afforded, and ranged themselves on the side of their friends. The battle continued long doubtful, till victory at last declared in favour of the towns-people. On the part of the town Thomas Kerr and his servant were slain and several others wounded. On the other side there fell Robert Turnbull of Beulie, John Middlemost, brother to William Middlemost of Lilliesleaf chapel. James Douglas of Todd Hill was shot through the

bowels, James Douglas broke in the nose, Davidson of the Kaims had his right hand cut off, Mark
Turnbull of Beulie lost his thumb, and William
in the Townhead was shot in the groin.   For this
affray several of the actors were tried, condemned,
and suffered death.*   But this feud did not end
here ; two years after the bloody transaction above
narrated occurred, George Turnbull of Belses way-
laid Walter Turnbull of Rawflat, and his servant
Adam Turnbull, as they were returning from
Jedburgh, shot the master, laid hold of the
servant, and, after having bound him with fetters,
hung him by the feet and shoulders over a baulk
for the space of thirteen days, by which his feet
rotted off.   For this atrocious act Turnbull's right
hand was struck off at the cross.†

In 1606 took place a new dissolution of the kirk
of Dumaney from the abbey of Jedburgh, to enable
his majesty to grant the same to Sir Thomas Hamilton.   In the same year the cell and priory of
Restenet were dissolved from Jedburgh, that the
same might be granted to Viscount Fentown.‡   In
the same year, also, Jedburgh and Coldingham
were erected into a lordship for Alexander Earl of
Home, for the payment of a blench duty of
£266 13s. 4d.   Next year the estates of the king-

---

* Pitcairn's Criminal Trials.   † Ibid.
‡ Acta Parl. vol. iv. p. 351.

dom, considering the extraordinary dearth and price of shoes, appointed the magistrates of Jedburgh, Douglas of Bonjedworth, and Rutherfurd of Hundalee, commissioners, to take trial of the prices of rough hides and barked hides, and fix reasonable prices of boots and shoes, with penalties upon the shoemakers who should take a higher price.* In 1612 William Rutherfurd was commissioner to the Parliament. In 1617 Alexander Kirkton and John Rutherfurd were commissioners.† In the same year the Lord of Jedburgh was ordained to convene his feuars, vassals, tacksmen, and pensioners, at the burgh of Jedburgh, and collect the taxes imposed to meet the expenses of his Majesty's visit to Scotland.‡ At the election of magistrates in 1618 Sir Andrew Kerr attended, and gave out the leets of provost " according to custom," when George Moscripe was elected provost, and Robert Rae treasurer.§ After the election the council enacted that the provosts should only continue in office for three years. John Penman was *de novo* elected clerk. In 1619 the provost, bailies, and councillors bound themselves to assist the possessors of property on the south side of the Canongate in obtaining the same privileges as the inhabitants of

---

* Acta Parl. vol. iv. p. 467.   † Ib. p. 525.
‡ Ib. p. 581.   § Burgh Records, vol. i. p. 1.

the royalty.* The possessors of property in Richmond ordered to watch. This year an act was passed imposing penalties from £40 to £100 on any persons guilty of disobedience or want of due respect to the magistracy.† At the general election this year Sir Andrew Kerr appeared, and produced his majesty's warrant for the election. The same magistrates were continued, and the whole council swore to observe and give due obedience to the acts of kirk and council, as authorized by his majesty.‡ John Penman was confirmed in his office of clerk for life. A green cloth ordered to be purchased and laid before the provost at court and council. In the same year the council enacted that every evil-disposed person found drinking after nine o'clock was to be liable in a penalty of £10, and laid in the stocks fifteen days. At the election in 1620 Sir Andrew Kerr again appeared and gave out the leets for the provost, when Alexander Kirkton was elected provost. This year an act was passed by the council forbidding all opprobrious words or blasphemy to be used against any of the magistrates, before their faces or behind their backs.§ In the same year an act was passed ordaining the members of council to wear hats at the kirk and council, and

---

* Burgh Records, p. 5.   † Ib. p. 7.
‡ Ib. p. 10.   § Ib. vol. i. p. 11.

not blue bonnets, under the pain of ten shillings for each offence.* This year James Ainslie mortified £200 for poor householders. Thomas Dickson, Newcastle-on-Tyne, appeared before the magistrates, and enacted himself to leave the burgh and never return, under the pain of drowning without an assize.† All persons charged, and failing to attend the magistrates to St. James's Fair, to be fined. The drummer ordered to go through the town at *four* o'clock in the morning and *eight* at night, under the pain of forfeiture of his wages. A person of the name of Gladstone banished never to return, under the pain of hanging without an assize. In 1623 Andrew, Master of Jedburgh, appeared and gave out the leets. This year William Jeffrey was elected to the office of master of the grammar school by the magistrates, with the advice of John Bishop of Caithness— salary £100; £20 to be paid by the Kirk-session, besides the augmentation by the bishop, the quarter's fees, and a cartful of peats laid down at his door by the parent of each bairn.‡ This year an agreement was made between Andrew, the Master of Jedburgh, and the town, for establishing a perpetual annual race—the town to put out a silver cup of £40, and to be won by the first horse, and

---

* Burgh Records, vol. i p. 17.
† Ib. p. 21.   ‡ Ib. p. 31.

the master a velvet saddle, to be won by the second horse.* In 1625 it was enacted that all persons absent from the weapon-shawing pay £20, and forfeit their liberty; and any one committing a riot, either by word or deed, on such an occasion, pay £100 to the common good, without abatement, and banished the burgh for ever.† In 1628 every person who kept hens ordered " to clip their wings and cut their *taes*." At the election of this year the new council was for the first time chosen before the election of the magistrates. In 1629 Alexander Aikenhead, agent for the burghs, attended the council, and demanded that the new council should be elected before the election of the magistrates. Andrew Lord Jedburgh appeared, and produced a commission from King Charles. At the election in 1630 David Aikenhead, the agent for the royal burghs, directed the procedure, when the council for the first time voted the leets for provostry. This year Alexander Kirkton represented the burgh in the parliament held at Holyrood House. In 1632 the *swasher* and piper ordered to go through the town morning and night.‡ This year Bessie Turnbull, spouse

---

* These races were run on Jedburgh Edge.

† Burgh Records, p. 45.

‡ "*Swasche.*" Dr. Jamieson, in his Dictionary and Supplement, says that *swasche* is a trumpet. The learned editor of the Old Criminal Trials of Scotland defines it to

to Andrew Crombie, sheriff clerk, appeared before
the magistrates, and swore that she had only sold
one tun of wine during the year.   In 1633 John
Rutherfurd was provost, and Alexander Kirkton
commissioner to the Parliament.   Next year
Kirkton was provost.   In 1635 an act was passed
by the council, ordering all the old deacons and
quartermasters of every craft on fair-days to con-

---

be an alarm drum, and, with reference to the doctor's defi-
nition, remarks, that in all the instances he can recollect of
having met with the word, in ancient records and other
MSS., reference is uniformly made to its being *struck*, not
sounded or blown.   It is thought that the entries in the
records of Jedburgh clearly show that *swasche*, or *swesche*,
is a drum, not merely an alarm drum, but applied to the
common drum of the town, for in some entries the drummer
and piper are ordered to go through the burgh morning and
night, and in others the word *swascher* is used to denote the
drummer.   The two words are synonymous.   It will also
be observed from the text that the instrument used in
Jedburgh was struck ("rap of the swasche"), not sounded or
blown.   Mr. Pitcairn hesitates as to the meaning of the
word "*swascher*," but if *swasche* be a drum *swascher* must
be the person who used it.   All the royal burghs seem to
have kept a *swascher* for warning the inhabitants, and the
city of Edinburgh two, who appear also to have performed
the additional duty of attending upon the Parliament when
it met in Edinburgh.   In the burgh of Culros the *suyse*
was ordered to be struck at four in the morning and *eight* at
night, under the penalty of ten pounds.—Pitcairn's Criminal Trials, vol. ii. pp. 30, 245 ; Lord Treasurer's Accounts,
1542, 1544, 1548; Burgh Court Books of the Canongate,
1576; Records of Culros, 1596 ; Records of the City of Edinburgh, anno 1600.

vene in the high kirkyard, "with hats on their heads," upon the first rap of the swash, to "convoy the magistrates through the town." In 1636 John Rutherfurd of Bankend was provost. Every inhabitant of the town was this year forbidden to keep swine, under a penalty, and if found in their neighbour's "skaith," to be killed. Husbands were made answerable for their wives, and to pay £20 for their disobedience, and eight days in the stocks or ward. Next year a number of acts and regulations were passed in regard to the plague, which had broken out in various parts of the burgh,—*inter alia* no sick person to be concealed, under the pain of death, to be inflicted on the master of the house "without favour;" ports to be shut and guarded; all dogs and cats to be destroyed; and the sick to be visited at the door. Supplication and remonstrance to the Lords of the Privy Council against the books of common prayer and the canons and constitutions of the Church. In 1638 Alexander Kirkton was provost. The provost and Rutherfurd elected commissioners to the burghs and convention of the nobility. In 1639 John Rutherfurd was commissioner to the Parliament.* The markets of Jedburgh, which were formerly held on Mondays, ordered to be held on Tuesdays. In September of the same

* Acta Parl. vol. v. p. 249.

year the Parliament ratified the act granting two new fairs to the burgh.* This year Provost Rutherfurd attended the Assembly at Dunse. In 1640 the markets for the sale of all kinds of goods were discharged by the Parliament from being held on the Monday, with the view of preventing Sunday travelling.† In 1641 Adam Broune represented the burgh.‡ In the same year ratification passed, in favour of William Earl of Lothian, of the lands, lordships, and barony of Jedburgh.§ In 1643 John Rutherfurd was commissioner to the Parliament, and was one of those persons who were appointed to fix the proportion to be paid by each shire of the £800,000 voted by the Convention of Estates, to be advanced by the kingdom as a loan.|| This year the council at their head court enacted that all persons having horses without a plough, or half a plough, to lend them to honest men having occasion to ride, for eight shillings a day, and when to Edinburgh or further, thirty shillings the first three days, and six shillings every other day. In 1644 the Earl of Wigton's regiment of eleven hundred men was in Jedburgh. Adam Broune commissioner. Same year markets were prohibited from being held on Saturday as well as Monday, with the view of

---

* Acta Parl. vol. v. pp. 256-9.   † Ib. p. 301.
‡ Ib. p. 332. ·   § Ib. p. 546. || Ib. vol. vi. p. 19.

preventing Sabbath desecration.* In 1645 a number of men and women were ordered to go to service or be banished the town. Of these nineteen lived in the Townhead, eight in the Highgate, three in the Blackquarter, and three in the Canongate. This year the estates of Parliament found Jedburgh liable to maintain eighteen men of the army, at a monthly pay of £162.† A committee appointed by the magistrates to fix on eighteen dragoons, as the town's proportion of the five hundred dragoons to go out under Colonel Scott. On the 20th of November Francis Earl of Buccleuch, in virtue of a commission from the Privy Council, held a justice court here, and ordered the magistrates to detain and keep in gaol three thieves of the name of Armstrong. On the 28th March, 1646, a justice court was held at Jedburgh by the magistrates conform to a warrant from the committee of estates, for the trial of Donald M'Vandiller, Hutcheson M'Donald, and Foga Hart, charged with having been out with the rebels at Kilsyth and Philiphaugh. In the same year Rutherfurd of Bankend was elected provost. This year the burgh paid £162 for soldiers. In 1647 the burgh paid £126.‡ In February, 1648, a committee for every quarter of the burgh ap-

---

* Acta Parl. vol. vi. p. 127.   † Ib. p. 171.
‡ Ib. p. 207.

O

pointed, to make up a roll of soldiers. Each quarter of the town ordered to furnish four horses to carry meal to Carlisle. Pistols, swords, and belts belonging to Colonel Hume kept by Andrew Crombie for payment of two hundred merks, as the price of a sorrel mare and grey nag taken by the colonel and his officers as baggage-horses. The soldiers of the burgh, both horse and foot, ordered to march to the army, and to make choice of any horse within the town, and appraise the same. The committee to ride to Ancrum Bridge with the soldiers, and absentees to be punished. In October, 1648, John Haswell produced an act of the committee of estates, inhibiting all those who were accessory to the late engagement with Charles in aiding, or assisting, or voting in that Parliament, and alleged that Robert Rutherfurd, the burgh commissioner, did vote and consent to the said treaty, but which was denied by Rutherfurd. In December the council passed an act ordaining the middingsteads to be removed from the streets every Saturday night. In February, 1649, a proclamation was made at the cross of the burgh acknowledging the right of Charles II. to the throne,—Charles, before exercising royal power, to give satisfaction to the kingdom for the security of religion, common good, and peace of the kingdom, according to the National Solemn League and Covenant. This year the town was charged by the Lyon herald to hold a just accounting with Exchequer. In June of this year an act and dispensation authorized the justice court to sit at Jedburgh during the summer. Same year Lieutenant-Colonel Kerr, Captains Scot and Greenhead's troops were paid by the burgh and county.*

In 1651 a committee was appointed by the council to ride to Selkirk and declare the town's innocence of the outrages committed by the moss-troopers on the Friday previous, and to speak with Lord Howard and others drawn together. A court-martial of the English officers was however held, and the burgh fined in £500. On the result of the court-martial being intimated to the council, a meeting was called of the whole inhabitants, when it was unanimously determined not to pay the fine imposed on them, " and to stand by one another." The English court-martial, learning the resolution of the burgh, despatched a body of horse to the burgh, who took the provost, bailies, and several of the councillors prisoners, and put them in gaol. In this emergency another meeting of the inhabitants was called, at which it was agreed to pay the fine and charges agreeably to a stent roll to be made up.† A committee was also appointed to assist

---

* Acta Parl. vol. vi. p. 491.   † Burgh Rec. vol. i. pp. 202-3.

the magistrates in such troublous times, and four common posts were named to be ready on call "to run at all times for two shillings per mile," and to be free from town's burdens. Fleshers ordered to furnish beef for 3d. and pork at 4d. per pound to the regiment in the town. In October an act was passed by the council for the proper quartering of the English regiments in future. Major-General Lambert having imposed a monthly cess on the burgh, the council supplicated for relief. John Rutherfurd was commissioner to the Parliament this year.

In 1652, in consequence of an order having been received from the English commissioners requiring the burgh to elect a commissioner to meet them at Dalkeith in the month of February current, the council and inhabitants met, and, upon a vote, agreed to send a commissioner to Dalkeith; and accordingly James Forrest was sent as commissioner, but he was instructed not to agree to anything without the advice and consent of the magistrates. The English commissioners, however, refused to accept a commissioner so qualified. Robert Rutherfurd was then elected, with full power to act with the commissioners from the Parliament and Commonwealth of England at Dalkeith. At this meeting the following propositions were submitted to the consideration of the Scots commissioners :—

1st. Whether they would accept the declaration of the Commonwealth of England that Scotland should be incorporated and made one commonwealth with England. 2nd. That they would declare in the mean time to live peaceably under and give obedience to the authority of said Parliament. 3rd. That the commissioners should offer what objection they had against the union and settlement taking place with speed, and to suggest what would be most for the satisfaction of the people of Scotland. The burgh having sent an answer agreeing to these propositions, and suggested the condition on which they wished the settlement to take place, were granted protection by the English commissioners, dated March 1, 1652.* In 1653 the council received a letter from Colonel Lilburn ordering the magistrates to continue in their offices until further orders from the Council of Estates in England. In 1654 Andrew Kerr of Chatto, one of the principal sheriffs, ordered the town to send him arms to Berwick, but the council refused on the ground that they had not any more arms than were necessary for their own defence or to oppose the moss-troopers. The council also resolved not to send a commissioner to the burghs, on account of the dangerous state of the country.

---

* Burgh Records, vol. i. p. 216.

General Monk this year abated the monthly cess. In 1655 the council passed an act prohibiting all tradesmen not bearing portable charges, and not raising "reek" within the burgh, from voting at the deacon's election, or enjoying any other privileges. A regulation was made, forbidding "*muck*" to lie in "*the fore street*" longer than a week. In 1656 a charge was made by the treasurer against the bailies "for pocketing fines for theft." Persons forbidden to brew in houses without a chimney. At the election this year Rutherfurd of Wells was objected to on the ground that he was under bond to the English. In May, 1657, Francis Hager, son of Colonel Hager, of the county of Nottingham; John Greaves, son of Humphrey Greaves, Esq., of the county of Salop; Edward Mosely and Henry Goodsir, two of his highness's judges in Scotland, and a number of other gentlemen, admitted burgesses. In the same year an application was made by the burgh to the Earl of Roxburgh to allow St. James's Fair to be removed from the "Burrass or Tarrass," near Kelso, to Roxburgh muir. In May an order was made by the council to provide "coals and other necessaries for the execution of the witches on Tuesday next." In 1658 Major Smithson's troop was quartered in Jedburgh. Council-house of three stories built this year. In November, 1659, a letter

ROXBURGHSHIRE, ETC.   199

was received by the council from General Monk desiring a commissioner to be sent to Edinburgh, as he was anxious to speak about affairs which concerned the country. Robert Kerr was elected commissioner, and a committee appointed to frame an answer to General Monk's letter, which was ordered to be subscribed by all persons in the burgh. In a few days after the commissioner reported that the general had exempted the burgh from excise duty. In June, 1660, the magistrates and council "resolved to make a show at the cross on Thursday next, being the thanksgiving for his majesty's home-coming, and six out of every trade to keep the people off." In the same year the council resolved to bestow a testimonial on John Rutherfurd, bailie, as one of the Committee of Estates, bearing that he had acted "in nothing contrary to his majesty or to the liberty of the kingdom." The clerk elected during pleasure. Andrew Rutherfurd to go with Mr. Peter Blair to Edinburgh to speak with the Chancellor and the Judge Advocate about the escape of a prisoner from the gaol. In 1661 John Buchan, trier of the witches at the town, to try several persons suspected of witchcraft. In the same year a petition was presented to the estates of Parliament by Sir Walter Riddell of that ilk, and John Rutherfurd of Edgerstone, mentioning that John Oliver, having made his escape out of

the prison of Jedburgh, to which he was committed for several thefts, did shortly thereafter
steal sixty sheep from a tenant belonging to the
said Sir Walter Riddell, and, being apprehended
with the sheep in his possession, was sent back
to the prison of Jedburgh, where he then remained,
and desiring a commission to try him and
William Fletcher, accused of stealing four oxen
and a cow from Edgerstone. The estates of Parliament granted commissions to Lord Mordington,
Sir Archibald Douglas of Cavers, John Murray of
Philiphaugh, Sir Thomas Kerr of Cavers, and John
Scot of Gornbery, to hold courts, and to put the said
John Oliver and William Fletcher to the knowledge of an assize.* Commissions were also
granted in the same year for trying a number of
witches in Jedburgh tolbooth.† It seems that
these poor creatures had confessed their guilt.‡
On the 19th July, 1662, the council ordained
the deacons to warn six of every trade to attend
the commissioners appointed for trying and
judging the witches on Wednesday next.§ On
the 4th of August the provost produced a letter ordering him to appear before the burghs on Tuesday
next to answer the complaint of George Moscripe,
when the council authorized him to send a letter

---

* Acta Parl. vol. vii. p. 268. † Ib. app. p. 78.
‡ Burgh Records, vol. i. p. 287. § Ib. vol. ii. p. 1.

of excuse, as his presence was necessary at the execution of the witches on that day. In July, 1663, Thomas Porteous, a burgess, was fined in £50, besides imprisonment during the magistrates' pleasure, for speaking rudely to the treasurer. On the establishment of episcopal government the magistrates and council met on November 7th, and subscribed a declaration that the National Solemn League and Covenant was unlawful.* In 1668 the council enacted that, for the future, " no houses be let to persons not able to bear portable charges, and no fires be kindled in a house without a chimney or lum, and that no servant man in cases of fire come out without graip or fork, and no serving woman without pan cog or barrel." This year the burgh paid the sum of £108 as its proportion of the £72,000 to the king.† This year there were twenty-two brewers in the town.‡ In July the council ordered all the gates of the town to be kept shut night and day, and no strangers admitted into the town and no person allowed to go to England without leave of the magistrates, on account of the plague said to have broken out at Newcastle. Same year Sir George M'Ken-

---

* Burgh Records, vol. ii. p. 31.
† Acta Parl. vol. vii. p. 541.
‡ Burgh Records, vol. ii. p. 48.

zie was advocate for the town in a number of causes with the Marquis of Lothian. The council enacted that for the future the clerkship should be rouped. It was bought for a year by Thomas Rutherfurd for £144. The council subscribed 2,500 merks for building the kirk. In 1667 the council appointed two men to search for coal at Hunthill. This year the Rood-day fair was altered to the 17th September. The council agreed to furnish the third part of the timber and lime for building the kirk in the ruins of the abbey. A silver cup, worth £6 17s. 6d., was given by the council to be run for at this year's races. In 1670 and 1672 John Rutherfurd was commissioner to the Parliament. In 1672 circuit courts ordered to be held each year at Jedburgh in the month of April or May.* This year a correction-house was ordered to be built in the town. In 1674 the provosts of Jedburgh and Aberdeen were fined in £1,000 and 1,000 merks for being the most active in representing their grievances and rights and privileges in answer to the king's letter.† In 1686 forty bags of lime were brought home by the councillors, and sixteen other persons in the town, as their contribution towards converting part of the ruins of the abbey into a kirk. In 1689 Adam Ainslie and Robert Ainslie

---

* Acta Parl. vol. viii. p. 88.
† Ib. vol. ix. app. p. 77.

were returned as commissioners to the meeting
of the Estates, and both claimed a right to sit.
A committee was appointed to inquire into the
matter, who reported that they had heard parties,
and examined witnesses, and found "it proven
that the magistrates threatened and menaced
those who offered to protest against the clandes-
tine marking of the votes for Robert Ainslie, and
those who voted for Adam Ainslie were threatened
by these magistrates to have their heads broken;
and that it is acknowledged by Robert Ainslie
that Porteous, whose name is subscribed at full
length to the said Robert's commission, could never
write, and therefor it is their opinion that Robert
Ainslie's commission is null and illegal, and that
Adam Ainslie's commission ought to be pre-
ferred. The Estates do approve the said report and
interpone ther authoritie thereto."* In April of
the same year warrant was granted for giving out
extracts for new elections, in all the royal burghs
of the kingdom, of magistrates and councillors,
by poll of the whole inhabitants. Jedburgh
election was appointed to take place on the 2nd
of May following—Lord Newbattle, overseer.†
This year the Earl of Mar's regiment was quartered in the burgh. In 1696 the burgh paid
£102 monthly of supply. In 1698 a petition

* Acta Parl. vol. ix. p. 18.
† Ibid. p. 51.

from the town was presented to Parliament praying for a small custom on goods passing Ancrum Bridge, for the repairing thereof, and remitted to a committee of trade. In 1700 Walter Scot was commissioner to the Parliament. In 1704, when the act of security was passed, the town of Jedburgh was put in a posture of defence, and officers appointed to command the militia. The trades raišed 100 men, well armed, for the good of the burgh and support of the magistrates. Next year a proposal was made to the burgh by Thomas Rutherfurd of Wells to the effect that if the town would bind themselves to pay him a certain sum of money within four months he would grant an obligation for its re-payment out of the first free profits of the coal if found at Hunthill. The council agreed to the proposition, and hazarded for Rutherfurd's encouragement £50. In November, 1706, the magistrates and council addressed the Parliament against the union with England. At this time the town was represented in Parliament by its provost, Walter Scot. In 1707 the royal burghs of Scotland were formed into fifteen districts, of which Jedburgh, Lauder, Haddington, Dunbar, and North Berwick made one district.* This year internal discords ran so high

* Acta Parl. vol. xi. pp. 421-5.

in the burgh that a petition was presented to the
Convention of Burghs craving its interference.
The convention appointed the commissioners of
Edinburgh, Selkirk, Peebles, and Annan to meet
at Jedburgh on the 15th October following, to try
and compose the differences between the inhabitants in relation to the public welfare. The
commissioners met with the magistrates and
Blackhill and dealt seriously with them, advising
that all differences should be buried and matters
accommodated, for the peace and quiet of the
place, and to prevent further trouble and expense;
but Blackhill would not yield, and the commissioners left without accomplishing their object.
In 1714 the magistrates received notice of the
dangerous state of Queen Anne, and calling upon
them to protect the peace of the district. After
her majesty's decease the burgh addressed her
successor, King George, and on the day of his
coronation invited all the neighbouring gentry
to dinner. The trades walked through the town
with their colours; a large bonfire blazed at the
cross, and eight pounds of powder was furnished
to the dragoons for firing "in the time of the
solemnities."

On the 15th of October, 1715, the provost
represented to the council that, hearing a considerable body of men had gathered together on
the borders, he thought it necessary that all the

arms that could be got should be kept ready for use. The council ordered the different ports of the town to be watched by forty men day and night. On the 17th a portion of the rebel army, under Lord Kenmuir, arrived at Jedburgh on their way to Kelso; but on hearing from that place that it was defended, they marched for Rothbury, in Northumberland. During their stay in Jedburgh they called up the September stent, amounting to £30, and though it was not collected, the rebel officers threatened to lay waste the town if their demand was not complied with; on which William Robson, merchant, at the request of the magistrates, advanced the money, and received a receipt from John Dunbar and Lewes Grant, under the hands of W. Macintosh, brigadier-general to the rebels. On the 27th of the same month the rebels, learning that the royal troops were advancing, left Kelso, and retreated towards Jedburgh, which place they entered in the evening. While there a party, under the command of Captain Erskine, rode up to the council-house, and carried away nineteen guns and a carbine, for which he tendered a receipt, which the magistrates thought fit to accept, to ensure, as they said, "their own and the town's safety." The magistrates also furnished oatmeal to the Highlanders on their retreat to the amount of £133 1s. 8d., and wine to the old brigadier,

£61 10s. For these advances, and for damages sustained, the burgh was afterwards compensated by the Parliament.* After the rebel army left Jedburgh, Sir W. Bennet wrote the provost that the Duke of Roxburgh, Lord Lieutenant of this shire and Selkirk, with the advice of his deputy-lieutenant, was raising a force in the district, and requesting the burgh of Jedburgh to provide a man and horse, well mounted, with broad-sword, pistols, and carbine, at Caverton Edge at ten o'clock on the Friday following, or else to pay £18 10s., being forty days' pay at 1s. 6d. The magistrates applied to their tacksman of the mills to provide man and horse, and, on his refusing, a protest was taken by the town, holding him liable in the outrigging of the militiaman and horse, conform to obligation contained in the tack, and also for any damage the burgh might sustain through his default. The magistrates provided a man and horse, and the provost, on the recommendation of the council, accompanied him to Caverton Edge, and met with the leaders of the shire, to whom he presented the man and horse, fit for service as required.† In 1727 Sir James Dalrymple of Hailes represented the burgh. In the same year the lands of Broomhall and Tempendean were relieved from customs levied on

---

* Burgh Records, vol. iii.   † Ibid.

the burgh.   In 1729 each inhabitant was ordered
to causeway the front of his door to the "rig" of
the street.   In 1730 brandy and foreign wines were
prohibited from being sold in the burgh.   In 1734
Captain Faa was elected M.P. for the burgh.   In
1736 Provost Robinson mortified £100 for cha-
ritable uses in the burgh and parish.   Owing to the
House of Peers having declared the previous election
illegal, a poll of the whole inhabitants living in the
town and contributing towards its burdens took
place by virtue of a royal warrant, when the Marquis
of Lothian was elected provost.   The council so
chosen elected Archibald Crombie, sheriff-clerk of
the county, clerk of the burgh.   The election was
confirmed by his majesty in council in September following.   In 1739 the committee appointed
to inquire after and demand the council books of
John Haswell, reported "that they understood that
these books were put into the hands of Andrew
Chalmers, writer in Edinburgh, during the plea
betwixt the two contending sets of magistrates,
and that ten or eleven of the books were still in
his hands, and that he was willing to deliver them
to any one authorized by the council."   The
same year the magistrates resolved to ride St.
James's Fair as usual, and ordered the inhabitants
to be warned to attend upon them; but they
" agreed to take no dinner at the fair, and allowed
the water-bailie 7s. 6d. for his breakfast, and

ordered the treasurer to advance the same." In 1740 Sir John Scott of Ancrum's house, in the Backgate, was purchased for the purposes of a poor-house and a manufactory. This year a committee from the council waited on Captain Faa at Dunbar, reminded him of his promises to the burgh, and required him to perform the same; he promised to be at Jedburgh in the following week, when the provost and magistrates "should receive every satisfaction." Gaoler ordered to clean the streets around the market-place once a week. Lord Robert Ker was provost at this time. In 1741 the inhabitants of the burgh were in great poverty, and were liberally assisted by Lord Robert Ker, and also by gentlemen of the county. This year William Davidson was appointed carrier, or town's post, at a salary of £2 10s. per year, out of which he was to pay for the newspapers weekly. In 1744 the council agreed to allow the magistrates " to spend 20s. at St. James's Fair." In 1745 the rebel army, whose rear left Dalkeith on the 3rd of November, marched southward in three columns, by Lauder, Selkirk, and Hawick, and the eastern column, of between three and four thousand, by Kelso. On the 4th the prince arrived at Kelso at night, from whence orders were sent to Wooler 'to prepare quarters for 4,000 foot and 1,000 horse; but, notwithstanding, he crossed the Tweed and marched

P

for Jedburgh. On arriving at the burgh he was met by a great number of people, one of whom mounted the parapet of the bridge at the Town-foot, and exclaimed, " God prosper Prince Charles, our lawful king !" While the prince remained in Jedburgh, he slept in the house of Ainsley of Blackhill, now Nos. 9 and 11 Castlegate.* In 1747 the Earl of Ancrum was provost. In 1748 the burgh contributed towards building a stone bridge over the Rule at Spittal, erected by Cavers Douglas. Next year the council unanimously resolved that it would be for the good of the burgh to sell St. James's Fair, and ordered the conveners of trades to call the deacons and trades, lay the resolution of the council before them, and report. In 1750 the council agreed to be at one-third of the expense of repairing the kirkyard dykes. This year the convention of burghs allowed Jedburgh £20 to assist in repairing the town. In 1751 Andrew Fletcher of Saltoun was elected M.P. In 1766 James Haswell was provost. In 1767 Thomas Winterup filled the office of provost. In 1768 the Court of Session appointed managers of the burgh. In 1769 the cross of the burgh was repaired. In 1770 Dr.

---

* An ample account of the proceedings of the rebels within the county will be found under the head of " Annals of the County," vol. iii.

McKnight, minister of the parish, allowed to set up his haystack at the south side of the abbey door, but in such a way as to leave a passage into the kirk, on payment of one penny yearly. The clock taken down from the old steeple and put up in the new. On the magistrates being restored in 1777, William Elliott was elected provost. In 1779 Robert Lindesay filled that office. In 1785 the inhabitants held a public meeting for the purpose of petitioning for parliamentary reform. In 1792 the burgh sent up a strong petition to parliament for the abolition of the slave-trade. In 1817 the inhabitants exerted themselves to obtain reform in the burghs. In 1830 a public meeting of the inhabitants was held, and parliament petitioned to pass a most liberal measure of reform. At this meeting the provost presided, supported by the other magistrates and the town-clerk. On the 21st March, 1831, a meeting of the freeholders of the shire was held in the burgh to take into consideration the question of reform. This meeting Sir Walter Scott attended, and proposed one of the tory resolutions. The Town Hall was crowded chiefly by the reforming inhabitants of the town and district anxious to hear the arguments of the leaders of the tories and whigs on the all-absorbing question of the day. The whig speakers were loudly cheered by the auditory, while the advocates of the existing system of representation met with a very different reception. The speech of Sir Walter Scott in particular drew down the ire of the audience, and he was repeatedly interrupted by loud hissing, especially in the passage where he compared the reformers to a parcel of schoolboys taking to pieces a watch which used to go tolerably well for all practical purposes, in the conceit that they could put it together again far better than the old watchmaker. I was present at the meeting, and while I deeply regret that any hooting or hissing should have occurred during the speech of Sir Walter Scott, I am satisfied that these interruptions were directed not against the man, but against the sentiments which he uttered. The audience was composed for the most part of those not possessing the franchise, and who had no other way of expressing their feelings upon the subject which was being discussed than by a noisy disapproval of the views of those speakers opposed to the rights claimed. If the populace were more violent during the address of Sir Walter Scott, it was a compliment paid to his great genius, and a proof that the illustrations used by him were fully understood ; but they did not love the *man* the less. I am convinced there was not a man in all that assembly who would not have risked his life for Sir Walter. In no place had his genius more admirers than in Teviotdale, and even at this day there is scarcely a peasant in the district who has not made repeated pilgrimages to "Dryburgh's sacred shrine" to gaze upon the grave which contains the dust of him "whose fame has shed a lustre on our age." But while the men of Jedburgh delighted to wander in fairy regions with Sir Walter as their only guide, they did not think themselves bound to follow him in matters regarding their political rights and privileges.

During the three days that Earl Grey left the helm of affairs, the inhabitants of the burgh met, and addressed his majesty to recall the ministry, and in case such advice should not be acted upon prayed the House of Commons to withhold the supplies. On the Reform Bill becoming the law of the land, the reformers gathered together to solemnize the occasion by a jubilee. Old and young of both sexes marched in procession under different banners, and after perambulating the streets partook of a sumptuous banquet. During the whole period of this important struggle the inhabitants of Jedburgh conducted themselves in a manner becoming those who claimed such high privileges. It is to be hoped that they will long hold the position they now occupy as a body of sober, peaceable, and intelligent men; bearing always in mind that the dearest birthright of a British subject is freedom of opinion, and any attempt to prevent such an expression of feeling is unworthy of a great and a free people.

PROPERTY OF JEDBURGH.—As stated before, the territory of Jedburgh belonged, at the dawn of record, to Ecgred Bishop of Lindisfarne, who bestowed it upon the see of which he was bishop. On the death of King Edgar it became the property of David I. It was settled on Queen Johanna in 1221 by Alexander II. In 1282 Gilbert Marescal was in possession of the territory, and delivered it over to the English king. John Comyn was steward of Jedworth in 1288, the rents of which amounted to £96 13s. 4d. In accounts rendered by Comyn to the crown he credits himself with £5 10s. 6d., being the cost of constructing nine hundred roods of hedge and ditch around the woods and meadows.* The same Comyn acted as steward to the English king, and while he held the office fell into an arrear of £1,563 14s. 6½d., which was forgiven him by Edward.† In 1296 Edward I. bestowed the mains of Jedewurth upon Thomas of Burnham, the keeper of the castle.‡ Previous to 1320 the town and manor were conferred by Robert Bruce on his bastard son Robert.§ In 1320 it was conferred on the good Sir James Douglas.‖ In 1328 Henry Baliol, sheriff of Rox-

---

* Compota Camerar. vol. i. p. 68.
† Rotuli Scotiæ, vol. i. pp. 12, 17.   ‡ Ib. vol. i. p. 23.
§ Robertson's Index, p. 12, No. 50.
‖ Ib. p. 10, No. 17.

burgh, levied from the freeholders of the bailiewick and burgh of Jedburgh £169 5s. 7½d. In
1356 Edward granted the lands to Percy. The
notices of property held by individuals are scanty.
In 1610 Andrew Gourlay was possessed of a piece
of land called the five rude and two *mercatorium*
of Glenislands. In 1616 George Moscripe, provost of Jedburgh, was proprietor of a third part of
these lands. In 1618 Andrew Ker, burgess of
the burgh, was possessed of fifteen acres lying
in Hyndhousefield in the barony of Ulston.
In 1623 John Wallace, burgess of Jedburgh,
was proprietor of two acres of land in Glenislands called Braiddail. In 1625 Thomás Alison,
burgess of Jedburgh, was proprietor of five acres
of land called Doomshill, and two acres of land
in Hyndhousefield called Broomhill. In 1626
William Stewart, merchant, burgess of Jedburgh,
possessed the Cruketdail. In 1627 Andrew
Rutherfurd was the owner of the Aickiebräe and
haugh. In 1628 George Lawsoun was proprietor
of Mowisclois; about the same time Margaret
Olipher, in Jedburgh, was possessed of six acres of
land in Hyndhousefield within the barony of Jedburgh. In 1629 James Dundas of Arnistoun
was proprietor of the mills and granaries of Jedburgh, viz., the Abbey Mill, Town Mill, and East
Mill, and the fulling-mill of Jedburgh, valued at
£96 6s. Lady Anne Ker and Lady Jane Ker,

daughters of Robert Earl of Lothian, were in possession of the same subjects in 1642.   In 1654
James Fulton, burgess of Jedburgh, was the owner
of lands in Glenislands.   In 1670 Bessie Scott and
Anne Scott, daughters of Scott of Whitslaid, possessed the Manor Place of Jedburgh, with the mills
and granaries of the burgh.   In 1693 John Ker of
Cavers, son of John Ker of West Nisbet, possessed
Rottenrow and Headfaulds, several tenements
in the burgh, and the garden called the " back of
the friars."

The town seems to have been possessed of a common of considerable extent, of which not a vestige
now remains.

OF THE FAMILIES OF THE BURGH.—Very little
information exists as to the families inhabiting the
burgh at an early period.   Originally surnames
were unknown in Scotland, and even for more than
a century after the Norman era individuals were
known chiefly by their Christian name and that of
their place of abode, their calling or appearance,
and frequently by a *sobriquet*.*   When Jedburgh
submitted to Edward I. the individual members of

---

* I have seen letters of horning in which the Provost
of Jedburgh was charged as John Robison *alias* "*Lous*" Jack.
From an early period there has always been a sobriquet of
the Green; at present the possessor of the surname is *Will of
the Green.*

the corporation subscribed the oath of fealty by their Christian names only, with the addition of the name of their place, trade, or occupation; for example, John Dameson, alderman; Symon of Ramington, Heue of Lindsay, Hugh of Watton; Robert and Stevene, stablers; Rauf the grocer; Thomas and Symon, tailors; Richard the clerk; Ewy, the clerk of Jedworth. In like manner, when the aldermen and burgesses of Roxburgh swore fealty to the same king at the same time, the Christian name was subscribed, and the trade added to distinguish the individual, *i.e.* Walter the goldsmith; Richard the cutler; Michael the saddler; Austyn the mercer.* In the course of the fourteenth and near the end of the fifteenth centuries John is seen designed as of Rutherforde of Hundole, showing even at that comparatively late date the use of the Christian name only, with the name of the territory added to distinguish the person.† Several individuals also were called by the surname of Jedworth. In 1296 Robert of Jedworth took the oath of fealty to Edward I. He appears to have filled the office of parson to the church of Kermighel.‡ Vedastus of Jedworth was a tenant of the monks of Melrose, and Thomas of Jedworth

---

* Prynne, iii. p. 653.   † Lib. de Chalchou, p. 425.

‡ " Robs de Geddeworthe psona de ecclie de Kirmyghel vic de Lanark."—Rotuli Scotiæ, vol. i. p. 25.

was a monk of Melrose between 1296 and 1343.* About the middle of the same century Robert of Jedworth and a person of the name of Tailfer, of the same place, got a safe-conduct for themselves and four horsemen from Edward III. to remain in England for a year.† Before 1291 John Comyn or Cumyn was steward of Jedburgh, and held considerable possessions in Jedburgh and neighbourhood. He greatly improved the burgh and vicinity by constructing hedges and ditches around the woods and meadows; he is the same person who competed for the crown of Scotland, and who was slain by Robert Bruce on February 10, 1306. The family of Comyn originally belonged to Northumberland, and came into Scotland during the reign of David I. Richard Comyn obtained from Earl Henry, the son of King David, the manor of Linton, in Easter Teviotdale, which is thought to have been the first possession of the family in Scotland. By his marriage with Hexild, daughter of Bethok, who was the daughter of King Donalbane, he obtained considerable property around Jedburgh and in the valleys of the Teviot and Rule. About 1296 the family of Stewart appears in connection with "Jeddeworth." During that year Johan *le seneschal* (the steward) of Jeddeworth swore fealty

---

* Lib. de Mel., pp. 424, 684.
† Rotuli Scotiæ, vol. i. p. 823, *a*.

to Edward I.; he is thought to be the same Stewart who fought on the Scots' side and fell at the battle of Falkirk in 1298.* His son John Stewart of Jedworth married a daughter of Turnbull of Mynto, who bore to him Sir William Stewart, who in time became one of the sheriffs of Roxburghshire, greatly beloved by his sovereign Robert III., and much employed on the borders. It was this Sir William Stewart who was taken prisoner at the battle of Humildon on the borders of Northumberland, and executed under the illegal directions of Percy, the Hotspur of Shakspeare. In 1390 John Turnbull of Mynto granted to his nephew, Sir William Stewart of Jedworth, the lands of Mynto, which donation was confirmed by Robert III.† The family of the Stewarts of Jedburgh became merged in the family of the Stewarts of Dalswinton by a marriage between Marion Stewart, of the latter family, and a son of the celebrated sheriff.‡ It is thought that the family of Stewart conferred the name of Stewartfield on an adjoining property which now bears the name of Hartrigge.

In the course of the thirteenth century the name of Rutherfurd is also seen flourishing in the burgh and surrounding territory. Jedburgh

---

* Nisbet's Heraldry.   † Robertson's Index.
‡ Nisbet's Heraldry.

and the district around it may be said to have
been for centuries the land of the Rutherfurds
as vassals of the Douglas.   At the present day the
name still exists in connection with the land; but
as the origin of the family will require to be fully
treated of in the subsequent pages, I shall only
further notice here, as an illustration of the
number and importance of the Rutherfurds, that
the whole space of the choir of the abbey was,
during the fifteenth century, divided amongst them
for interring their dead.*

In the fourteenth and fifteenth centuries the
names of Fossard, Moscripe, Burrel, Pyle, Brand,
Walas, Hall, Clerk, Dun, Lorymer, Vauch, Smith,
Bell, Adamson, Olieure, and Cant appear.   The
name of Cant was about this time of considerable
importance in the county.   In 1434 John Cant
was one of the bailies of Jedburgh, and in 1564
Henry Cant was warden of the place of the
Minorite friars of the burgh of Roxburgh.   One
of the same name is at present living in the village
of Fairnington, in the parish of Roxburgh.   The
Olivers of Jedburgh and its forest increased greatly
in number, and during the fifteenth century were
noted thieves.   Their principal place of abode
seems to have been at Stryndes in the forest.

In the sixteenth and seventeenth centuries the

---

* Map in possession of Rutherfurd of Fairnington.

names of Rae, Ainslie, Alison, Walker, Bruce, Elliot, Brown, Kirkton, Scot, Gray, Scougal, Young, Jerdan, Porteous, Douglas, Henderson, Haswell, Crombie, &c., appear in the records. In the course of the last century, Winterupe, Young, Johnstone, Spinnie, Smail, Wright, White, Gibson, Lindsay, Pott, Madder, Borthwick, Fair, Hilson, &c., are noticed as taking a lead in the affairs of the burgh.

CHAPTER IV.

OF THE DISTRICT OF JEDBURGH.

THE territory included within the district of Jedburgh comprehends the parishes of Jedburgh, Crailing, Oxnam, Southdean, Hobkirk, Bedrule, Minto, and Ancrum. My intention is to treat of the district as a whole, without reference to its parochial divisions. I have been induced to follow this plan, as these parishes make one of the modern divisions of the county, and in ancient times, with the exception of Minto, formed the regality of Jedburgh Forest. This district is bounded on the south by the mountains of the Cheviot range. In these water-sheds the rivers Rule, Jed, and Oxnam have their rise, and flow in a parallel direction northward into the river Teviot, which takes its rise in the western part of the county, and runs through the beautiful dale bearing its name. These three rivers are at about equal distances from each other, with high grounds between. The division contains within its extent the greater portion of the hunting-ground known in early times by the name of Chevy-chase, the possession of which caused much strife between the houses of Douglas and Percy. It is thought that the whole of this territory formed a part of the great forest which extended all along the borders of Scotland and England. The trees consisted chiefly of oak interspersed with the birch and pine ; but of the former the capon-tree and king of the wood, described in the first volume of this work, and of the birch a few clusters occasionally met with on the mountain-sides, appear the only representatives existing at the present day.

It is very difficult to ascertain with any degree of precision the manner in which this district was occupied from 1020 to the death of Edgar in 1107, when it became the property of the Prince of Cumberland. After that time glimpses are obtained of the state of possession from the grants made by the prince to the eminent persons who followed him from England, or who were driven to seek shelter within the Scots' border from the oppressions of the English kings. The town of Jedburgh and the forest in its immediate neighbourhood seem to have been retained by the prince and his successors, under the management of a *stewart*. As already noticed, one of these early stewards was *Comyn*, who was also one of

the sheriffs of the county.*   On King Robert
Bruce obtaining possession of Teviotdale he conferred Jedburgh and its forest on his natural son
Robert, and, at his death, upon the good Sir
James Douglas.   From the words of the grant it
would appear that the grateful Bruce conferred
upon Douglas the *"mercat-town of Jedburgh,
castle, forest, and mains thereof."* † Considering
that Jedburgh was at that time erected by the
same king into a burgh royal, it is not easy to
see how it came to be included in the grant of
regality.

The place selected by Douglas as capable of
being defended against almost any force was
Lyntalee, on the left bank of the Jed, about a mile
and a half from Jedburgh. This afterwards
became the first dwelling of the Douglas in the
south of Scotland, but it must have been a place
of note long previous to that day; at least, its
British name would indicate that it had—*the fort
or manor place at the pool or lyn.*   A more beautiful and secure retreat could not have been
chosen.   On the east is a precipitous rock of about
one hundred feet high, washed at its base by the
Jed.   On the north a deep ravine runs up from
the table-land between the Jed and the Rule.   On

---

* Rotuli Scotiæ, vol. i. p. 17.
† Robertson's Index, p. 10, No. 26.

LINTALE

the south a deep glen winds from the river Jed to the Sueney moor, which, about three or four hundred yards from its source, sends off a deep branch in the direction of the ravine on the north, and approaching so near it as to leave only a neck of land between them. To the east of this neck, and surrounded by the Jed and the two ravines, is an open space of ground, and upon it the Douglas built a house for himself, and huts for his men. The house of the chief occupied the site of the modern cottage between the ridges on the west and the precipice. The situation far exceeds in beauty anything to be met with in the forest. Standing between the cottage and the Scaur, and looking south, the eye wanders among the dark oak woods of Fernieherst, in the middle of which appears the grey mansion of the Kers, the scene of many a contest. The course of the river is seen from this spot at great advantage, as it winds down its narrow valley from the mountains of the border. As it bends from side to side of the valley it forms numberless little haughs, surrounded by hanging woods, each one a picture of quiet and simple beauty. It is not easy to conceive the equal of such scenes as are to be met with on the river Jed. While the Douglas occupied this locality, he must have felt perfect security from the attacks of the forces of England. In addition to the natural strength of the ground, an almost impenetrable forest enclosed him for miles on every side, through which it was impossible to convey an army in the face of any serious opposition. Several attempts were made to disturb him in his stronghold, but without success. Sir Robert Neville and Cailou, a Gascon, governor of Berwick, who had previously plundered the Merse and Teviotdale, led their army in 1315 against him, but were defeated. The Earl of Arundel next entered the forest with a numerous army, but Douglas, warned of their approach by Adam Gordon, the warden of the marches, placed his bowmen mong the hazel bushes and brushwood, and then drew the English into the ambuscade, forced them to fight at a disadvantage, and drove them back with great slaughter. To revenge these losses Thomas Earl of Richmond led 10,000 men against this secure retreat, and provided his men with axes to make a road through the forest itself, but the address and valour of the Douglas prevailed, and the English leader fell by Douglas's own hand. The peerage writers state that there was added, in 1325, to his armorial bearings, "a wreath of stakes, in commemoration of his having wreathed in the English in the said forest, so that they could not escape, and then defeated them;" but I am inclined to think that the compartment added to the armorial bearings of the Douglas was meant to represent the retreat in the forest

so encircled by wood as to be impregnable.   Even
at the present day the woody banks of the river
and the glens form a girdle of wood around the
early home of the Douglas.   Now that the extinc-
tion of the thick forest exposes its secrets, it is
interesting to notice camps in almost every direction around this stronghold, not only showing
the care with which it had been protected, but the
extent of the armies which the forest sheltered.
On two *tongues* of land, formed by the glens on
the south, are distinct remains of ancient strengths
and forts, and in *Sueney* moor a number of the
same kind of strengths are to be seen.   The
names of both these places, as well as other circumstances, lead to the conclusion that a considerable settlement of the Danish people existed
in this locality.

While my limits will not permit me to enter
into anything like a history of the house of Douglas,
yet in a work of this kind I cannot avoid bestowing
particular attention on this remarkable family,
which for centuries exercised so great an influence
on the borders.

According to tradition the name of Douglas
is said to have originated after the battle in which
the usurper Donalbane was vanquished by the
king's forces.   It is said that Donalbane, being
enclosed in a wood with a narrow outlet, turned in
desperation upon the forces which surrounded him,

and threw them into confusion, when at this critical
juncture a chieftain with his sons and retainers
appeared upon the field, rallied the troops of the
king, and gained the victory.   The king, who was
at some distance, on hearing of the danger in which
his army was placed, hastened to the scene of strife,
but on his way thither was informed of the successful efforts of the chieftain.   On asking for the
hero, the answer was, " Sholto Duglas" (See that
dark man). " Ay, Sholto Duglas," said the king,
and by that name he was ever afterwards distinguished.*

Wyntoun says, " that of the beginning of the
Murray and Duglas divers men speak in divers
ways, so that he can affirm nothing for certain ;
nevertheless, as both bear in their arms the same
stars set in the same manner, it seems likely to
many that they have come of the same kin either
by lineal descent or by collateral branch."†   The
historian of the house of Douglas, who wrote two

---

* Buchanan, vol. i. p. 260.
† Wyntoun's Chron. book viii. cap. vii. The house of Mur-
ray owes its origin to Frisken, a Fleming, who received from
David I. several grants of land in the most fertile districts of
Moray, for assistance in putting down an insurrection of the
Moray men. The first William *de Duglas* married a daugh-
ter of this Frisken. The family took the surname of *de
Moravia*, or Moray, during the beginning of the 13th
century.

centuries ago, thus expresses himself:—" We do not know them in the fountain, but in the stream; not in the root, but in the stem; for we know not who was the first *mean man* that did raise himself above the vulgar."*

Douglas, in his Peerage, adopts the tradition that the name originated in consequence of the seasonable assistance rendered to the king by " the dark or swarthy-coloured man" in the battle with Donalbane, and adds that the king, as a reward for his gallant conduct, granted him a tract of land on the Douglas water in Lanark.†

The indefatigable Chalmers, in his Caledonia, traces the family of Douglas to its origin in a person, *Theobald, a Fleming,* who before the middle of the 12th century obtained a grant of lands on the Douglas water from Arnold the abbot of Kelso.‡ *William* the son of Theobald, according to the custom of the period, assumed the name of the lands as his surname : *William de Duglas.* The editor of a late valuable work on the origin of parishes, and also in the preface to the Chartulary of Kelso, published by the Bannatyne Club, declares the view of Chalmers, that the family of Douglas sprang from the honest Fleming, " to be wholly untenable," and that " there is neither

---

* Godescroft's History of the Douglas, preface.
† Peerage, 180. ‡ Caledonia, vol i. p. 579.

proof nor reason to believe that the Flemish Theobald was in any way connected with the Douglas, and it is beyond doubt that the lands on the opposing bank of the valley which he acquired from the monks of Kelso were no part of the ancient domain of the Douglas."*   But the editor fails to trace the family further than the *William de Duglas* referred to by Chalmers as the son of Theobald, concluding his search with the remark that the old conjecture of the prior of St. Serf's Inch, in Lochlevin, "still stands as the limit of our knowledge, beyond which no research has been able to pass."†   It seems clear to me that the family did not acquire the name in the manner stated by tradition, but from the waters on which their lands lay,—Duglas, "the dark blue" stream. It is equally certain that the family made no figure in the annals of the country till the end of the 13th century, when *William de Duglas*, the father of the good Sir James, succeeded to the family estates, under the name of *William de Duglas :* he was present at the parliament held at Brigham, and, in 1291, swore fealty to Edward in the chapel of Thurston. A weighty circumstance against the early importance of the Douglas is the fact that the grant by King Robert Bruce to Sir James

---

* Origines, vol. i. p. 155 ; Lib. de Calchow, pref. pp. 27, 28.
† Wyntoun, *ut supra.*

Douglas of Jedforest appears to be the first royal grant to the family. It is also instructive to notice that, with the exception of a charter of William the Lion, and another of Alexander II., the name of Douglas does not appear as a witness to the numerous royal grants of that early period, and, as observed by Chalmers, not one of the first three lairds of the *Duglas* appears among the great men of Scotland who acknowledged Margaret of Norway as the heiress of Alexander III., in 1284.* None of them was among the associators at Turnberry in 1286 for maintaining the pretensions of Bruce. But while the Douglas are not found in the company of kings and the great men of the land, they may be seen mixing in the transactions of the church of Glasgow and Kelso between 1175 and 1199; and William de Duglas, about the same period, is a witness to a grant to the monks of Arbroath by Thomas the son of Tankard, a Fleming who was settled in Clydesdale. The grandson of William de Duglas the son of Theobald obtained in 1270 a second grant from the monks of Kelso of a considerable tract of land along the rivulet Pollenel, and adjoining his demesne of Duglas.† In 1288 the same Douglas is seen granting an

---

* Rymer Fœd. vol ii. p. 266.

† Lib. de Calchow. This grant was made to the Douglas in consideration of aid afforded by him to the abbey of Kelso in troublous times.

acknowledgment to the abbot of Kelso for all his charters which were in the custody of the abbot.* To show still further the close connection between the monks of Kelso and the lairds of Douglas, it may be mentioned that when Bricius, one of the younger sons of the first William de Duglas, chose the church, the abbot of Kelso became his patron, and under his benign influence Bricius rose to be the prior of Lesmahago in his native vale, and dean of Moray.† At the death of Richard in 1203, the same influence obtained for him the appointment of Bishop of Moray.‡ In gratitude to the abbot of Kelso, the bishop granted to him the church of Birnie, in Moray, with the pertinents and lands thereof.§ Had the family been so eminent at an early date, as contended for by the peerage writers and others, they must have been seen taking a part in the important transactions

---

* Lib. de Calchow.

† In 1144 David I. granted to the abbey of Kelso, by the advice of the Bishop of Glasgow, the church and territory of Lesmahago for instituting a cell for the monks of Kelso, and for receiving poor travellers ; he granted his peace to all fleeing to the said cell, or who came within its four crosses, to escape peril of life or limb. The prior had a seat in parliament. It is said that Lesmahago derived importance from its affording a retreat to the monks of Kelso during the ravages of border war.

‡ Chron. Melros. "Obiit Ricardus Episcopus de Moravia cui succedit dom Brecius prior de Lesmahago."

§ Lib. de Calchow.

of the kingdom; and the fact that they do not so appear shows clearly that, however respectable the race was as lairds of Douglas, they were *not eminent men of the kingdom* till Sir James arose in the beginning of the fourteenth century.*

At the time of his father's death in 1302 Sir James was in France, but on his return to his country he fought under the Bruce for the independence of Scotland. He commanded the left wing of the army at Bannockburn, and greatly contributed to the victory. By his vigour the English were expelled from Teviotdale, excepting Jedburgh, Roxburgh, and some other places. In 1318, as noticed above, Bruce granted to him the town of Jedburgh, the castle thereof, and the forest of Jedburgh, with Bonjedworth. So high did he stand in the favour of this good king that in 1325 a new charter was granted him, by which all his lands, wheresoever situated, were erected into a free regality, and possession or sasine thereof given by investing him with the king's emerald ring—a symbol of kingly power—and from which circumstance it is said the charter has been since called "THE EMERALD CHARTER." This grant included Ettrick forest, which had been won by his valour from the English. It also comprehended the

---

* It is said that the family of Douglas up to this period never parted with an acre of land which they acquired by marriage.

town and territory of Lauder, which had formerly belonged to the family of Morvilles, which in early times supplied constables to Scotland. In 1196 the vast estates of the Morvilles passed by a female to the Lords of Galloway, and from them, by other female heirs, to Roger de Quincey, William de Fortibus, and John Baliol, whose son competed for the crown. Baliol represented the Morvilles in Berwickshire, and after his forfeiture the territory of Lauder passed to Douglas by the Emerald Charter.* This gallant warrior fell at Theba on the frontiers of Andalusia, on August 25, 1330. His remains were conveyed to Scotland and interred in the church of St. Bride. Sir James, not having been married, was succeeded by his brother Hugh, who, in May 1342, resigned the estates of the family (excepting Jedburgh forest) into the hands of David II., who renewed the grant to William Douglas, nephew of the said Hugh, and his heirs male.† His father was Archibald, who was created Lord of Galloway by King Robert Bruce, and who fell at Halidown hill in 1333.‡ On his return from France, where he had been for his education, he was, in 1342, by David II., appointed leader of the men of Roxburgh and Selkirk. After

---

* Robertson's Index, No. 10.   † Ib. p. 55, No. 18.
‡ Ib. p. 31, No. 42. He was called the Tynman on ac-count of his never having been engaged in a battle without losing it and also some part of his person.

the fatal battle of Nevil's Cross, the English, who had been in 1338 driven out of Teviotdale by the knight of Liddesdale, invaded the country, retook the castle of Roxburgh, and again seized Teviotdale and the forest of Selkirk. At this epoch William Douglas of Douglas appeared upon the scene, and the men of Teviotdale, recognizing in the young chieftain the spirit of his uncle the good Sir James, gathered around him, and by their bravery enabled him to defeat Coupland, the governor of Roxburgh Castle, in a pitched battle, and expel the English from the shires of Roxburgh and Selkirk. During these conflicts the knight of Liddesdale, another William Douglas, said to be a bastard son of the good Sir James, was prisoner in England with David II., and entered into an intrigue with the King of England, whereby Edward agreed to give the knight his freedom, with Liddesdale, Hermitage Castle, and other lands, on condition that the knight should hold the whole from the English king, and allow free passage to his armies into Scotland. Both parties immediately entered upon the fulfilment of this contract, but William Douglas, the leader of the men of Teviotdale, being informed of the treason, ordered the knight to be slain while hunting in Galeswood in the forest in 1353.*

---

* This William Douglas, who was slain, is celebrated by historians and poets as the Knight of Liddesdale, the *flower*

Edward III. took the widow under his care, and married her to a brother of the Lord Dacres; but the Castle of Hermitage was seized by William Douglas. In 1357 he was created the first Earl of Douglas. He died in 1384 in his castle of

---

of chivalry. Considerable difficulty exists in identifying the Knight of Liddesdale in consequence of there being two knights of that name whose fathers were both named James. Godescroft says the knight was a bastard son of the good Sir James. The genealogists Crawfurd and Douglas are of opinion that the knight was the son of Sir James Douglas of Lothian, second cousin to the good Sir James. Lord Hailes also takes the same view; but Chalmers produces decisive proofs that the real Knight of Liddesdale was William Douglas of Polbothy, the bastard son of the good Sir James. He is so named by Edward III. when taken prisoner by Sir Anthony Lucy in March, 1333. He remained a prisoner in England for two years, and could not be present at the battle of Halidown hill, fought in July, 1333; but the other William Douglas of Lothian was present and taken prisoner at that battle. William of Lothian's wife was Margaret Graham; the wife of the knight who transacted with Edward was called Elizabeth, and when he was set at liberty the English king ordered the lands of Polbothy to be restored to him which had been granted by Robert I. to the good Sir James. It may therefore with safety be held that the true Knight of Liddesdale, who made so conspicuous a figure on the borders, was Sir William Douglas of Polbothy, bastard son of the good Sir James Douglas. It is said that jealousy influenced the Douglas to seek the death of the Knight of Liddesdale; but, be this as it may, the murder of Sir Alexander Ramsay and the intrigue with the King of England were sufficient grounds for putting him to death. The weakness of the king prevented him

Douglas, and was buried in the abbey of Melrose. From 1342 to his death he bore a decisive sway upon the borders, and to such a degree of power did the family rise that " nae man was safe in the country unless he were either a Douglas or a Douglas man." When he went abroad his escort consisted of 2,000 men; he kept a kingly court, and created knights.

The first Earl of Douglas was, at his death in 1384, succeeded by his gallant son James, who terminated a short but glorious career on the field of Otterburn. This celebrated battle was, fought upon St. Oswald's-day, August 5, 1388. It is said by many writers, as I think erroneously, that the beautiful ballad of " Chevy-chase" is founded upon this great battle. But the ballad describes a conflict between the Douglas and Percy for possession of a hunting-ground, while the battle of Otterburn was the termination of an inroad in which the forces of both nations were engaged. It is necessary to attend to a few facts. The King of England having entered Berwickshire with a large army, and laid it waste, the King of Scotland assembled his nobles at Aberdeen, and by their

---

from punishing the knight at the time of Ramsay's cruel murder. It must also be kept in view that Douglas of Jedforest was both warden of the marches and the king's justiciar, and within the bounds of the two forests he had regal power.

advice it was resolved that the whole force of the realm should be raised to revenge the injuries done by the English.   An army of between thirty and forty thousand men, under the command of the Duke of Albany, marched for England. While in the forest of Jedburgh the duke detached the Earl of Douglas, the Earls of Dunbar and Moray, with 15,000 men, to enter England by the eastern border, while he himself penetrated the western frontier.*   Both divisions laid the country desolate as they passed through with fire and sword, and met about ten miles from Newcastle.   To repel this invasion all the chosen men from York to the borders were soon in arms under the command of Henry and Ralph Percy, sons of the Earl of Northumberland, who, from extreme old age, could not follow the steps of the Scottish leaders.   Before the gates of Newcastle the famous

---

* It is said by Sir Walter Scott that the Scots army met at Yetholm, but his statement is not warranted by the fact; and it is thought that he has mistaken *Yetholm* for Southdean, the early spelling of the two being much alike.   The army could not have collected at Yetholm, for at that time the English had possession of a line of forts from Berwick to Jedburgh, *i.e.* Berwick, Norham, Cornhill, Wark, Roxburgh, and Jedburgh.   The forces of Scotland would require to keep to the west of Jedburgh, and it is probable that they crossed the valley of the Rule above Bonster and met in the neighbourhood of Southdean, from whence they could conveniently pass either to the west or east by old Roman ways.

Hotspur was unhorsed by the gallant Douglas, and also lost his "*staffe.*"* The English forces having been greatly increased in numbers, Douglas retreated towards Redesdale, pursued by the Percies with an army of chosen troops, who again were followed by the Bishop of Durham, with all the yeomanry of the bishopric. The armies met at Otterburn, and a terrible battle ensued. The victory fell to the Scots, but it was dearly purchased by the death of Douglas, who fell in the front ranks covered with wounds. The two Percies were taken prisoners by the Scots, and the English retired from this memorable conflict. Such was the battle of Otterburn. It has not the least resemblance to a skirmish between two gallant men and their followers for possession of a certain territory; on the contrary, the inroad was planned by an assembly of nobles presided over by the king, a king's son was the chief leader of the army, and with him were associated not only nearly all the leading nobility, but the wisest and

---

* The spear and pennon of Percy were carried with the body of Montgomery to Eglinton Castle, and when a late duke asked their restoration, the Earl of Eglinton replied, "There is as good lea-ground here as on Chevy-chase; let Percy come and take them." Froissart says this encounter happened accidentally. Other writers say that the two chieftains met in consequence of a challenge given by Percy to fight the Douglas man to man—a practice common in those days.

bravest of Scotland's generals. But while Otter-burn was a national event, the ballad of Chevy-chase touchingly describes one among a thousand of the skirmishes which took place between the Douglas and Percy for possession of that land which both claimed as their own by grants from their respective kings, and it is probable that the bard who recorded it shared in the fray. Of a portion of the Chase at least Percy was the earliest owner. For the better understanding of this matter it is proper to notice the connection the family had with this district in early times. When David took possession of this part of the kingdom at his father's death, *Allan de Perci* appears as one of those whom the prince loved to honour. He is one of the witnesses to the *Inquisitio Davidis* in 1116, and he is also a witness to a charter by David, when he became King of Strathannan, in favour of Robert Bruce.* He obtained a grant from David of the baronies of Oxnam and Heiton. In 1138 he was present with the king at the battle of the Standard, where he acted with the impetuosity of his race. He granted a ploughgate of land in Oxnam, and ano-ther in Heiton, to the monks of *Whitby*.† About

---

* Chart. Antiq. Bibl. Harl.

† These grants were for the salvation of his own soul, for the salvation of the souls of *his lord King David*, and his son Earl Henry, and for the souls of his father. Allan de

1153 Geoffrey, his brother and heir, granted, with the consent of Henri de Perci, his brother and heir, to the monks of Kelso, for the souls' health of David I. and Henry his son, a ploughgate of land in Heiton, containing *one hundred and four acres,* next to the land belonging to Roxburgh hospital.* He also gave to the monks of Jedburgh the church of Oxnam and two ploughgates, and two bovates near the church, with pasture and fuel in the common. Henry de Percy, who succeeded Geoffrey, confirmed the grant in the presence of Malcolm the Maiden, and added to it the lands of Newbigging, with pasture and fuel, as enjoyed by the other inhabitants of the village of Oxnam.† These grants were confirmed by William the Lion before 1174.‡ From the Percy the barony of Oxnam and Heiton passed into the family of Colville at the death, it is thought, of the said Henri de *Perci* without issue. Such was the early connection of the Percy with an extensive portion of the Chase. For 150 years the family are not seen

Percy, and of his mother. This grant was witnessed by his brothers Malcolm, Walter, Geoffrey, and Henry. Dugdale's Monasticon, vol. i. p. 74; Charlton's Whitby, p. 81.

* Lib. de Calchow, pp. 286-7.

† Henry seems to have been much in the company of Malcolm. He witnessed two charters about 1159. Dug. Monasticon, vol. i. p. 851; Diplom. Scotiæ, pl. 24.

‡ Chart. Jedburgh. Original at Dalkeith.

possessing any part of the forest.   When Baliol in
1334 ceded to Edward III. the town and forest of
Jedburgh, that king granted the castle, con-
stabulary, and the towns of Bonjedworth and Hassendean to Henry de Percy, in exchange for
Annandale.*   So firmly was it believed by all that
the territory belonged to Percy, that when Hugh,
the brother of the good Sir James, resigned into
the hands of the king the estates of the Douglas,
in favour of William Douglas his nephew, Jedburgh forest and town were not included in the
deed.†   But the young Douglas boldly laid claim
to the forest and the whole territory thereof, as
described in a charter of the Bruce, as the heir,
not only of his uncle Hugh, but of his other
uncle the good Sir James.   It was still in the
hands of the English in 1363, although included
in the treaty between David II. and Edward III.‡
In 1367 Henry Percy was in possession.§   In
1374 a commission was appointed by Edward III.
to settle the disputes between the families of Percy
and Douglas as to this territory.‖   But in 1384
Douglas succeeded by his gallantry in getting
possession of the territory which belonged to his
uncle Sir James, except Jedburgh and Roxburgh,

* Rotuli Scotiæ, vol. i. p. 793.
† Robertson's Index, p. 55, No. 18.
‡ Acta Parl. Scot. vol. i. p. 135.
§ Rotuli Scotiæ, vol. i. p. 911.   ‖ Ib. p. 965.

which remained in the hands of the English. In 1403 the whole of Teviotdale was bestowed on Percy.* Two years after Jedburgh and the whole of the neighbouring country was claimed by the English king as his own property.† From these notices it will be seen that when the English power prevailed Percy was owner of Teviotdale, and when the star of the Douglas was in the ascendant, Douglas enjoyed his own again. These grants by the kings of Scotland and England to their favourite warriors were the true causes of the enmity of the two houses of Douglas and Percy. The ballad of Chevy-chase describes a conflict which occurred between them when the *Douglas* held the forest. In the spirit of these chivalrous times—

> " The Persé owt of Northombarlande,
> And a vowe to God mayd he,
> That he wolde hunte in the mountayns
> Off Chyviat within dayes thre,
> In the mauger of doughtè Dogles,
> And all that ever with him be."

This vaunt being reported to the Douglas, no doubt by the order of Percy himself,

> " Be my feth, sayd the doughtè Dogles agayn,
> I wyll let that hontyng yf that I may."

Into Scotland, with fifteen hundred chosen

---

* Rotuli Scotiæ, vol. ii. p. 174.   † Ib.

archers and greyhounds for the chase, Percy
marched on a Monday morning.

> " The dryvars thorowe the woodes went
> For to reas the dear;
> Bomen bickarte uppone the bent
> With ther browd aras cleare.

> " Then the wyld thorowe the woodes went
> On every syde shear,
> Grea-hondes thorowe the groves glent
> For to kyll thear dear."

By the hour of noon a hundred fat harts lay
dead, and as Percy, with his men assembled around
him, stood and gazed on the fallow deer and harts
of grice,

> " He sayd it was the Duglas promys
> This day to meet me hear;
> But I wyste he wold faylle verament:
> A gret oth the Persè swear.

> " At the laste, a squyar of Northomberlonde,
> Lokyde at his hand full ny,
> He was war ath the doughtie Doglas comynge
> With him a myghtè meany,

> " Both with spear, byll, and brande:
> Yt was a myghti sight to se;
> Hardyar men, both off bart nar hande,
> Wear not in Christiantè.

> " The wear twenty hondrith spearmen good,
> Withouten any fayle;
> The wear borne along be the watter a Twyde
> Yth boundes of Tividale."

Percy saw that stern work was at hand, and
ordered his men to leave off the sport and look to
their bows being in a serviceable state for the
coming conflict. When Douglas approached " on
his milk-white steed, mist like a baron bold," he
demanded to know whose men they were that,
without his consent, did hunt in the chase and kill
his deer. Percy was the first man who spoke, and
replied that he would not say whose men they
were, but they would hunt in the chase in spite of
him and those who were with him. The Douglas
then swore by St. Bride that one of them should
die, and proposed to settle the dispute by single
combat, and save the lives of their men who were
guiltless. But a squire of Northumberland inter-
posed, and declared that his leader should not fight
on a field while he stood looking on, for while he
could a weapon wield he would fight with heart
and hand. The bows of the Englishmen were
then bent, and discharged a shower of arrows upon
the Scottish force. But the men of Teviotdale
were not dismayed ; they levelled their spears " off
myghtie tre," and rushed on the English archers.
A general battle then ensued, the result of which
is not given in the old ballad, but in later copies
the victory is declared in favour of the country in
which the ballad happened to be printed.

It is impossible to read the two ballads of Chevy-
chase and Otterburn and believe that they relate the

same event ; they are entirely different. The ballad of Chevy-chase makes Percy the invader of
Scotland ; Otterburn makes Douglas the ravager of
England. The conflict of Chevy-chase was fought
on a *Monday*, Otterburn took place on a *Wednesday*. In the ballad of Chevy-chase two earls are
the leaders ; the one army composed of men of
pleasant Teviotdale, and the other of the hardy
sons of Northumberland. At the battle of Otterburn the Earl of Northumberland did not head
the English army, which was made up of the
soldiers of all the northern shires, with the yeomanry of the bishopric ; while the Scots army consisted of the whole forces that could be raised in
Scotland. In short, the ballad of Chevy-chase
must either be taken as describing a conflict between the Douglas and Percy for possession of
ground which each claimed as his own, or rejected
as pure fiction. I believe the ballad to be history
and truth ; " but history exalted, elevated, in-
spired ; truth, all life, spirit, and heroism."*

---

* A writer in the *Penny Magazine*, while treating of the
English historical ballads, says of Chevy-chase :—" We
shall not attempt to vindicate our admiration of this ballad
by quoting the praise of Sydney, the criticism of Addison,
or the commendations of Scott. There are, we believe, few
memories without a portion of it. We have heard it quoted
by the dull as by the bright, by the learned as by the
illiterate ; nay, we once heard an accomplished lady sing it
to the harp, while the greatest genius of our isle since the

James was succeeded by his brother Archibald,
surnamed the *Grim*, who long enjoyed the estates
and influence of the family. He died of fever at
Restalrig in 1400, after returning from the pursuit

---

days of Milton witnessed to its beauty by his tears. Nor
was it the heroism and chivalry of the ballad which called
forth such testimony ; it contains bits of tenderness which
our painters as well as our poets have felt.

> " ' Next day did many widows come
>   Their husbands to bewail ;
>   They washed their wounds in brinish tears,
>   But all would not prevail.

> " ' Their bodies bathed in purple gore
>   They bore with them away,
>   And kiss'd them dead a thousand times
>   Ere they were clad in clay.' "

Fifty years ago scarcely a cottage on the borders of Scotland but contained on its window-shelves copies of "Chevy-
chase," "Sir William Wallace," "Sir James the Rose," and
other historical ballads, alongside the well-worn family
Bible and the works of Boston, Erskine, and other Scots
worthies. Almost every mother delighted to recite and sing
to her children the productions of Scotland's ancient minstrels ; and few there were of the young who could not talk
of the deeds of their forefathers. But things are sadly
changed : the works of the old divines are pushed into a
corner, where they lie musty and moth-eaten ; the ballads
which celebrated the deeds of Wallace, Bruce, the fiery
Douglas, and heroic Percy, have entirely disappeared. Instead of the Bible and the works of the old fathers trashy
tracts are to be found, and the place of the ballad literature
is filled by weekly and monthly serials of a very doubtful
kind.

of Hotspur and the Earl of March, who had invaded Scotland, leaving behind him "a memory of his high prowess and noble valiancy showed in many and sundry enterprises by him luckilie achieved for the wealth of his countrie. He was surnamed, from his terrible countenance and dreadful look, *the Grim Douglasse.*" His second son, Archibald, was the next Earl of Douglas. Sore displeased at the loss of many gallant men in a conflict between Hepbourne of Hailes and Hotspur, assisted by the Earl of March, the Earl of Douglas led 10,000 men into England, and slept not till he reached Newcastle, burning and destroying the country on his way. But on returning with a great booty, Hotspur and March, with a large force, met him on the Cheviot hills at a place called Homildon, and, after one of the bloodiest engagements of that day, the Scots were worsted with great slaughter. Many of the nobles of Scotland fell, and the earl himself, and the most part of the Barons of Fife and Lothian, were taken prisoners. The battle was fought on the Rood-day and on a *Tuesday*. This earl carried the Scottish auxiliaries to France, where he was created marshal of her armies and Duke of Touraine. He commanded at the battle of Verneuil, where he fell with many a Scotsman, in August, 1424. Archibald, his next son, succeeded. He assisted the French from 1419 to 1424, when he

returned home. In 1424 he was one of the am-
bassadors sent to England to treat of the ransom
of the king, which they accomplished, and returned
home with the king. He died in 1438. His daughter, the Lady Margaret, was celebrated as " the
fair maid of Galloway." The power of the house
of Douglas now rivalled that of the king, and their
possessions in Scotland and France equalled in
income the revenues of the crown. William, his
son and heir, succeeded at the age of seventeen,
and immediately assumed all the state and independence of a king. His personal attendants consisted of 1,000 men, and he could bring into the
field at any time an army of well-disciplined
troops. The Chancellor Crichton, having resolved
to cut off the Earl William and his younger
brother David, invited them to Edinburgh Castle,
where they were beheaded, and shortly after their
friend Malcolm Fleming, of Cumbernauld, shared
the same fate. It is said that this murder was
committed by the connivance of James the *Gros*,
who succeeded and who died in 1443. His son
William was the eighth Earl of Douglas, and
married his cousin, " the fair maid of Galloway."
The king at the age of fourteen assumed the
government, and chose him for his favourite. In
attempting to revenge the wrongs of his family,
the earl raised a civil war. He was stabbed by
the king in Stirling in 1452 for refusing to break

the Grahamslaw league.*   James, the ninth earl, flew to arms to avenge the death of his brother; and had he possessed only a small portion of the decision of his race the Stewarts would have at that time ceased to reign in Scotland.   Procrastination ruined his cause, and his partisans placed themselves under the standard of the king.   In June, 1455, the earl, his mother, brothers, and his adherents were forfeited by parliament; he died in monastic seclusion in 1488.   He was the last of the race called the " Black" Douglas.   The lands reverted to the crown, but were in a short time conferred on the Earl of Angus, the head of a younger branch of the old family, descended from George, the only son of William the first Earl of Douglas.   He was the first of the " Red" race, and did what he could to destroy the old house. From the accession of this line the possessions of the family were held in uninterrupted succession till the death of the Duke of Douglas in 1761, when the ducal title became extinct.   The Duke of Hamilton got the title on account of his descent from the first Marquis and eleventh Earl of Douglas.   The real and personal estate of the last Duke of Douglas passed to his sister's son Archibald Stewart, Esquire, who was served heir to him in Septem-

---

* This league is said to have been signed in the coves at Grahamslaw on the Cayle Water.

ber, 1761,* and created Baron Douglas in 1796. The last heir male of this race died in 1857, while the sheets of this work were passing through the

---

* This gentleman was a party to the celebrated " Douglas cause." As mentioned in the text, the Duke of Douglas died childless in 1761, when the title became extinct, but the real and personal estates were claimed by his nephew Archibald Stewart as the lawful child of Lady Jane Douglas, sister to the duke, by a secret marriage with Mr. Stewart, afterwards Sir John Stewart, of Grandtully, in 1746. Lady Jane was at the time of her marriage forty-eight years of age, and is said to have been one of the handsomest women of her day. They resided abroad till 1749, when they returned to London, bringing with them two male children, of whom they said Lady Jane had been delivered in Paris in 1748, when her ladyship was fifty years old. The youngest twin died in May, 1753, and the Lady Jane died in the November following in Edinburgh. At the Duke's death the guardians of the surviving twin sought to put him in possession of the estates by serving him heir to the deceased Duke; but this service was opposed by the Duke of Hamilton and the Earl of Selkirk, who claimed the estates as heir male. The jury having unanimously served him heir to the Duke, the tutors of the Duke of Hamilton and Sir Hew Dalrymple, of North Berwick, raised a reduction of the service on the ground that the pretended delivery of her ladyship was a fiction, and that the alleged twins belonged to poor persons in France. On the other hand, Mr. Stewart raised an action of declarator against all persons claiming as heirs of line of the Duke of Douglas. The actions were conjoined, and a long proof led. In the month of July, 1767, the case came on for judgment. The fifteen judges took eight days to deliver their opinions, the result of which was that seven voted for the legitimacy of

press ; he was the third son of the said Archibald Stewart Baron Douglas.

FERNIEHERST.—On .the right bank of the river, nearly opposite the stronghold of the Douglas, stands Fernieherst, in early times the mansion of the Kers, the vassals of the Douglas, and the bailies of the abbey of Jedburgh. It is thought that no part of the present structure is older than the end of the sixteenth century. It occupies the site of a baronial fortress, erected in 1410 by Thomas Ker, a person distinguished in border warfare, and called by him Fernieherst. No information exists as to its form, but, according to Earl Surrey, it " stode marvelous strong, within a grete woode."* There can be little doubt that the name was given to the house as descriptive of the locality in which it stood—on a terrace or bank in the middle of an oak wood. The situation was well chosen for beauty and strength. The nearly impervious forest surrounded it on every side, and formed a perfect security from surprise. From the bank on which the castle stands there is a view of the valley, beautified by the numerous

---

the children, and seven against it ; the Lord President gave his casting vote against the legitimacy. The cause was carried to the House of Lords and reversed in 1769. It is a strange story.

* Surrey's letter to Henry VIII.

FERNIEHIRST CASTLE.

G.B

windings of the Jed, bounded on both sides by
shady banks and impending precipices clothed
with wood; these again bounded by distant mountains, composing a justly admired landscape. Some
time ago the remains of this baronial abode were
converted into a farm-house for the occupant of
the surrounding lands, and *the beautiful chapel
into a stable for his horses.* It may have been
necessary to turn the dwelling of a " baron bold"
into a farm-house, but surely the chapel might
have been spared!

This place has been the scene of many a fray.
Not a spot around the mansion but has been
drenched in blood. The day after Earl Surrey
had taken Jedburgh, in 1523, he despatched Lord
Dacre with eight hundred men to assault Fernieherst; but the besiegers were severely handled by
the defenders, commanded in person by its owner,
and it was only " with long skirmishing and moche
difficultie gat furthe the ordynance within the
house, and threwe down the same." Ker was
taken captive.* It is said by Surrey that the

---

* " The next daye I sente my seid Lorde Dacre to a
stronghold called Fernherst, the lorde whereof was his
mortal enemy; and with hym Sir Arthur Darcy, Sir Mar-
maduke, constable, with DCCC. of their men, one cortoute,
and dyvers other good peces of ordynance for the field (the
seid Fernherst stode marvelous strongly within a grete
woode); the seid two knights, with the moost parte of their

house was thrown down, but it seems to have been afterwards repaired and strengthened by the English, for in 1549 it stood a severe siege by the French general who was then in possession of Jedburgh, aided by Sir John Ker himself and the inhabitants of the district. The garrison defended themselves with great skill and courage, not only repelling the besiegers, but sallying from the castle and showering their arrows down the steep ascent leading to it, and also from the outer wall by which it was surrounded. The besiegers, however, won the "lims" of the house, and forced the English into the keep, where they were kept so hotly engaged as to afford opportunity to the besiegers to . mine a hole in the wall capable of admitting a man. After this was done, a great number of Scots broke open the gate of the base-court and burst on in heaps, thirsting for vengeance, on the

---

men and Strickland your grace servaunte, with my Kendall men, went into the woode on fote with th' ordynance, where the seid Kendall men were soo handled, that they found hardy men that went noo fote back for theym; the other twoo knightes were alsoo soo sharply assayled that they were enforced to call for moo of their men, and yet could not bring the ordynance to the fortresse unto the tyme my Lorde Dacre, with parte of his horsemen, lighted on fote ; and marvelously hardly handled himself, and fynally, with long skirmyshing and moche difficultie, gat forthe th' ordynance within the house, and threwe down the same."—*Letter of Earl Surrey to Henry VIII.*

Englishmen, especially the captain, who had committed such excesses of lust and cruelty "as would," says a chronicler of the event, " have made to tremble the most savage Moor in Africa." The captain, aware of his peril if he fell into the hands of the Scots, presented himself at the hole which the Frenchmen had made by the mine, and yielded himself a prisoner to the commander of the French troops, and implored his protection, which that officer readily granted, and attempted to take him out of the strife ; but a marcher coming behind him, whose wife it is said he had ravished, smote off his head so just from his shoulders that it leaped four or five yards from his body. Many of the Scots then rushed forward and washed their hands in the blood of their oppressor, tossing the head from hand to hand as if it had been a game at ball. Every prisoner was put to death in the most cruel manner, the victors, it is said, " contending who should display the greatest address in severing the legs and arms before inflicting a mortal wound. When their own prisoners were slain, the Scots purchased those of the French, parting willingly with their very arms in exchange for an English captain." An officer of the French band, in relating the tale of horrors, says, " I myself sold them a prisoner for a small horse. They laid him down upon the ground, galloped over him with their lances in rest, and wounded him as they

passed. When slain they cut his body in pieces
and bore the mangled gobbets in triumph on the
point of their spears.   I cannot greatly praise the
Scots for this practice; but the truth is, the English
tyrannized over the borders in a most barbarous
manner, and I think it was but fair to repay them,
according to the proverb, in their own coin."*

In 1569 the Earl of Northumberland, Sir Egre-
mont Ratcliffe, and other leaders of the English
insurgents, found shelter at Fernieherst. The Earl
of Westmoreland retired to the tower of Hector
Armstrong.   Next year the Earl of Sussex penetrated into Teviotdale, and not only laid in ruins
this stronghold, but other fifty towers and peels,
plundered and destroyed three hundred towns,
villages, and hamlets, belonging to Ker and Buc-
cleugh, in revenge of an inroad made by the two
into England the year previous, as well as for their
having afforded hospitality to the leaders of the
English insurgents.†

---

* Hollingshed, vol. ii. pp. 252-3. Compegnes de Beauge.

† LEGEND OF FERNIEHERST.—A lady of the place, *not*
famed for piety and good works, was in the habit of walking
in the dark oak woods surrounding the castle. In one of
her rambles it is said she met a gentleman in black, whose
appearance and conversation made such an impression on
her at the first meeting, that she consented to meet him at
the same place next evening. They accordingly met, and
the gentleman so gained upon the lady, that he became her
lover, and many a time and oft at night they wandered in

The castle continued the chief residence of the family till they obtained the honours of nobility. Newbattle, in Lothian, then became the principal seat of the family, and latterly Mount Teviot Lodge, on the soft margins of the Teviot, where a new mansion was begun about thirty years ago, by the father of the present marquis, upon an elegant and commodious plan, becoming the residence of this ancient race; but it is not yet finished.

The precise period at which the surname of Ker first appeared in Scotland is involved in obscurity. Several antiquarians trace the origin of the family to France, and allege that the first of the name who arrived in England came in the army of William the Conqueror, as one of his principal officers. Others, again, are of opinion that the name is local, and first assumed by the possessors of the lands and baronies of Ker and Ker's Hall, in Yorkshire. Sir George Mackenzie, who is followed by

---

the woody glens of Fernieherst. At last the lady felt herself to be "as ladies wish to be who love their lords," but before the time of her confinement it became known to herself and friends that her lover was " no earthly man." When the time of her delivery arrived a great cauldron of boiling oil was provided, for the purpose of scalding to death the fiend-begotten birth at its first appearance, but on seeing the light the "ill thing" managed to evade the cauldron, made its way through the attendants, and escaped by the chimney, leaving, however, the marks of its claws on the chimney brace, which marks are said to be visible to this day.

S

Douglas in his Peerage, says that the Kers first settled on the borders in the year 1330, and that the settlement was made by two brothers, Ralph and Robert, and presumes that Ralph, the ancestor of the Kers of Fernieherst, was the elder brother, because they carried the same arms with the Kers in England and France, without any difference either in tincture or charge. Robert, the younger, is said to be the progenitor of the Cessfurd Kers, who now enjoy the ducal honours of Roxburgh.* Later peerage writers fix the first settlement of the Kers in Scotland in the end of the thirteenth century. Chalmers also concurs in this view.† But it is evident the name must have existed before the period referred to by the peerage writers. At the end of the twelfth century " John Ker, the hunter of Swynhope," is one of twenty-eight witnesses who were present at the perambulation of the marches of Stobo.‡ But while this fact puts the existence of the name previous to the thirteenth century beyond doubt, it is certain that no traces of the name have been as yet discovered

---

* It may be noticed that the two houses became amalgamated in the persons of William, eldest son of Robert, first Earl of Ancrum, and Lady Anne, the eldest daughter of Robert, second Earl of Lothian, and Lady Annabella Campbell, daughter of Archibald Earl of Argyle.

† Caledonia, vol. i. p. 543.

‡ Register of Glas. p. 89.   " Johes Ker uenator aput Swynhope."

in the borderland till about 1330, when it appears in conjunction with the Douglas, the favourite warrior of the Bruce.*　At that period Ralph settled in the forest of Jedburgh, on lands obtained from the Douglas, lying between the waters of Jed and Scraesburgh. The locality was afterwards called by his own name, which it retains to the present day. Since that time great changes have taken place in the face of the country. The waters of Jed still roll over their rocky channel, through scenes of surpassing loveliness ; but nothing now remains of the old forest, excepting a few clumps of oak and birch on the hill-sides, and here and there a solitary oak in the vale below. One of these, the capon-tree noticed above, stands on a beautiful haugh, through which flow the waters of the Jed. The land on which the tree stands formerly belonged to the monastery of Jedburgh, being called by the name of the prior of that house, Prior's-haugh. In the first volume I hazarded a conjecture that the name of this tree

---

* On referring to the history of the kingdom during the latter part of the thirteenth century and beginning of the next, it will be seen that one of the name of Ker followed the fortunes of the patriotic Wallace, and aided in the war of independence. The Douglas and Ker were fellow-soldiers in the gallant struggle which ended in the emancipation of Scotland from the thraldom of the English king. From this a reason may be found for the Kers selecting the margins of the Jed.

was derived from the monks, " who delighted to
wander amidst such lovely scenes, and linger beneath the shade of the wide-spreading oaks."*   I
am now satisfied that the tree derives its name
from its remarkable resemblance to the hood worn
by the monks of Jedburgh, and which was called
a *capon*.   On the opposite page will be found an
engraving of the tree and also a monk of Jedburgh
hooded.   The king of the wood stands on the
property of the Kers, and within the first grant.†

Thomas the son of Ralph is said by Douglas, in
his Peerage, to have purchased the lands of Crail-
ling from the Humes, and married a daughter of
Sir Thomas Somerville of Carnwath, and widow
of Kilpatrick of Closeburn in Nithsdale.   Her
mother was daughter of Alexander Stewart, Lord
Darnley, ancestor of King James VI.   His son
Andrew rose to be cupbearer to Robert III.
Thomas his son and heir was one of the gentlemen
of rank who accompanied the Earl of Douglas to
Rome.   He married the eldest daughter of Sir
Thomas Home.   Ralph his son succeeded and
died about 1460, leaving two sons, Andrew his
heir, and Robert afterwards of Yair.   Andrew
married a daughter of the first Lord Herries, who
bore to him two sons, Thomas, who succeeded, and
John Ker, the stem of the Kers of Greenhead.   He

---

* Vol. i. p. 48.   † Ib.

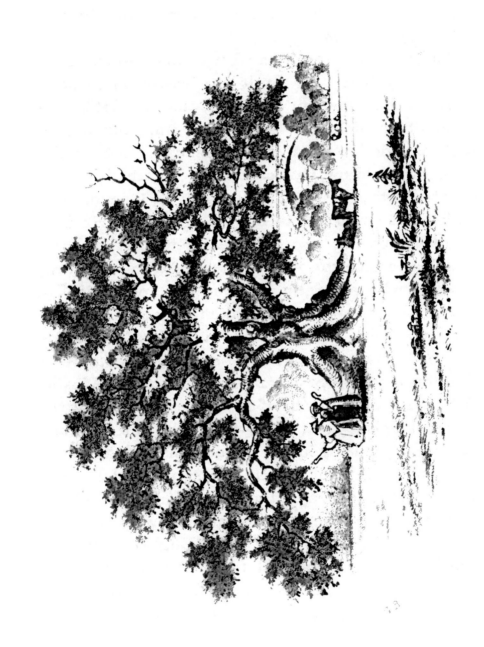

was the last of the Kers who were called by the title of *Kersheugh.*

Thomas the eighth laird was distinguished in border warfare. He built the castle as noticed above in the middle of the wood, and called it by the name of Fernieherst. From this time the family took the designation of Fernieherst. About the time of building the castle he obtained a new charter from Archibald Earl of Angus, the superior, which was confirmed to his son in 1511. He died in 1499, leaving two sons, Andrew, his heir, and Ralph, the ancestor of the Kers of Cavers. Andrew, his son, who generally went by the appellation of *Dand Ker,* seems to have taken an active hand in border affairs previous to his father's death.* Under that name he appears at the justice ayre at Jedburgh in 1493 as cautioner for Ralph Ainslie, for treasonable stonthreif and hereship made at the place of Spittal, of twenty-four oxen and cows and six horses, with goods and utensils belonging to the tenants thereof.† He is also marked as cautioner at the same ayre for Adam Kirkton of Crailing-mill, "for the treasonable carrying off of a shoemaker in Jedeworthe to the English, and causing him to be redeemed for £40 sterling." He

---

* He is erroneously called David in several histories and other works.

† Pitcairn's Criminal Trials, vol. i. p. 17.

was also cautioner for Simon Young of Rouchlee, for stealing from the farm of Hundalee. In all the entries Andrew and Dand seem to be synonymous.* He also appeared at the justice ayre of 1502, and became cautioner for the Olivers in Stryndes, charged with many thefts and the resetting of rebels.† He was one of the assize who sat at Edinburgh in 1512 on the trial of several parties accused of theft and treason.‡ In 1515 Dand Ker marched to Kelso with a body of his retainers, and, having assaulted the abbey, took it and turned the superior out of doors. About the same time he was, along with Lord Hume and Mr. William Hume, arrested and imprisoned that better rule might be kept on the borders. The two Humes were convicted of treason, and both beheaded, but Dand Ker escaped. Drummond says, " that David Ker, either by the jury being declared not guilty, as some have recorded, or by the corrupting of his keepers, escaped this danger."§ In 1524, when Archibald Earl of Douglas was appointed to the office of wardenry and lieutenancy of the borders, Andrew Ker was one of those who appeared and swore that he would by himself, kin, friends, servants, and " pairt-takeris," and all

---

* Pitcairn's Criminal Trials, vol. i. p. 18.   † Ib. p. 28.
‡ Ib. p. 88.
§ Drummond's History of the Jameses, p. 222.

that he may raise and stir up, loyally and truly
serve the Earl of Angus " ryde gang," and serve
at their possible power in the office of wardenry
and lieutenancy for " stanching of theft, reif,
slauchter,"· and for the execution of justice, and
furth·bearing of the king's authority.   On the same
day he appeared before the lords, along with Ker
of Cessfurd, Scott of Buccleuch, Mark Ker of
Dolphinstone, the Laird of Hundalee, the Laird of
Hunthill, the Laird of Bethroull, the Laird of
Wells, Ker of Mersington, Murray of Fallohill,
William Kirkton, the Laird of Haldane, Scott of
Synton, Scott of Allanhaugh, Hoppringell in Gal-
lowshiels, Scott of Tushielaw, Scott tutor of Howpaslet, and of their own consent bound and obliged
themselves to rise with their kin, friends, servants,
and all that they could influence, to assist the
lieutenant in the " furthputting of all Liddisdale
menne, Eskdale and Ewisdale, thare wiffis and bar-
nys, now dwelland within the bounds of Tevidale,
Ettrick forest and boundis adjacent thairto, and
hald thaim furth of the samyne in tyme to cum;"
and the said parties also became bound for every
person that lived upon their lands, under the pain
of " tynsale of lyf, land, and guddes," to produce
them to the lord-lieutenant or his deputies within
twenty days, to underlye the law for any crime
committed by them; or otherwise, within the said
twenty days, to put the transgressors, their wives,

and bairns, out of the county, and keep them out of the same, and deliver over their goods to the party who had suffered damage.* In 1520 he had a dispute with the Earl of Angus as to the bailiary of Jedburgh forest, but which was compromised. In 1530 he was, along with the Lords Maxwell and Home, the Laird of Buccleuch, Polwarth Johnson, and Mark Ker, as chiefs of the broken men of the borders, imprisoned by the king, because, as narrated by Sir James Balfour, " they had winked at villanies and given them way, quheras they by their power and authoritie might have restrained them." ˙ Better rule was thereafter kept upon the borders during the king's life.† He commanded the attack on the castle of Wark, and he was present at the battle of Melrose in July 1526, when Ker of Cessfurd was slain by Elliot of Stobbs, a follower of Buccleuch. He got a new charter of the lands of Fernieherst and others from James V., the superiority of the forest being then in the crown in consequence of the forfeiture of the Earl of Angus. He also acquired the barony of Oxnam through his mother, who was the daughter of the Lord of Ochiltree, the proprietor thereof. In 1542 he obtained a grant of the bailiary of Jedforest. He married a daughter of Sir Patrick Hume of Polwarth, who bore to him three sons

---

* Pitcairn, vol. i. p. 127.   † Lesley.

and a daughter, the eldest of whom died before his father, and the succession was taken up by John the second son, who had during his father's lifetime acquired the lands of Lanton. In most peerages he is called Sir Andrew, but I can find no trace of any of the family obtaining that honour till John was knighted by the Governor of Scotland at Jedburgh along with a number of other gentlemen of the borders.

John married a daughter of Ker of Cessfurd. In 1549 he retook, with the help of the French, as already noticed, his Castle of Fernieherst. In 1552 Fernieherst, Cessfurd, Ker of Littledon, Cowdenknowes, Greenhead, and Buccleuch, with many other valiant men, were knighted by the governor at Jedburgh as deserving "well of the commonwealth, to the end that their virtue, adorned with such honourable recompence, might be more enlarged towards the care of their countrie."* In the same assembly David Panter was consecrated Bishop of Ross. Sir John seems to have been a rebel, and at the king's horn,† shortly afterwards, it is thought for the share he had in the slaughter of Sir Walter Scott of Branxholm in the streets of Edinburgh, but for which he got a remission under the Great Seal. Sir Andrew was taken

---

* Hollingshed, vol. ii. p. 266.
† Pitcairn's Trials, vol. i. p. 379.

prisoner by the English in a skirmish near the Cheviots. Two years after the Humes invaded Crailing and the other lands of Fernieherst. Sir Thomas his heir succeeded about 1562. He was a great royalist and a steady friend of the unfortunate Mary, whom he never deserted even in her greatest distress. In her behalf Buccleuch and he entered England in 1570, but without any beneficial results to their royal mistress. Owing to the burghers of Jedburgh espousing the cause of the king, they were brought into collision with Fernieherst and Buccleuch from having maltreated a herald sent by the Queen's party to make a proclamation at the cross. Sir Thomas was present at the attack on the Earl of Lennox and the Parliament at Stirling in 1571. For his share in that gallant exploit he was forced into exile and his estates forfeited; but on James ascending the throne he was recalled, his estates restored, bailiary of Jedforest confirmed, and a remission under the Great Seal obtained for all past offences. It is said that he witnessed the execution of the Earl of Montrose and appeared to take great delight in the spectacle. He was twice married, first to a daughter of Kirkaldy of Grange, by whom he had one son, Sir Andrew, and two daughters; secondly to Jane eldest sister of Sir Walter Scott of Buccleuch, in 1569, by whom he had three sons and one daughter—Sir James Ker of Crailing, Thomas

Ker, and Robert Ker, who was afterwards created Earl of Somerset, Baron Brancepeth, and Viscount Rochester.* Sir Thomas died in ward at Aberdeen, where he had been placed to appease the wrath of Elizabeth for the slaughter of Lord Russell, the eldest son of the Duke of Bedford, at a border meeting. The broil was no doubt accidental, but Elizabeth feigned it to be premeditated on the part of Fernieherst with the view of involving the two kingdoms in war, and ordered her ambassador Wotton to demand that Fernieherst and Arran should be committed to ward. The king was greatly moved at this demand; he threw himself upon his bed and wept, declaring that "it

---

* This person was the corrupt favourite of his royal master, whom he accompanied to England, and had for a long period unlimited power at court and the absolute disposal of all the royal favours. In 1611 he was created gentleman of the bedchamber and Lord High Treasurer of Scotland; Viscount Rochester and Knight of the Garter in 1612; Earl Somerset, Baron of Brancepeth, Chamberlain of the Household, and a Privy Councillor, in 1613. He married the divorced Countess of Essex, and in 1616 both were convicted for the murder of Sir Thomas Overbury. In reference to this murder the king swore that, "*If I spare any that are guilty, God's curse light on me and my posterity for ever!*" In the face of this awful imprecation the king granted the murderers a pardon under the Great Seal in 1624. This infamous person died in 1645, and was buried in St. Paul's. It would be difficult to determine whether the master or servant was worse. The curse certainly took effect on the king's posterity.

had not grieved him so much if ten thousand men had entered the country and spoiled to Edinburgh."[*] Elizabeth commanded Randolph, who succeeded Wotton, to insist upon Fernieherst being delivered up and tried in England; but his death settled the dispute.

Sir Andrew his son and heir succeeded. While his father lived he had acquired the lands of East and West Nisbet. The charter is said to be dated in 1584. In September 1592, Fernieherst, John Rutherfurd elder of Hunthill, William Rutherfurd younger, William Rutherfurd, provost of Jedburgh, and William Kirktoun, bailie of Jedburgh, were ordered to be denounced rebels for failing to appear that day to answer a charge of treasonable reset, intercommuning, and intelligence with the Earl of Bothwell. In December following they were ordered not to approach nearer the royal presence than *ten miles*, and a warrant was granted to the magistrates of Edinburgh to arrest Andrew Ker of Fernieherst, Watt Scott of Harden, and others who could not produce a licence to remain in the city.[†] In 1600 Sir Andrew was provost of the burgh of Jedburgh. His period of office is remarkable for a riot between the clan Turnbull and its dependants on the one side, and the Kers and

---

[*] Calderwood, vol. iv. p. 380.
[†] Pitcairn's Criminal Trials, vol. i. part ii. pp. 380, 381..

the townspeople on the other.* In December 1601 Sir Andrew and a number of others were tried before the justiciary at Edinburgh for the slaughter and demembration of a number of Turnbulls, Middlemases, and Davidsons. At the trial William Earl of Angus, lord of the regality of Jedburgh Forest, appeared and claimed Sir Andrew and others as dwelling within the bounds of the regality, and produced his infeftment containing express privilege of regality. But it was answered for Turnbull of Beulie and Mynto that the sasine in favour of the Earl of Angus did not prove Fernieherst to be within the regality, and he was not therefore entitled to repledge the persons charged. Angus urged that Fernieherst and the lands thereof were part and pertinent of the lordship of Jedburgh Forest, and held of him. Ultimately the indictment was departed from in so far as concerned Fernieherst, and the cause was continued to the justice ayre of Roxburgh for trial of the other parties concerned. Sir Andrew and Sir John Ker of Hirsel were amerciated for several of the parties charged not appearing to answer the indictment made against them.† In 1662 Sir Andrew was raised to the peerage by the title of Lord Jedburgh.‡ Sir Andrew had only one son

* *Ut supra*, p. 183.   † Pitcairn, vol. ii. p. 378.

‡ The estates of the monastery were before this time erected into a lordship. It is certain that the estates of the

by a daughter of the Master of Ochiltree, who died before his father without issue. At the death of Sir Andrew in 1631, his half-brother, Sir James

---

abbey were in the family of Home at the Reformation. Jedburgh, along with Coldingham, was erected into a lordship for the Earl Home under the title of the Lordship of Coldingham. During the regency of Albany the monks of Coldingham placed themselves under the Earl Archibald Douglas, who again appointed Alexander the Laird of Home *under-keeper* of the house, with a pension of £20 Scots yearly. Ultimately the Homes got Coldingham to themselves. In 1610 a second charter was granted to the Earl of Home, of Hobkirk, Nisbet Crailing, Spittal, and Cunizerton. At this time the Kers were proprietors of Hirsel, and it was agreed on between the two families to excamb the property of Hirsel and the estates of the monastery. A contract of excambian was accordingly executed, and Home also executed an instrument of resignation the same year. Before the transaction was carried through, Home died, and some years after the Countess of Home and Ker entered into a contract whereby she bound and obliged herself to obtain a gift from the crown of the benefice and abbey of Jedburgh, the right having fallen by Home's death, to the effect that his majesty might erect the same into a temporal lordship for the Earl of Home, and enable the family to carry out their agreement with Ker. A new dissolution of the abbacy took place by act of Parliament in 1621 to enable his majesty to grant the same to Home, that the estates might be erected into a free barony, to be called the barony of Jedburgh, and to be holden free blench of the crown. The crown accordingly granted it to Home, and he again, in accordance to the previous contract, made over the barony of Jedburgh to Ker, who afterwards abtained a charter under the Great Seal of said barony of Jedburgh.— *Paper on Local Antiquities by the Author.*

Ker of Crailing, succeeded as second Lord Jedburgh. He had married Mary Rutherfurd, heiress of Hundalee. Charles II. confirmed the peerage to him. With consent of the crown he made in 1670 an entail of his estates in favour of William Lord Newbattle, son of the then Earl (afterwards Marquis) of Lothian, his nearest heir male, and after him to the eldest son of the house of Lothian, as a distinct peerage for ever. In virtue of this patent the eldest sons of the family have a right to sit and vote in Parliament as well as their fathers. Dying without issue he was succeeded by William eldest son of Sir Robert Ker of Ancrum, who had been, in 1633, raised to the peerage by the title of Earl of Ancrum, Lord Ker of Nisbet, Neuton, and Dolphingstone. He married Lady Anne, eldest daughter and heiress of Robert Ker Earl of Lothian, by Lady Annabella Campbell, daughter of Archibald Earl of Argyle. Having no male issue he, with consent of the king, made over his estate and titles in favour of Lady Anne. He died in 1624, and Lady Anne succeeded to the title and estates. In 1631 William her husband obtained a grant of the lands and lordship of Newbattle, which had been erected into a temporal lordship in 1589, and an earldom in 1606, in favour of Mark Ker, the grandfather of Lady Anne, who was commendator of the abbey of Newbattle at the Reformation. By the grant in favour of Wil-

liam the peerages of Lothian, Ancrum, and Jedburgh were all vested in this family.   During the
troubles of Charles I. Earl William took his seat
in Parliament, and protested against the treatment
which the king received from the Parliament of
England.   In 1648 he was one of the commissioners appointed to treat with the English for the
monarch's safety; but his efforts were fruitless in
securing the king, while their nature so displeased
those in power that the commissioners were imprisoned, and only relieved on a remonstrance
from Scotland.   Even when released from confinement, they were guarded till their embarkation.
In 1650 he was one of those who went to Breda
to invite Charles II. to Scotland.   He had three
sons and seven daughters.

Robert his son succeeded, and married Jean
daughter of Archibald Duke of Argyll.   He was
one of the privy council to King William, justice
general, and high commissioner to the general
assembly.   By the death of his uncle, Charles
second Earl of Ancrum, he succeeded to the earldom, and was created Baron Ker of Newbattle,
Oxnam, and Jedburgh, Viscount Buin, and Marquis
of Lothian, with remainder to his issue male, failing which to the other heirs of entail succeeding
to the estates.   He died in 1703.   William the
second marquis was one of the commissioners appointed by Queen Anne to treat of the union

between the two kingdoms.   He married his cousin Lady Jean Campbell, by whom he had a son, William, and four daughters.   He died in 1772, aged sixty years.   William, the third marquis, was one of the representative Scotch peers for three British parliaments, and for seven years was his Majesty's high commissioner to the general assembly of the Church of Scotland.   William Henry, the fourth marquis, entered early into the army, was aide-de-camp to the Duke of Cumberland, and was severely wounded at the battle of Fontenoy.   At Culloden the cavalry was commanded by him, and he attained the rank of general in the army in 1770.   His brother Lord Robert was killed at Culloden.   His son William John also attained the rank of general, and died in 1815.   William, the sixth marquis, succeeded, and died in 1824.   His son John William Robert, seventh marquis, was born in 1794 and died in 1841.   During his lifetime he annexed to the estates on the border Bonjedworth, Timpendean, Crailing Tofts, Ormiston, and Harden Peel.   His eldest son William Schomberg Robert Ker, born 1832, now enjoys the title and estates.

The burial-place of the family is in the north transept of the abbey; in it are to be seen the tombstones of Dand Ker, Sir John Ker his son, and Sir James Ker of Crailing, but they seem to

T

have been of modern erection.   The dates on the stones are incorrect.

HUNDOLE.—This ancient seat of a branch of the Rutherfurd family is situated upon the left bank of the Jed, within a few hundred yards of the Douglas stronghold.   The situation is very lovely. It commands a fine view of the vale of Jed, and of the distant mountains of Cheviot.   The name is thought to be derived from its having been the place where the hounds for chase and war were kept.   The ancient Britons were keen followers of the chase, and it is thought they also used the same kind of dogs in war.   While the Romans occupied the country they loved the same amusement, in which they were assisted by the native dogs.   The Roman classics are loud in their praises of the British dog, the breed of which, it is said, excelled that of any other country.   On the remains of Roman pottery left in the island, there are representations of these dogs, some of which resemble the mastiff of the present day, but in the greater majority of the hunting scenes a dog similar to the *gre*-hound appears.   It is thought that the dogs used by the Romans in hunting were of the same kind as were used, after that people left, in hunting the wolves with which Britain and Ireland were infested, and afterwards for following the deer.   *Strabo* mentions a *gre*-hound in use among the native people, which, he states, was held in high esteem, and imported into Gaul for the purposes of the chase. *Silaus* also calls the dog a *gre*-hound, and asserts that it was during the days of Roman grandeur used in the combats of the amphitheatre at Rome. *Campian* speaks of the dog as " a greyhound of great bone and limb." *Pliny* relates a combat in which these dogs took a part, and describes them as much taller than the mastiff. According to Evelyn the greyhound was a stately creature, and beat the mastiff in a fight. These dogs were only permitted to be kept by princes and chiefs, and in the Welsh laws of the ninth century, heavy penalties were enacted for the maiming or injuring of them, and the value set upon them was double the price of the ordinary hound. It is said that these dogs when sitting measured about five feet; their hair long, rough; and it seems that white was the colour most in repute about 250 years ago; but the breed is now nearly if not altogether extinct. Dogs were also used for following thieves at a very early period, and are called in the old laws " *cane traciente.*"* When James VI. ascended the English throne, " *slough doggs*" were ordered to be kept on the borders, at the expense of the inhabitants, to let loose at the ravaging parties or to

---

* R. i. 7 ; R.M. iv. 28.

track them. The Scots borderers also used dogs in battle. The first of the Turnbulls was attended by a mastiff at the battle of Halidon Hill in 1333. *Stowe* relates that Turnbull and a large mastiff approached the English army, and gave a challenge for single combat, which was accepted by Sir Robert Benhale, a young Norfolk knight, much inferior in stature to Turnbull, but of great strength and adroitness in military achievements. The mastiff made the first attack, but was received by the English knight with a stroke upon the loins with his sword, which severed his body. The combat was ultimately decided by Turnbull losing his arm, and afterwards his head.*

The family of Rutherfurd is one of the most ancient on the borders. According to tradition the family obtained the name of Rutherfurd from a man of distinction on the borders having conducted Ruther, King of the Scots, safely through the river Tweed, in an expedition against the Britons, at a place from that event called Rutherfurd. The king, after the expedition was over, bestowed some lands contiguous thereto upon his faithful conductor, from which his posterity assumed the name of Rutherfurd as soon as surnames became hereditary in Scotland.† While

---

* Hutchinson's Northumberland, vol. ii. p. 70.
† Douglas's Peerage, p. 597.

there is no information to point out the first man who bore the name of Rutherfurd, there can be no doubt that he derived it from the name of his property. There can be as little reason to doubt that the place referred to is the present Rutherfurd on the Tweed. The name is derived from the British, *Ruth-thir-ford*, signifying the ford of the Tweed at the *red-coloured land*. The British name exactly describes the locality, the land where the river is passed being of a red colour. I am not aware of any other ford on the Tweed possessed of this quality, and I have no doubt that the early people meant the name to point out a place where the river Tweed might be passed, *i.e.* the ford at the *red-land heights*, or the *red ford*. Although out of place in this chapter to enter upon a description of the locality of Rutherford, I may remark, in passing, that it appears to have been a place of great importance long before it formed a part of the kingdom of Scotland.

The name of Rutherfurd or Ruderforde first appears in a charter of William the Lion, confirming a grant by Hugh de Normanville and Alina his wife to the monks of Melrose, of a ploughgate of land and other easements in the lands of Morhus, shortly after the commencement of his reign in 1165.* In 1226 the name is also seen in

* Lib. de Melros, pp. 77, 79, 81.

a grant by John de Normanville, Lord of Maxton, a portion of which territory is said to be bounded by "that part of the moor which lies between Suthside and Arewes, and on the east is contiguous to the moor of Rutherford."* These grants were confirmed by Alexander II.† During that period (1165—1249) the names of Gregory and Nicholas of Retherford, or Rutheford, are to be seen. In 1260 Nicholas of Rutherford is witness to a deed by Malcolm de Constabletun and his wife, of a carucate of land in Edulfistun to the church of Glasgow. The witnesses who subscribed the deed along with Rutherford were Henry of Candela, Robert of Polworth, Nicholas of Glendonewyning, the Vicar of Peebles, John the Hunter, Hugh of Persby, Reginald of Lacu, Erchibald of Hopekelioch, and seven others. Hugh and Sir Richard of Rutherford also appear before 1285. Within ten years afterwards William of Rutherford of that ilk.‡ In 1296 Nicholas of Rotherford, his daughter Margaret, and Aymer of Rotherford, took the oath of fealty to Edward I.§ It is said that this Sir Nicholas was a near relative of Sir William Wallace, whom he joined before the battle of Biggar. While Wallace abode in Ettrick Forest, Rutherforde brought to

---

* Lib. de Melros, pp. 223, 224.　　† Ib. pp. 220-7.
‡ Lib. de Calchow, p. 387.　　§ Ragman's Rolls.

his aid a band of sixty gallant men. His son Robert is said to have done good service to the Bruce. In 1338 Richard of Routherford, of that ilk, is a witness to a charter of William de Felton, King Edward's sheriff of Roxburghshire, to the monks of Dryburgh.* About 1358 William of Rutherford, of that ilk, is a witness to a charter by Roger of Auldton to the chantry of St. James', Roxburgh, along with the abbots of Mailross, Geddeworth, and Dryburgh.† His son Richard of Rotherfurd is a witness to a charter by Robert III. to John Turnbull of Minto. In 1398 he was ambassador to the court of England, and in 1400 was one of the wardens of the marches. He had three sons: James, who succeeded him; John of Chatto, ancestor of the family of Hunthill; and Nichol, the stem of the Hundole family.

NICHOL obtained charters of the lands of Grubbet and Makerston between 1426 and 1430. In 1467 John designed of Rutherfurd of Hundole (probably the son of Nicholas), and John of Aynislie of Dolphington, were appointed by parliament to take up a valuation of the shire.‡ In 1475 the same John of Rutherfurde of Hundole and Elizabeth his wife appear as tenants of two lands

---

* Lib. de Dryburgh, pp. 261-2.
† Reg. of Glas., pp. 257-8-9.
‡ Acta Parl. vol. ii. p. 90.

in the Castlegate of Jedburgh under the monks of
Kelso.* In 1484 John Rutherfurd was charged
to leave the abbey of Jedburgh, void and red, and
allow Thomas Cranstoun, the abbot, to take possession thereof, under pain of rebellion. In 1492 the
seven-mark land of Samieston was resigned by
Walter Ker of Cessfurd, and the whole lands of
Rowcastel were resigned by Thomas Dickesoun
into the hands of the king, who granted them to
John Rutherfurd of Hundole.† In 1494 the
grandson of the said John is pursuer of an action
before the Lords of the Privy Council against
William Douglas of Cavers, Archibald Douglas of
Cavers, and John of Gledstaines, and obtained
decree against them for one hundred marks due
to his grandfather.‡ In 1502, at the justice ayre
of Jedworth, John of Hundole and Thomas his
brother became sureties, to satisfy the parties, for
Nicholas Rutherfurd of that place for theft.
George of Hundole, his son, was one of the border
barons who entered into a bond to support the
Earl of Angus on his appointment to the office of
lieutenant and warden of the marches in 1524.§
In 1530 he and his son Nicholas, along with nineteen barons and lairds of Roxburghshire, found

---

* Lib. de Calchow, p. 425.
† Reg. Mag. Sig., lib. xii. No. 321.
‡ Acta Dom., p. 189.
§ Pitcairn, vol. i. p. 127.

surety to enter when required before the justice to underlye the law for all crimes imputed to them.* In 1538 George Rutherfurd of Hundole, Ker of Cessfurd, Douglas of Cavers, John Rutherfurd of Hunthill, and Andrew Ker of Dolphinston, were convicted of art and part of the favour and assistance afforded to Robert Rutherfurd, George Rutherfurd called *Cockburne,* and John Rutherfurd called *Jock of the Greene,* and their accomplices, in violation of their bond to the king.† In October, 1545, Nychol Rutherfurd appeared before the lords of council at Linlithgow, and took burden upon himself for his kin, friends, tenants, servants, allies, adherents, "pairt-takaris," and all others depending upon him, to resist the English enemy, defend the realm, and prevent thieving and reving. This bond was subscribed by Walter Ker of Cessfurd, John Ker, son and heir of Fernieherst, John Rutherfurd of Hunthill, William Douglas of Cavers, and William Scott, son and heir of Walter Scott of Branxholm. Nychol was also present at the parliament held at Stirling in the same year, and was one of those who subscribed a resolution to defend the kingdom and invade England, as thought expedient by the government and council of the realm. In 1575 Nychol Rutherfurd was

---

* Pitcairn, vol. i. p. 147. † Ib. p. 208.

present at the battle of the Redswyre, and, according to the ballad,

> "Bonjeddart, Hundlie, and Hunthill
> Three, on the laid weel at the last."

The edition of the ballad as given in the Minstrelsy of the Scottish Border says—

> "The Rutherfurds with gret renown
> Convoyed the town of Jedburgh out."

Walter Rutherfurd, a member of Congress, United States of America, in a letter to his nephew at Edgerston about the beginning of the eighteenth century, quotes the verse of an old ballad in reference to this battle :—

> "Bauld Rutherfurd he was fu' stout;
> Wi' his nine sons him round about,
> He led the town o' Jedward out ;
> All bravely fought that day."

Sir Walter Scott, in a note to the ballad in the Minstrelsy, states that the Rutherfurds " were ancient and powerful border clans, chiefly on the river Jed; hence they very naturally convoyed the town of Jedburgh out." But I am inclined to think that the *bauld Rutherfurd* who convoyed the burghers to the battle was the provost of the burgh. At that time *Richard Rutherfurd* was provost, a bold and gallant man, and it is not probable, while such a person was at the head of the burgh, that the *staffis* would be led by any

other chief. Ignorance of the fact that a Rutherfurd was provost of the burgh has led to the erro-
neous supposition that the *bauld Rutherfurd* was
one of the border families in the neighbourhood
of the town. In 1563 Nicholl Rutherfurd and
James Cowdene, notary public, were convicted of
forging a deed in favour of George Rutherfurd of
Hundole for the purpose of restoring to him, as
heir-at-law of Janet Rutherfurd, the lands of
Woodhall in the shire of Edinburgh.* In 1608
Rutherfurd of Hundole and Douglas of Bonjedworth were appointed by parliament to meet
twice a year in the burgh of Jedburgh and fix the
price of shoes.† In 1616 Sir Nicholas Rutherfurd
of Hundole and James Langlands of that ilk were
named arbiters for the Laird of Ormistowne in the
contract for settling the feud between the Scotts
and Kers. Sir Nicholas is the first who subscribes
the bond entered into in the same year by the
barons, landed men, gentlemen, inhabitants of
the sheriffdoms of Berwick, Roxburgh, Selkirk,
and Peebles, the provosts and bailies of burghs and
towns within the bounds, in name of the inhabitants of the same, against the thieves of Liddesdale, Eskdale, Ewisdale, and Annandale.‡ At the

---

* Pitcairn thinks that Nichol was a relative of George of
Hundole ; it is probable that he was his son.

† Acta Parl. vol. iv. p. 404.

‡ Pitcairn, vol. iii. pp. 394-5-6.

death of Sir Nicholas, it is thought, the male line of this ancient family became extinct and merged in the family of Ker by a marriage between Sir James Ker of Crailing Hall (ancestor of the Marquis of Lothian) and Mary the heiress of Hundole. In 1672 an act was passed in favour of Sir Andrew Ker of Cavers of *inter alia* the lands of Samieston which formerly belonged to Nicholas Rutherfurd of Hundole.*

The arms of the Hundole family were—Argent, an orle gules, voided or, and in chief three martlets sable.

The Rutherfurds of Fernylie in Selkirkshire were descended from the Hundole family. They carried the same arms, and for a crest a horse's head and neck : motto, *Sedulus et Audax.*

SCRAESBURGH, OR HUNTHILL.—This manor is situated on the right bank of the river Jed, to the east of Fernieherst, and extends from near Jedburgh to the valley which runs from the Jed to the Oxnam. As early as the beginning of the twelfth century it was the property of Richard Inglis, who was also the owner of Lanton in the neighbourhood of Jedburgh. Previous to 1165 the said Richard granted to the church of " Mary of Jedworde" two oxgangs of land in Scraesburgh.

* Acta Parl. vol. viii. p. 125.

This grant was confirmed by William the Lion on his ascending the throne in 1165. In the thirteenth century it was the property of John Comyn. On the 7th of July, 1296, John Comyn of Scraesburgh, with a number of other Comyns, swore fealty to Edward I.* It was included in the grant by Robert Bruce to the good Sir James Douglas in the beginning of the fourteenth century. In the subsequent century it became the property of Robert Rutherfurd, son of John Rutherfurd of Chatto, who was the son of Sir Richard Rutherfurd of that ilk, and brother of Nichol first of Hundole. In 1466 Robert obtained a charter under the Great Seal to him and his wife Margaret of the middle parts of the town of Scraesburgh.† His son Andrew is said to have been first designed *de Hunthill.* He acquired the lands of Kephope in 1529. He was succeeded by John Rutherfurd. In 1538 he was convicted along with many others of breaking their *bond* to the king in permitting rebels to oppress the poor lieges. In 1545 John Rutherfurd, William younger of Hunthill, and a number of other chiefs on the borders, bound themselves to put down stealing and resist the English.‡ In 1575 John Rutherfurd, called the " Cock of Hunthill," was present at the battle of

* Ragman's Rolls.
† Mediæ partes villæ de Scaresburgh.
‡ Acta Parl. vol. i. p. 461.

the Redswyre.   In 1588 his sons were hanged for treason.   In 1593 John Rutherfurd elder, and Thomas Rutherfurd younger of Hunthill, were charged with treasonable practices against the king, invasion of his palaces, and intercommuning with Bothwell.   In 1616 John Rutherfurd and other principal men of the borders subscribed a bond at Kelso for the repression of theft and the keeping of good rule on the borders.   His son Sir Thomas Rutherfurd had the honour of becoming Lord Rutherfurd in 1668 by a deed of settlement of Lieutenant-General Andrew Rutherfurd, created Lord Rutherfurd in 1661.   Lord Rutherfurd was the son of William Rutherfurd of Quarry-holes, by Isabel, daughter of Stewart of Traquair.   He served with great reputation in France, and came to Britain at the restoration of Charles II., who conferred upon him the dignity of Lord Rutherfurd by letters patent dated January 19, 1661, which honours were to descend not only to the heirs of his body, but to whoever he should nominate.   The patent was produced and read in the parliament on July 12, 1661, by the Lord Commissioner, and, the estates acknowledging his Majesty's favour to the said Lord Rutherfurd, the Lord Commissioner delivered the patent to Lord Traquair, who, in the absence of Lord Rutherfurd, received the same on his knees.*   His lordship

---

* Acta Parl. vol. vii. p. 317.

was appointed to the government of Dunkirk. After the sale of that place he was created Earl of Teviot in 1662, and shortly afterwards he got the command of Tangier. Before proceeding thither he executed a deed of settlement, whereby he nominated Sir Thomas Rutherfurd of Hunthill, his eldest son, and whom failing his nearest heirs male, to succeed to the estates under the title of Lord Rutherfurd. He was slain at Tangier in 1664. Sir Thomas Rutherfurd, in terms of the above deed of nomination, succeeded to the whole estates and honours of the late Andrew Lord Rutherfurd. In 1666 King Charles II. granted a charter to Lord Rutherfurd and his heirs male, whom failing to his nearest male heirs whatsoever, of the barony of "Scraesburgh, *alias* Hunthill," excepting the ten-mark land of old extent lying in the town of Langton; as also the lands of Nether Chatto, Gidlescleugh, Sharplaw, and Hangenshaw; as also the lands of Capehope, lying within the barony of Hownam, together with the right to the patronage of the parish kirk of Hownam. The charter also contains an erection of the said whole lands and patronage into one barony, to be called the barony of Scraesburgh, *alias* Hunthill, with an erection of the town of Rutherfurd, formerly called Capehope, lying in the said barony, to a free burgh of barony to be called the Burgh of Barony of Rutherfurd, with power to name bailies and magistrates, and of having trades and mechanics, a *mercat cross,* and a weekly mercat upon Thursday, with two free yearly fairs, the one on the Thursday immediately preceding Whitsunday, and the other on the 18th of September, with tolls, customs, and privileges, and with power to erect a tolbooth, and all liberties and privileges competent to any baronial burgh in the kingdom ; paying yearly for the said burgh of barony, fairs, mercats, and customs, one penny yearly at the feast of Whitsunday on any part of said ground ; and for the right of patronage one penny Scots yearly at the parish kirk at the term of Whitsuntide yearly if asked.   The charter also declared that it should be lawful for the said Lord Rutherfurd, his heirs male and successors, to sell and dispose of the lands, barony, and others, or any part thereof, in favour of any person they should think fit.*   In 1667 Sir Thomas Rutherfurd took his seat in parliament as Lord Rutherfurd.†   Dying in 1668 without any issue of his body, he was succeeded by his brother Archibald, who attended the parliament held at Edinburgh in 1669, when the letter from the Prince of Orange was produced and read. He died in 1685 also without having any issue, and the title devolved upon Robert his younger brother.   He executed a conveyance of the lands

---

* Acta Parl. vol. ix. p. 314.   † Ib. p. 536.

of Nether Chatto, Capehope, and others, and of
the patronage of the parish kirk of Hownam, in
favour of Sir John Scott of Ancrum. In 1693
the parliament passed a ratification of a charter
granted by the king to Sir John Scott.* He also
executed a settlement conveying his whole estates,
title, and arms in favour of Thomas Rutherfurd of
that ilk, chief of the name. His lordship was
present at the second session of William and
Mary. In 1690 his name is attached to the bond
of association for the defence of the Protestant
religion. He died in 1724. At his death Captain
John Rutherfurd, great grandson of Richard
Rutherfurd of Littlehaugh, claimed the title and
was served heir male to Robert the fourth lord in
September, 1737. The title was also claimed by
George Durie of Grange, as the lineal descend-
ant of Christian, daughter of William Rutherfurd of Quarryholes and sister of the first Lord
Rutherfurd. No one as yet has been able to
make good a claim to the title.

SCRAESBURGH, like all the other towns of Teviotdale, shared in the miseries of border warfare.
The town seems to have been of considerable
extent and strength in ancient times. At a very
early period a chapel was founded here, and
described in the charter as " lying in a recess of the

---

* Acta Parl. p. 346.

U

forest to the east of the water of Jed."* It is probable that the principal part of the town was near the west end of the lake of Scraesburgh, near to where the present Mossburnford stands. On the east of the town there was a village called Orchard, which also belonged to the Rutherfurds, and on the margin of the lake stood *Fendy Hall*, formerly the abode of the kindly tenants of the abbey of Jedburgh. It consisted of about nine or ten cottages, and the occupants thereof were called the *peat lairds* of *Fen*dyhall, in consequence of their obtaining their chief subsistence by cutting peats in the fen or moss, and conveying them to Jedburgh and other places for sale. On the high grounds are the remains of an encampment said to be Danish, but, from the changes made by successive occupants, it is not easy to form an opinion of the age of this and many places of strength on the borders. It is more than probable that nearly all the camps in the neighbourhood of Jedburgh owe their origin to the wars between Scotland and England.

DOLPHINSTON.—The manor bearing this name lies to the south of the Lake of Scraesburgh, with the river Jed for its western boundary. It is said

---

* Et de Scarisburgh capellam etiam, quod fundata est in saltu memoris super acquam Jed.

that part of the present farm onstead occupies the
site of the old strength. It was of old the property of one of the sons of Gospatrick, who came
to Scotland in 1072. The first Gospatrick had
three sons, Gospatrick, Dolphin, and Waldef. All
the three appear in the inquisition of David as to
the churches of Teviotdale, in 1116.* When it
became the property of Dolphin, it was called by
his name, *Dolphinston*—the *tun* or dwelling of
Dolphin. In the course of the next century it
belonged to the family of Ainslie. In 1221 Thom.
de Anesl. was present within the chapel of the
castle of Roxburgh, and was one of the witnesses
to a friendly settlement of a dispute between the
monks of Kelso and the Bishop of Glasgow.†
There were also present William of Greenlaue,
Stephen of Lillescliue, Alexander de Hersell, John
de Mackswelle, Robert his son, William Mautelet,
and many others. Seven years after, R. de Anesl.,
miles, was present at Nisbet, and witnessed,
along with many others, the settlement of a dispute between the Bishop of Glasgow and the
rector of Morebattle.‡ Between 1231 and 1249 he
is witness to a charter of Earl Patrick of Dunbar.
In 1296 Johan de Anesleye took the oath of fealty
to Edward I. The fortalice of Dolphinstone was
destroyed by the Earl of Northampton. It was

---

* Reg. Glas. pp. 5, 6, 7.　　† Ib. p. 101.　　‡ Ib. p. 107.

afterwards taken possession of by the Scots, and rebuilt. In 1361 Edward III., on the petition of Robert de Colville, commanded the sheriff of Roxburgh to assemble the whole force of the sheriffdom, and assist Colville in destroying the fort, which was held by the Scots to the grievous injury of the whole country.* In later times a guard of sixty men was stationed here to protect the neighbouring country, and watch over the forces of England. In 1377 the lands of Dolphinstone were granted by Robert II. to William de Anesleye, forfeited by his father John.† In 1467 John of Ainslie still possessed the lands.‡ He married a daughter of Sir William Douglas of Cavers, the sheriff of Teviotdale. In November, 1493, Ralph Anysle appeared at the justice ayre at Jedworth, and produced a remission for being treasonably with the Duke of Albany; also with Richard Reed, an Englishman; also for art and part of the treasonable stouthreif and heirschep, made at the place at Spittal, of twenty-four oxen and cows, and six horses and mares, with utensils worth £30, from the tenants thereof. Andrew Ker of Fernieherst became his surety. About the beginning of the sixteenth century, the barony of Dolphinstone was acquired by Mark Ker,

* Rotuli Scotiæ, vol. i. p. 857.
† Reg. Mag. Sig. p. 134, No. 37.
‡ Acta Parl. vol. ii. p. 90.

second son of Walter Ker of Cessfurd, by his marriage with Margery, the daughter and heiress of the said John Ainslie. A branch of the family possessed Clethaugh, and another Falla, down to the end of the seventeenth century.

OLD JEDWORTH.—The place which bears this name is situated on the left bank of the river Jed, about four miles from Jedburgh. It is thought by many that a large town existed here at an early period, of which a farm onstead and the ruins of a small chapel are the only remains. Chalmers states, that " on the west bank of the Jed, in the middle of a vast forest, Ecgred, the Bishop of Lindisfarne, who died A.D. 845, built a village, which he named Gedworth, and a church for his village. Even before the age of the beneficent David I., another village of the same name, with a church and a castle, a few miles lower down on the Jed, had arisen, and had eclipsed the ancient hamlet. At New Jedburgh David founded a house for the monks of St. Augustine."* But I doubt if there is any authority for holding that the hamlet on the Jed is older than the burgh. It is no doubt true that the locality of the ruined chapel is called Old Jedworth, but that appellation has been conferred on it in modern

---

* Caledonia, vol. ii. p. 133.

times, without reference to its being founded
anterior to the existence of the royal burgh.   It
is believed that long before David's day Jedburgh
was a *weorth*, or town, of considerable importance,
with a religious establishment presided over by a
prior, who was afterwards worshipped as a saint.
On David succeeding to the territory at his brother's death, the town was fortified by a castle.
In his charter to the monks, granting them the
multure of his mill of Jedworth, he takes care to
distinguish the town by the castle : " *ubi castellum
est.*" The same expressions are used in Earl
Henry's grant, and in the charter of King William.   When Edward of England granted the
forest of Jedburgh to Percy, he also distinguished
the town with the castle from the other Jedde-
worthe and Bonjedworth.   It seems probable that
the town at the castle was first founded, and on
account of its situation became at an early period
a royal residence, while the place *now* called Old
Jedworth consisted merely of a few houses
gathered together in the neighbourhood of the
" chapel, which was founded in the forest glade,
opposite to Zernwingslawe."   The situation is one
of great beauty, in the middle of one of the little
haughs formed by the windings of the river Jed as
it flows down the valley from the border mountains.   The only remains of this little chapel, in
which the rude forefathers of the hamlet wor-

shipped, are part of the foundation-stones, which have escaped being carried away to repair the farm onstead or dykes, by a number of ash-trees growing on the line of the wall. The form and dimensions of the chapel cannot now be ascertained. The traces of small buildings are still to be seen on the south side of the chapel, and about forty yards from it, in the same direction, a large solitary ash-tree stands as a sad memorial of the houses which once existed near it. It is probable that this tree marks the limit of the chapel buildings on the south. It is about eight feet in circumference. The little graveyard on the north can be distinctly traced by a line of ash-trees. There are no tombstones to tell the names of those who sleep in this holy place, but certain is it that within the line of ash-trees repose the ashes of many a gallant man who has made his way resistless among a thousand foes. No doubt the tombstones have met the same fate that befel the stones of the chapel. On the opposite side of the river, and at the foot of a steep bank, stood Dolphinston mill, for the use of the foresters in former days, but it is now silent, and, like the chapel, its foundations can only be traced. Of this early grange in the forest nothing now remains. At the head of this little haugh the river runs against a steep bank, called, in the common language of the district, *Hellsheugh*, and by some persons *Earlsheugh.*   It seems clear that *Hellsheugh* is the proper name, which it has obtained from its proximity to the graveyard, *hell* being the Saxon word for a grave, or hole in the ground—*Hellsheugh : the heugh at the graveyard.*

EDGERSTOUNE, OR EDGARSTOWN.—This seat of the family of Rutherfurd stands upon the margin of a rivulet which descends from the Cheviot ridge and joins the river Jed a short way above the old chapel of Jedworth.   The barony of Edgerstoune now includes the barony of Broundoun, which consisted of the lands of Eddelshead and Elfin-shop, called Easter and Wester Broundounlaws, part of the lands of Overtoun called Stotfield and Marrow,* the Moit and Pierrig.†   All these lands were, about the end of the seventeenth century, united into one barony under the name of Edgerstoun.   The derivation of the name is doubtful; it is possible that it may have been one of the towns built upon the Jed by the Bishop of Lindisfarne, but it is more likely to have obtained its name from some early occupant of that part of the forest. The name of *Edzare* was common in the thirteenth and fourteenth centuries.   It is thought by some that Edgerstoune was the scene of the

---

* These places are called *Stotfold* and *Narrow* in the act of parliament ratifying the charter of Charles II.

† Retours.

great battle fought in 603 between the king of Scots, and the Dalreods and Northumbrians. In the Anglo-Saxon chronicle the battle-field is called *Egesanstonne*, of which Edgerstoune is supposed by them to be a corruption.* Chalmers thinks this battle was fought at Dawstonerig, and the editor of " Bede's Ecclesiastical History" suggests Dalston near Carlisle, or Dauston near Jedburgh.† But it is more probable that this battle was fought on the estate of Dinlebyre on the Liddel.‡ Still there is room for doubt.

In the beginning of the fifteenth century the barony of Broundoun was the property of a person of the name of Haswell. In 1492 Edgarstoun was granted by James IV. to James Rutherfurd of that ilk, who was the grandson of the Richard Rutherfurd of that ilk, who was the father of John of Chatto, the ancestor of the Rutherfurds of Hunthill and of Nichol the first of Hundole. This James Rutherfurd was named one of the conservators of the peace with England in 1457 and 1459.§ In 1471 he got a charter of the lands of Hownam, Capehope, Swinset, and others. In the same year the lords ordained James Rutherfurd of that ilk to restore and deliver again to Adam of Pringell the complete stand of harness which he had borrowed

---

* Anglo-Saxon Chron., Bohn's edition, p. 315.
† Bede, book i. chap. 34.   ‡ Vol. i. p. 265.
§ Rotuli Scotiæ, vol. ii. pp. 383, 399.

from him, in as good a state as he received the same, or else to pay to him the sum of £20 for the said harness.*   In 1482 he acquired the patronage of the church of Bedrule.   In the same year he was pursued before the Lords of Council by Robert Colville of Ochiltree for the wrongous destruction and demolition of Maxton, and carrying away the timber thereof.   The defence set up by Rutherfurd was that the place belonged to himself.†   In 1493 the lords ordained James Rutherfurd to enter his person in ward within the castle of Edinburgh until he released James Lowrey, servitor to the Earl of Bothwell, warden, who was lying in England with Sir Thomas Gray, captain of Norham, in pledge for the payment of a bill for the burning and heirschip of Wark.‡ About the same time he obtained a charter of confirmation from the king of a grant by Douglas of Cavers, superior of the lands of Rutherfurd and Wells, to himself and his grandson Richard Rutherfurd and his heirs male, whom failing to his second son Thomas, and Robert his son.   He died in 1493, leaving two sons, Philip and Thomas, and a daughter, who married Sir Robert Ker, only son of Sir Walter Ker of Cessfurd.   Philip, who died before his father, married a daughter of Walter Ker of Cessfurd, by whom he had a son

---

* Acta Aud. p. 12.   † Ib. p. 101.   ‡ Ib. p. 1731.

Richard, and two daughters, Helen and Catharine. The former married Sir John Foreman, and, after his death, Andrew Rutherfurd of Hunthill. Catharine married James Stewart of Traquair. Richard Rutherfurd succeeded his grandfather, but died without issue. At his death his uncle Thomas Rutherfurd was served heir male to him, but Helen, the wife of Rutherfurd of Hunthill, and eldest sister to the deceased Richard, reduced the service as heir of line, but she having died without leaving any children, Sir William Stewart of Traquair, grandson of Catharine, served himself heir to his grandmother's sister Helen, and got the lands of Rutherfurd and Wells. The barony of Edgerston, however, remained with Richard the son of the said Thomas Rutherfurd. In 1559 he got a charter under the Great Seal of the said lands and barony. During the disputes about the succession of the lands, Robert son of Thomas Rutherfurd, mentioned in the charter of Douglas of Cavers, seems to have been in possession of the castle of Edgerston. In November, 1536, Walter Ker of Cessfurd, warden of the middle marches, the friend of Traquair and the enemy of Rutherfurd, bound himself to keep the castle of Edgerstoune on receiving the profits of the lands for his trouble, and also to apprehend Robert Rutherfurd the rebel.* But it appears that Cessfurd

---

* Pitcairn's Criminal Trials, vol. i. p. 179.

had met with greater difficulty than he had anticipated in getting possession of this border fort, for
in October, 1537, all the gentlemen within the
shires of Linlithgow, Stirling, Perth, and Monteith,
were charged to pass with the Lord Regent to the
besieging of Edgerstoune.   Similar warnings were
also sent to the master of artillery and to the
Laird of Cessfurd to lie about Edgerstoune, and to
cause oxen to be ready on the arrival of the guns
within their bounds.*   Thomas his son succeeded.
From his complexion he was called the Black
Laird of Edgerstoune; and, with his nine sons at
his back, made himself feared on the borders.   He
was present with his followers at the battle of the
Redswyre in the neighbourhood of his castle, and,
according to the ballad, " was not to lack" in the
fight.   His son Richard married a daughter of the
Laird of Larrieston, chief of the Elliots, a powerful
clan in Liddesdale, and noted moss-troopers.   Her
mother was a daughter of Buccleuch.   In 1616
he was one of those who subscribed the bond at
Kelso to the king to keep good rule on the borders.   He died early, and was succeeded by his
son Robert, who was a minor at the time.   He
united himself in marriage to Margaret Riddell,
daughter of Riddell of that ilk, by whom he had
five sons.

---

* Pitcairn's Criminal Trials, vol. i. p. 286.

It was now safer to live upon the borders. The Act of Union converted the swords of the borderers into ploughshares and reaping-hooks. Robert seems also to have partaken of the spirit of the times, for on his son and heir marrying a daughter of the Bishop of Caithness, he gave up the greater part of his estates, and retired to the Rig, a pleasant place on the river Jed, where he passed the remainder of his days in calm enjoyment.

John, his son and successor, was a man full of courage and energy. In 1638 he raised a troop of horse, and in the following year was with the army at the taking of Newcastle. He remained with the army till the king's surrender, on which he left, being greatly displeased at his majesty being delivered up to the English. In 1643 he was appointed by the estates one of the committee of war for the shire of Roxburgh.* In 1646 he was again placed on the same committee. In 1648 he was a member of the war committee, and concurred with those who raised an army for the relief of King Charles, who was then a prisoner in the Isle of Wight. He joined the Duke of Hamilton, and was present at the battle of Preston. In 1649 he was one of those who assisted in putting the country in a state of defence, and was appointed to a command in the army which was

---

* Acta Parl. vol. vi. p. 54.

raised for the purpose of the king's restoration. In 1650 he was present with his troop of borderers at the battle of Dunbar, in which he was severely wounded, his horse killed under him, and only five of his gallant troop left alive. In 1661 he was named one of the commissioners for raising the annuity of £40,000 to his majesty for maintaining an army.* He commanded an independent troop of horse for keeping good rule on the borders. It is said that his diligence produced great reformation in the conduct of the borderers. In the MS. notices of the family, it is said that he executed a number of mutual discharges of feuds with several families in the neighbouring county of Northumberland, which had been of long standing. In 1671 Charles II. granted a charter under the Great Seal to and in favour of John Rutherfurd, and his eldest lawful son John Rutherfurd, their male heirs and assignees whatsoever, of the lands and lordship of Edgerston, with towers, fortalices, manor-place, mills, lands, and multures; also the lands and barony of Broundoun, the lands of "Sellshead and Elvingshope," called Easter and Wester Broundounlaws; parts and portions of the lands of Overtoun, called "*Stotfold et Narrow,* the Mott et Peirrige," infield and outfield, with licence to the said John Rutherfurd the elder,

---

* Acta Parl. vol. vii. p. 91.

his son, and their successors, to hold two fairs in
the year upon any part of the barony, each fair to
endure for forty-eight hours, the one to begin on
the first day of July, and the other on the fifth
day of October, each year. In 1672 the charter
was ratified by the king and parliament.* In
1678 he was nominated one of the commissioners
of the shire of Roxburgh, to receive the voluntary
supply of £1,800,000 Scots to his majesty. He
is said to have died in 1682, and to have been
succeeded by his second son Andrew, in consequence of his eldest son, named in the charter of
Charles II., having died before his father; but it
appears from the Retours that Andrew was served
heir to his brother John on May 19, 1686.†
Andrew died in 1718 unmarried, and Thomas, the
third son, continued the line of the family. The
fourth son Robert became the head of the house of
Bowland. It was to this Thomas Rutherfurd that
Robert Lord Rutherfurd made over his estate,
title, and arms by disposition, with procuratory of
resignation, and who was then recognized as the
chief of the Rutherfurds; but it is said that Thomas, esteeming a Scots peerage after the union
rather a loss than an advantage, never claimed the
title, contenting himself with assigning it in like

* Acta Parl. vol. viii. p. 133.
† Retours, No. 289.

manner to John Rutherfurd, his son and successor, who, entertaining the same opinion of a Scots peerage as his father did, declined to claim the title. He was married to Susanna Riddell, daughter and heiress of Riddell of Minto. His son John succeeded his father in 1720. He had been knighted in 1706 by the command of her majesty to the Duke of Queensberry, who represented her as high commissioner to the parliament of Scotland. In 1710 he married Elizabeth, heiress of the ancient family of Cairncross of Colmslie. Under James V. Andrew Cairncross of Colmslie was Great Chancellor of Scotland. A younger brother was Abbot of Melrose, a second Archbishop of Glasgow, a third Abbot of Holyrood, and another Bishop of Ross. By this marriage he had nineteen children. His son John, born in June, 1713, succeeded. In 1734 he was chosen M.P. for the shire of Roxburgh. He was again chosen to represent his native county in 1741. He was killed at the battle of Ticonderoga in 1758. He married a daughter of Sir Gilbert Elliot of Minto, a lord of session. She bore to him three sons and four daughters. He again was succeeded by his son John, who married, in 1789, Mary Ann Leslie, only daughter of the Honourable Major-General Alexander Leslie. For two successive parliaments he represented the shire of Roxburgh. To John Rutherfurd the county stands indebted for many improvements, particularly in turnpike roads, and to his active exertions the building of Kelso bridge may chiefly be attributed. He took the lead in all matters connected with the county, and indeed so complete was his sway, that it was seldom he was opposed by the gentlemen of the county. Having no children, and finding he had the power to determine the succession to the barony of Edgerstone, he conveyed it to his nephew William, eldest son of William Oliver, of Dinlabyre, by his sister Jane Rutherfurd. The estate of Fairnington, to which he had succeeded through his uncle, Baron Robert Rutherfurd, passed by entail to the next heir male, Charles Rutherfurd, second son of John Rutherfurd, of Mossburnford, and at his death to his brother Thomas Rutherfurd, the present possessor. He died on May 6, 1834, aged eighty-six, and was gathered to his fathers in the chancel of the ruined abbey of Jedburgh, where a beautiful monument was erected by subscription to his memory. William Oliver Rutherfurd now enjoys the barony of Edgerstone, under the settlement of his uncle. He has been fifty years sheriff of the county of Roxburgh.

On the barony of Edgerstone is a small village called the *Camptoun*. The origin of the name may be traced to a camp on the promontory between the river Jed and the deep valley through which Edgerstone burn runs. The name is merely a

x

translation of the British *Catter-thun—Camptown.*
I have no doubt a strength existed here during
the British period, but its form has been considerably altered by more modern occupants. The
post has been chosen with great judgment. On
the north and west is a deep valley through which
the river Jed pours impetuously over its rocky
bed. On the opposite side of the river, Mervinslaw rises abruptly to a considerable height. On
the east are the steep banks of Edgerstone rivulet,
and on the south-west the swampy ground ascending to the Carter Fell. It is evident that the
original formers of this camp dreaded an attack
from the north, as it is situated on the nose of the
promontory running in that direction. Like all
the early strengths it commands a great view in
almost every direction. It is fixed about midway
between the Watling Street on the east, and the
Wheel Causeway on the west. The stronghold is
fully ninety-five yards in diameter. The entrance
to it appears to have been from the south, and I
thought I could trace a way in the direction of
Rink, where it is probable, from its name, another
post of the same kind existed, although I failed
to discover it. It is possible that this place may
have been the original *Rink.*

On the ridge of hills forming the east side of
the glen of Edgerstone, my attention was directed
to a number of terraced lines on the Stotfield

farm, very near the summit of a lofty hill. The
same appearances exist in many places among the
Cheviots. Widely different views are entertained
as to the origin of these terraces or baulks. Gordon, in his "Itinerary," conjectures them to have
been Roman itinerary encampments. Wallis, in
his "History of Northumberland," thinks that
they were places for the militia to arrange themselves in time of war, that they might show themselves to advantage thus placed rank above rank,
in which opinion the learned tourist Pennant
concurs. Bruce imagines that the terraced lines
on the mountain-sides of the Cheviots and other
places resemble a mode of cultivation practised in
Italy, and thinks that the terraces on Reid-water
have been made by the Roman cultivator for the
purposes of growing corn. I concur with Mr.
Bruce in thinking that these baulks have been
used for agricultural purposes; but the period of
their first formation cannot be ascertained. Before
the Roman people arrived the natives had corn
farms, and after that era they were forced to grow
corn in abundance to supply the granaries of the
conquerors. After the Romans left the Saxons
had granges throughout the whole district, and
it is more than probable that they took possession
of the lands which were under cultivation at the
time. The same kind of terraces are to be seen
on the Cayle and Capehope waters, near Hownam,

and at Belford on the Beaumont. At all these places the monks had granges or farms, on which it is well known they grew corn. Higher up still than these terraces the ground bears unmistakable evidence of having been operated on by the plough.* Baulks something like these terraces are to be seen growing corn at the present day on the steep banks of Middleham-burn, where the monks of Kelso had one of their early granges. A number of short terraced lines are occasionally to be met with on the sides of the well-sheltered hopes which run into the Cheviot mountains, and imagined to be places of defence, but a careful examination satisfied me that they have been sheds where the cattle of these mountain granges were

---

* The appearance of cultivation high up in the Northumbrian mountains is explained by a legend of the district to have been made by the husbandmen while the kingdom lay under an interdict in the time of King John. The tillers of the soil imagined that the interdict only included the lands under cultivation at the time it was issued, and that the uncultivated parts were free, and they accordingly left the cultivated lands and ploughed the wastes and sides of the hills while the bull of his holiness continued in force. But I think the true reason for the husbandmen in early times resorting to the hill-sides to raise crops is to be found in the wet and marshy state of the level tracts that were not covered with wood. The greater part of the best land of the present day could not at that early period have been cultivated for wood and fresh-water pools. The hill-sides were free of wood and dry.

put for safety and shelter. But for the extent of these terraces at Edge-stone, they might be taken for the remains of these early cattle-sheds. The name *Stotfold* is very instructive.

On the same estate is a farm named *Arks,* a corruption of the Gaelic and Irish *ards,* high, and intended to describe a place at the high mountains or hills.

MERVINSLAW.—This hill is thought to be the *Zearwingnslawe* in the charters of David I. and William the Lion, and in earlier days extended from the river Jed on the east to near Rule water on the west; from the Jed on the south to the rivulet which enters Jed opposite Mossburnford, and the burn which rises near Kilsyke and runs by Westerhouses and Burnkinford into the Rule. At the present day the name is confined to the east wing of the law, on which the ruins of a peel bearing the name of the Hill stand on the lofty banks of the river Jed. The summit of this hill is now called the *Belling.* The name of Belling is thought by several to be derived from the *Beltein* fires which blazed on its summit, but I doubt the soundness of this origin. I think the whole hill was in ancient times called *Zearnwingslawe,* and that it may have got the modern name of *Belling* from a *bield* or shelter on its top near to where the road passes over it. It is thought that the old name was conferred on it on account of its being partly ploughed. In the commencement of the ninth century the eastern part of the *law* was a grange or farm belonging to the Bishop of Lindisfarne, and to distinguish it from other *laws* which abound in that locality, it was called *Earingslaw* or the ploughed law. The view from the summit of the law is one of the best and most extensive in the whole border district. The town of Jedburgh is seen lying in the middle of its beautiful hope surrounded with wood, through which the red scaur appears jutting out here and there among the trees. The view includes not only all the district between and the Cheviots, but also a considerable extent of these mountains; Woodenlaw and the pass down which the Roman legions poured upon Teviotdale; Hownamlaw, Cocklaw, the principal mountain of Cheviot, the hills in the neighbourhood of Yetholm, and so far as the *Yeveringbel.* On the north and west the Lammermuir and the Moffat hills bound the vision, while the whole of the lovely country lying between and Berwick is exposed to view. With the exception of the Dunion, the prospect from the summit of the Belling is unequalled in all the border land.

On the southern slope of the hill, lying in a quiet nook, is the farm of *Fallside,* once a place of considerable importance. In 1513, there were two towns of that name called Easter and Wester

"Fauside." The easter town had a strong peel built of "lyme and stane in it." Both towns were destroyed by Sir John Ratcliffe, after the disastrous battle of Flodden, with the tower of the easter town. The ruins of this "lyme and stane" fort are yet to be seen.* The town and peel of Hindhaughhead, on the same bank of the river, was also laid in ruins by the same party: a parts of its ruined walls still stands to tell the perils of other days. On the same farm, close on the water's edge, stood *Roughleanook*, the home of the father of the celebrated *Dandie Dinmont* and where the young Dinmonts were reared.† The place is now in ruins. About the end of the fifteenth century, a family of Youngs occupied Roughlea. Simon Young of Roughlea appears in

---

* The Olivers and Whites have occupied Fallside in succession, since 1611. In the early part of the seventeenth century there were seven Olivers of the name of Andrew or *Dand*, and who were distinguished by the part of the town in which they dwelt, and by their personal appearance. There is a powerful petrifying spring in the burn, a little below the farmhouse.

† Tradition relates that old Dandie was rough in expression, seasoning his conversation with oaths. One day the locality was visited by a severe thunderstorm, and while Dandie was making use of imprecations, too common with him, a thunderbolt struck the house and set it on fire. Dandie was so struck with the visitation that he became a changed man, and ever after during his lifetime kept that day as a fast, in remembrance of the preservation of himself and family from the storm that destroyed his house.

the early criminal trials. Further up on the south
bank of the river is Letham, which had at one
time right to two fairs in the year. Both banks of
the Jed were formerly in this locality covered with
broom equalling in height the broom of the Cowdenknowes on Leader.

SOUTHDEAN.—The name of this place was in
early times Sudhden, Sowden, Soudon, so called
from *Southdean,* a valley in which it is situated.
Suddenlaw, again, owes its name to its position at
the south dean or valley. *Sud,* in the Teutonic,
means south ; *dene,* in the Saxon, signifies a valley,
and law is the Saxon *lœaw,* a hill, *i.e. Southdene-
law,* the south valley hill, or the hill at the *South-
dene,* a name which exactly describes the locality.
The old church and town stood in the southmost
valley in that part of Scotland. At the west end
of the law, and between it and the river Jed, stood
the little church of Suddon. The editor of the
Origines Parochiales says, " the original site of the
church was on the right bank of the river Jed, at
the town or village of Sowdon, between two streams
named the Blackburn and the Inner Blackburn,"
and refers to Bleu's map as the authority on which
the statement is made. But the statement is not
warranted from the fact, as the ruins of the chapel stand on the east margin of the river close to
the west end of the hill, and not within three-

quarters of a mile of the nearest Blackburn. The chapel has been sixty-four feet long, and eighteen feet broad. The falling of the west gable has made a considerable mound of stones and earth, out of which several ash-trees grow. One ash near the centre of the chapel measures nine feet in circumference, and another at the little chancel is fully seven feet.* There are few tombstones to tell the names of those who rest in the graveyard, but on those existing I noticed the names of Douglas, Oliver, and Young of Roughleanook, with dates

---

* It is interesting to notice the number of ash-trees that are to be found in the neighbourhood of the ruins of the old chapels and graveyards, and also as marking out on the hill-sides and on the lonely valley the homesteads of a previous race. It is said that the ash was the first of trees which care was taken to plant and multiply, for no other was so useful in the construction of agricultural implements, nor would any other afford a wood so excellent for fuel. But the true reason for planting and preserving the ash is to be looked for in the belief of the old Saxons that it was the material used by *Odin* in creating the human race. They believed that Odin and his brothers formed the first pair out of two pieces of wood, the one of elm and the other of ash. In this belief of the old Saxons may be traced the origin of the ash plant-ations, and the reason why all the important vessels used by that people were made of the ash or ascien wood. The buckets which held the mead and wine at the festivals appear to have been of ash, and it is well known that ash tablets were used for writing at a very early period. This district bears its full proportion of this sacred tree, and the names of places evince that in former days, when the Saxon blood was purer than it is now, great woods of ash existed throughout its length and breadth.

about the beginning of the 17th century. It is said that a number of the tombstones have been carried away by the inhabitants of the neighbourhood and converted into hearthstones, which is very probable, considering the unprotected state of the little graveyard and the few memorials of the dead that are within it. From the register of Glasgow it appears that about 1260 Galford was vicar of Sowdon.* When Edward got possession of the district in 1272, he presented Adam of Osberneston to the church. The presentation is dated from Westminster, and addressed to William of Dumfries, the chancellor of Edward.† After the Reformation it was served by an exhorter and reader in succession, who had each a stipend of £13 6s. 8d. In Bagimont's Roll the *Rectorie de Sudon* is valued at £4 sterling. At this place, it is said, the Scottish army assembled in 1388, before proceeding into England on that memorable *raid* which ended in the battle of Otterburn. A short distance above the chapel the *Carter* burn flows into the Jed. The rivulet derives its name from the flat tract of marshy land through part of which it runs; *Car*, in the Saxon, signifies a marshy flat, and the Gaelic *tir*, land. The name of the *Carter* hill is intended to describe a hill whose top is flat and marshy as well as its situation at the tract of the flat marshy land;

---

* P. 183.　† Rotuli Scotiæ, vol. i. p. 6

a name very descriptive of the mountain and of a large tract of flat marshy land extending for several miles along its base. Some think that Carter is entirely from the Gaelic, signifying a turn in the land, but such a derivation does not truly describe the locality.* *Lustrother,* on the opposite side of the Jed from the church, owes its name to the same quality of the land which conferred its name on the Carter burn, and signifies the " manor-place situated on the marsh." *Lustrother* and *Dykerawe* were both taken and burned when Sir John Ratcliffe wasted the country in 1513. Each place seems to have been protected by a tower or fort. The occupants of Dykerawe defended it to the last extremity, and were only compelled to surrender by the English "laying corne and straw to the dore and burnt it both rofe and flore, and so smoked theym owt."

On the suppression of the parish of Abbotrule, half of it was joined to Sowdon, and for the better accommodation of the parishioners a new church was built in 1790 about a mile further north, at the village of Chesters. In the front wall of the church

---

* Sir Thomas Dick Lauder, in his article on Scottish Rivers (Tait's Magazine, vol. xiv, page 743), says that it is at the Carter Fell the scene of the ancient ballad of " The Young Tamlane" is laid, but he is mistaken. The scene of the ballad is laid at *Carterhaugh,* between Yarrow and Ettrick, in Selkirkshire.—*Ballad in Minstrelsy,* p. 224.

part of a pair of *jougs* is still fixed.   Near to the east end of the church the father of the poet of the "Seasons" is interred.   In another part of the graveyard I noticed a monument erected to the memory of William Scott, minister of the parish, who died in 1809, in the 74th year of his age and the 48th of his ministry.   The predominating names of those buried here are Oliver, Common, Turnbull, Telfer, Rutherfurd, and Crozier.   The modern *Cout* of Keilder lies interred near to the west entrance.   The view from the church and village is very wild, being confined to the tract of land lying between and the Carter Fell.   The village consists of a few straggling houses.   The patronage of the parish belongs alternately to the king, who came in place of the abbot for that part of it which was taken from Abbotrule, and the lords of Jedforest, who had formerly the patronage of Sowdon.

The *Wheel Causey*, which enters Scotland at Deadwater, can be traced to within two miles of the ruins of Sowdon chapel.*   It takes the name of Wheel Causey at Deadwater.   It is supposed by Chalmers and others, that it obtained its name from its being the only road on which wheel-carriages could travel.   But I think the origin of the name is to be found in the Saxon *woel*, a well or pool, and intended to describe the passage of the Causey through a land full of *woels*, or pools, and

* Vol. i. p. 247.

springs. Peel Fell ought also to be called Woel Fell.

ABBOTRULE.—This was the name of a parish
which was suppressed in 1777, and divided between
Southdean and Hobkirk. The early name of the
church and manor is said by Chalmers to have been
Rule Hervey, derived from the name of its owner
and the river Rule. In the charters of David I.
it is called *Herevei,* which, I think, is the Saxon
herewic, denoting the place where soldiers resided
or the quarters of the army. Now this place is
situated at the quarters of the army in early days.
On Bonchester hill, in the immediate neighbourhood of Abbotrule, are the remains of a Roman
post with numerous encampments, some square
and others of a round form. Considering the
nature of this post there can be little doubt that it
was permanently occupied by the Roman troops,
and by their Saxon successors. Between this place
and the river Jed on the east, the ground is full of
camps and entrenchments. Burnkinford and
Bairnkin seem to me to be a slight change on
Birnnkin, signifying the promontory or headland
on which the strengths are. I have no doubt the
name *Herewic* was conferred on this locality from
its being constantly occupied by an army. It may
also be mentioned in support of this view, that the
land between Bonchester and the river Jed was
selected in early times as a shelter for the Scottish

armies. When David I. founded the monastery of Jedburgh, he granted to the monks " *Rulam-Herevei,* according to its true boundaries in wood and plain, meadows, pastures, and waters, and in all things justly pertaining to the same town, in excambion for a ten-pound land which they had in Hardingstone."* On getting possession of the church, town, and lands, the abbot and his canons dropped the old name and called their place Abbotrule, to distinguish it from the other towns on the *Rule.* In 1165, William the Lion confirmed the grant of his predecessor. The barony remained with the monks till the Reformation, at which period it yielded, according to the Book of Assumptions, £40 yearly. The barony comprehended the lands of Abbotrule, Mackside, Fodderlie, Gatehousecot, Grange, Hartshaugh, Wolflee, Overbonchester, Langraw, Swanshiel, and Kirknowe. According to the rent-roll of the abbacy of Jedburgh, produced in a court held by Andrew, Master of Jedburgh, within the kirk of the burgh, in 1626, Abbotrule was occupied by one of the Turnbulls, at a rent of £5 ; other Turnbulls possessed lands beyond the burn of Abbotrule at the rent of £12 ; another Turnbull rented Macksyde at £5 ; and other

---

* " Rulam-Herevei, per suas rectas divisas in nemore et plano, pratis et pascuis et asqui, et in omnibus rebus ad eandam villam pertinentibus, datum in escambio decem libratarium terræ quas prefati canonici habuerant in Harding restorn."—*Confirm. Charter of William the Lion.*

Turnbulls rented Fodderlie for £2 2s. 4d.; Hartshaugh was also occupied by a Turnbull at 6s. 8d.
yearly; a Turnbull also rented Overbonchester at
a rent of £1 10s. A Rutherfurd paid a rent of
10s. for Wolflee; and Thomas Ker of Gatehousecot
at £1 16s. yearly; Scott of Todrig paid five
merks for the Grange; a person of the name of
Shields, rented Kirknowe and Langraw for £5;
and a Turnbull Swanshiel at £1 6s. 8d. The
church of *Rule-abbot* formed one of the grounds of
dispute between the bishop of Glasgow and the
canons of Jedburgh, which led to a meeting for a
settlement of differences between the two parties
in the chapel of Nisbet, in 1220. The canons
were found in the wrong, and obliged to cede the
whole dues to the vicar, he paying out of the fruits
the sum of 5s. yearly at the festival of St. James
as an acknowledgment.*

Stryndis.—A little to the east of Abbotrule
stood the Stryndis, called in modern times *Strange*,
the possession of a family of Olivers. † Not a stone

---

* Reg. Glas. p. 98.

† The name of Oliver belongs, it is said, to the Danish. A
celebrated chieftain of that race was named Oliver, and gained
the contemptuous surname of *Barnakel*, or the Preserver
of Children, from his dislike to the favourite amusement of
his soldiers, that of tossing infants on their spears. The
first of the name that settled in Scotland was David de
Olifard. He was the godson of David I., whom he saved
after the battle of Winchester, and accompanied to Scotland.

of it now remains.   Jedforest seems to have been the land of the Olivers in early times.   Even at the present day the name is found prevailing in many parts of the forest, and the old graveyards show the strength of the vassals of the ancient Lords of Jedforest.   The justiciary records also afford numerous instances of their activity, especially of the family of Stryndis, during the Michaelmas moons.   In 1502 there were six brothers of the name at Stryndis who were constant in their worship of the Goddess of the Borders, and were called David *na-guid Priest, Long* John Oliver, *Little* John Oliver, Robert, Martin, and Matthew, all noted moss-troopers.   They resetted rebels; stole horses, cattle, and sheep; committed slaughter; and were guilty of stouthrief.   At the Jedburgh justice ayre of 1502 David Oliver *na-guid Priest* was charged with stealing twelve oxen and cows from Sir David Hume, forth of Lammermoor; for thieving in company with Thomas and Andrew Grymslaw, and resetting them when put to the horn; for stealing a mare from John Douglas of Jedburgh; for taking two horses and a mare from

---

David I. granted to him the manors of Smalholm and Crailing.   He is thought to have been the first justiciar of Lothian.   He granted to the monks of Jedworth the tenth of the multure of his mail of Crailing.   His grandson, Walter, inherited the estates, and also acted as justiciar of Lothian. He died in 1142, and was buried in the chapter-house of Melrose.   The Oliphants are sprung from the same stock.

William Pavy, John Jamieson, and Billy Russell, in Nisbet, the price of each being *eight merks* ; and for stealing twenty sheep from Douglas of Trows, each sheep being valued at six shillings. David and Robert were charged with stealing thirty-six ewes and sixty-five sheep from William Kerr of Darnickmoor. Robert, John, and David were allowed to compound for the stouthrief of 200 sheep from the tenants of Jedworthe, Rewcastle, Lanton, Bethrouil; for the theft of six oxen and cows from Ormiston of Maxton ; Robert for the slaughter of John Moffat, and the stouthrief of 33 oxen and cows, 200 ewes and " wedderis," four horses and mares, from Barnisfader of Kilshop ; for the slaying of Robert Brig of the same place, and for treason old and new. *Long* John, and *Little* John, and David, were also allowed to compound for the stouthrief of six oxen, each valued at thirty shillings ; a mare, price ten marks; a pot, 34s. ; a gown of orange colour or rowen tawny, four pounds ; a *kirtill* of *braid red* cloth, three pounds ; a brown gown, 40s. ; four veils or scarfs, 30s. ; two pairs of linen sheets, 20s. ; two bed sheets, 10s. ; a covering, 5s. ; five ells of small white cloth, 20s. ; two *sarkis,* 10s. ; a doublet, 30s. ; a pair of kersey galligaskins, 10s. ; and other utensils valued at £7, belonging to Martin Wode of Whitefield. It seems that Robert, David, Martin, and Matthew had refused to find sureties according to law for the satisfaction

Y

of the parties whom they had injured.   Andrew
Lord Grey, the justiciar who presided at the ayre,
ordered the Sheriff of Roxburgh to take them into
sure keeping for the space of forty days, and at the
expiry thereof, without caution being found, they
were to *" be had to the gallowse and hanyit guhill
thai be dede."*   The sentence was carried into execution, and seems to have been a warning to the
rest of the family, as the name does not afterwards
appear in the records.   A family of Olivers, relatives
of the Stryndis family, possessed Lustrother on Jed
about the same period, and appear to have been ad-
dicted to the same practices as their kindred.   About
1546 a band, composed of Olivers, Crosiers, Halls,
and Turnbulls, while under assurance with the
English, took Edgerstone by storm, and left twenty
of their men to garrison the fort.

KILSYKE.—The only remains of this town is a
portion of the ruins of its keep.   It stands at the
head of a syke or burn which runs by Westerhouses.   Near to this place, and on the left bank
of the burn, is an oval fort or camp of about 200
yards long.   The burn forms the north side of it,
and on the other a trench or mound of about 14
feet high.   The road to Southdean passes near it.
The fort is planted with fir-trees.
On a small rivulet which rises in the table-land
a little above the peel of Kilsyke, and flows east-

ward joining the river Jed, opposite to Mossburn-ford, is the small property of Ashtrees, long the possession of a family of Scott. Between it and Woodhouse formerly stood the Bush and Thorter-wood. A little further to the east, and on the left bank of the Jed, is Clethaugh, an ancient possession of the Ainslies. Tradition fixes this place as the site of the battle between Richmond and Douglas, generally believed to have occurred at Lintalee.

BEDRULE.—The ancient name of this place was *Bethocs-Rule*. It was so called in the 11th and 12th centuries, and even so late as the 16th century it was occasionally written Bethrule. The early name was conferred upon the place by its owner, Lady Bethoc, daughter of King Donalbane, and wife of Rudolph, son of Dunegal. The territory extended from Jedburgh to the Rule on the west, and the valley of the Teviot on the north.

When David founded the monastery of Jed-burgh, Bethoc and her husband Rudolph granted to the canons a carrucate of land with common pasture, in the lands of Rewcastle, which formed a part of said territory. The grant was confirmed by William the Lion and Alexander II. The territory passed to Richard Cumyn, a nephew of William Cumyn, the chancellor of Henry I., who had obtained a grant of Linton, in Easter Teviot-dale, from David I. on his marriage with the

Countess Hexild, the daughter of Lady Bethoc and Rudolph. Richard died about 1189, leaving a son William, who lived to the age of seventy. He was twice married. By his first wife he had two sons, Richard and Walter.* Richard died about 1249, and was succeeded by his son John Cumyn, a powerful man of his day, and popularly known as the *Red* John Cumyn. He took part in all the great transactions of the period in which he lived. He was present with Alexander III., when he held his court at Jedburgh, in 1261.† As Lord of *Rulebethoc,* he granted to the bishop of Glasgow the whole lands of Rulehauch, described in the charter as lying on the north side of the river Teviot.‡ This grant was confirmed by Alex-

---

* His second wife was Marjory, only child of Fergus the ancient, Earl of Buchan. As Earl of Buchan, William Cumyn witnessed a charter of William the Lion, at Elgin, on 17 August, 1211. His son Alexander succeeded him as Earl of Buchan.

† Rymer's Fœd. i. 715. Fordun characterizes this John Cumyn as " vir ad rapinam et temeritatem expeditus:" lib. x. c. x.

‡ Reg. Glasgow, p. 195, " ex aquilonali parte aquæ de Teuyoth."—A change in the river's bed from the south to the north of the vale must have placed the haugh on the north side of Teviot. On examining an old map I found that the river Teviot, on arriving at the end of the bank at Spittal, turned and ran down close by Spittal and the south side of the haugh, and leaving a part of the Bedrule parish on the north side of the river. I have no doubt *Rulehalch* was situated at this place. It is now on the south of the Teviot. In 1393, a duel was fought here between Sir Thomas

ander III. in 1279. The next Lord of *Bethocrule* was William Cumyn, who was present at the parliament of Brigham. He died in 1291, and was succeeded by his younger brother John, commonly known as the *Black* John Cumyn, one of the most potent men of that age. He claimed the crown as heir of Donalbane, who died in 1097. He married Marjory, the sister of King John Baliol, by whom he left a son John, known as *Red* John Cumyn, who was chosen with general consent one of the guardians of Scotland. It was this John who joined Wallace, but deserted him soon after on the field of Falkirk. On the 10th of February, 1306, he was slain by Robert Bruce, in the church of Dumfries.* Robert I. granted to the good Sir James Douglas the lands of Bethocrule "in valle de Teviot," which had formerly belonged to the family of Cumyn, and which they had forfeited by their treason.† In 1389 it was still in possession of the house of Douglas. Next century it was in possession of the Turnbulls, who for more than two centuries were conspicuous in the district.

Strothers, an Englishman, and Sir William Inglis, a Scotchman, at which Archibald, Earl of Douglas, and Henry Percy of Northumberland, the wardens of the marches, acted as umpires. Sir Thomas Strothers was slain.

* Fordun, lib. xii. c. vii.

† Reg. Mag. Sig. p. 4. Robertson's Index, p. 5, No. 12; p. 10, No. 23.

THE CLAN TURNBULL.—It is said that the Turnbulls are descended from a family of *Roule* or
Rule, who derived their surname from the town of
Roule, situated on the left bank of the water of
Rule, and on the right margin of a rivulet which
rises in the slopes of Ruberslaw, and flows into
the Rule near Hallrule. It is thought to have
been originally the Kirktown, and of considerable
importance. All that now remains of the town is
a farm onstead and a few cottages belonging to the
farm. During the first half of the thirteenth
century, three Rules of the names of Thomas,
Richard, and Alan appear as witnesses to several
charters.* In 1296, Thomas and Adam Roule
swore fealty to Edward I. About 1300, *William*
of Rule is a witness to a grant by Adam of Roule
to the monks of Kelso.† This *William* is thought
to have been the first who bore the surname of
Turnbull, which he gained on account of a gallant
exploit, by which he saved King Robert Bruce
from the attacks of a wild bull while hunting in
the forest of Callander. The wild animal attacked
the king, unhorsed him, and would have killed
him but for Rule, who threw himself between the
king and the bull, seized it by the horns, and, by
the exertion of a strength which no other man
of the time possessed, overturned and killed it.

* Lib. de Mel. pp. 237, 244-5, 260; Reg. Glas. p. 126.
† Lib. de Cal. pp. 136, 458.

The gallant deed is beautifully described by a poet
of Teviotdale*:—

" Between red ezlarbanks, that frightful scowl,
   Fringed with grey hazel, roars the mining Roull;
   Where Turnbulls once, a race no power could awe,
   Lined the rough skirts of stormy Rubieslaw.
   Bold was the chief from whom their line they drew,
   Whose nervous arm the furious bison slew;
   The bison, fiercest race of Scotia's breed,
   Whose bounding course outstripp'd the red deer's speed,
   By hunters chafed, encircled on the plain,
   He frowning shook his yellow lion mane,
   Spurned with black hoof in bursting rage the ground,
   And fiercely toss'd his moony horns around.
   On Scotia's lord he rush'd with lightning speed,
   Bent his strong neck, to toss the startled steed;
   His arms robust the hardy hunter flung
   Around his bending horns, and upward wrung,
   With writhing force his neck retorted round,
   And roll'd the panting monster on the ground,
   Crush'd with enormous strength his bony skull:
   And courtiers hail'd the man who *turned the bull.*"

Such is said to have been the origin of the name
of Turnbull. The statement of Boece receives
considerable support, from the fact of King Robert
Bruce having granted in 1315 to William, called
Turnebull, that piece of land which lies on the
west side of Fulhophalch (Philiphaugh), as far into
the forest as it was ploughed in past times, for
a *reddendo* of one broad arrow at the feast of the
Assumption of the Virgin Mary.† The way in

---

* Leyden's Scenes of Infancy, p. 102.
† Reg. Mag. Sig. p. 6.

which Turnbull is designed in this grant is almost
sufficient of itself to establish the truth of the
account given by Boece. The charter not only
bears that the grantee was called Turnebull, but
the spelling of the name is descriptive of the
exploit, *Turn e bull* (*i.e.* turn the bull). The
account derives additional confirmation from the
circumstance that previous to the granting of the
above charter the name of Turnebull is not to be
seen on record. I have little doubt that the
manner in which the name of Turnbull was acquired is substantially true. William Turnbull
fell in single combat, fought between him and Sir
Robert Benhale previous to the commencement of
the battle of Halidon Hill.*   The exact period
when the name first appeared in Teviotdale is not
ascertained, but in the beginning of the fourteenth
century, a Walter Turnbull, probably a son of the
first Turnbull, is seen in possession of the lands
of Mynto. Before 1370, these lands were confirmed to him by David II.†   Between that time
and 1390, John Turnbull, called "*out wi' the
sword*," was in possession of the lands, and of that
date granted the lordship and lands to his nephew
Sir William Stewart of Jedworth, to be held in
chief of the king and his heirs in free barony.
This grant was confirmed by Robert III. In 1399
John Turnbull was in company with Sir William

---

* *Ut supra*, p. 276.   † Robertson's Index, p. 33, No. 48.

Stuart, when he 'was taken prisoner within the Northumbrian border. He went to France and fell gallantly fighting at the battle of Crevant. In 1423 and in 1429, another of the clan of the same name was knighted for his bravery at the famous siege of Orleans, under the constable Patrick Ogilvie. On the death of John Turnbull, his son Walter claimed the lands of Mynto, and in 1425 obtained the verdict of a jury, finding the grant to Sir William Stewart illegal, on the ground that he was a leper at the time it was executed. The sheriff of Teviotdale, under a writ from James II., perambulated the lands and divided the same between the claimants.* In the fifteenth century the Turnbulls obtained the barony of Bedrule. They are also about the same time found in possession of Hallrule, Bonchester, Fulton, Blindhaugh, Newton, Clarelaw, Firth, Beulie, Apoteside, Hoppisburne, Wauchope, Stanyledge, Whitehope, Belses, and several other places in the district. The clan became remarkable in a not over-scrupulous age for deeds of cruelty and thievish daring. They adjoined Liddesdale, and they were equal to any moss-trooper who lived within that thieving district. So formidable did they become about the beginning of the fifteenth century, that they defied the powers of the sheriff and lieutenant of the borders. The king,

* Vide New Statistical Account of the parish of Mynto.

informed of their excesses, and that the ordinary powers of the law were unable to deal with them, gathered together an army and marched to the water of Rule, in November 1510, while the court was sitting at Jedburgh, and executed summary justice upon the clan. Two hundred of them met the king at the water of Rule, holding in their hands their naked swords and having each a halter round his neck. A few were capitally punished, many imprisoned, and the rest dismissed, giving hostages for their future peaceable behaviour. It is said that the effect of the king's visit to Rule produced quiet on its banks for some years.* But in 1530 the clan seems to have resumed its old habits. In May of that year, David Turnbull of Wauchope, and Walter Turnbull of Howay, and others were denounced rebels for not entering to underlye the law for assistance given and afforded to thieves and malefactors in violation of their bonds. William Turnbull of Mynto, with twenty other barons and lairds of Roxburgh, found surety before the justice at Jedburgh to underlye the law for all crimes imputed to them, and for which they submitted themselves to the king's will. He also in the presence of the king bound and obliged himself to make Turnbull of Catlie to restore to Alexander Bartholomew a horse and other goods stolen from him, under silence of

* Hollingshed, vol. ii. p. 132.

night, by certain of the Turnbulls dwelling on the waters of Rule, and especially by Turnbull of Catlie, or to produce him in court, and "failing thereof, to burn his house, expel, and hold him forth of the country." The king attended the court in person, and the presence of a large army made the border clans humble and submissive. By the king acting as his own lieutenant on the borders and rigidly executing the laws, the clans were completely subdued. In 1545, the English entered the valley of the Rule, burned twelve castles and forts, with the towers of Crag and Barnhills. They at the same time harried the clan of their cattle and other means of subsistence, and carried off and destroyed nearly all their household gear. At the same time many of them were either slain or taken prisoners.

By such means they, as well as most borderers, were forced into taking assurance under the English, on which they were supplied with crosses of St. George, and compelled to accompany the English army in some of their inroads into Scotland. But when the two armies met on Ancrum Moor, the Turnbulls and others, seizing the opportunity to be revenged, threw away their red crosses, and turned their swords against the foes of their native land. By the aid of those Scots who were under assurance, the Douglas gained the battle of Ancrum. In 1561 Peter Turnbull, called the *monk*, was hanged for being a common thief. In 1565 Thomas Turnbull of Bedrule, along with a great number of nobles, barons, and gentlemen, attended at Edinburgh, on the summons of Queen Mary, and supported her upon her marriage with Darnley, and also assisted in putting down an insurrection by Murray the Duke of Chatelherault and others. Subsequently the Turnbulls and Rutherfurds espoused the side of Regent Murray, and kept in check the Scots and Kers, who then continued their adherence to the Queen. About this time the Turnbulls obtained military possession of the tower of Ker of Ancrum, their hereditary enemy; but the mother of Ker, a daughter of Home of Wedderburn, contrived to surprise them, and regained possession of the fort. At this time Ker was a fugitive for the slaughter of one of the Rutherfurds, then in alliance with the Turnbulls. At the Raid of Redswyre "auld Badroule" was present " wi' a' the Turnbulls at his back," and " did right weel, I you declare." In 1591, Bothwell and Home having rebelled, James VI. summoned all the fighting men to meet him at Edinburgh, to accompany him on an expedition against the rebellious lords. Amongst those who obeyed were " Wat o' Bedroul" and Turnbull of Mynto, with their retainers. In November of the same year, James Douglas of Cavers, Sheriff of Teviotdale, became surety for the said Walter Turnbull under the penalty of 1000 merks. Thomas of Bed-rule was one of the persons who subscribed the bond at Kelso, in 1569, for the repression of theft on the borders.* William his son succeeded; but the clan seems to have returned to its old practices in 1598. In 1601 Andrew Turnbull, brother to the guidman of Beulie, was beheaded at the cross, for the murder of Thomas Ker of Crailing. In May, 1603, George Turnbull of Belses was tried for being a common robber. James Waddell, a burgess of Jedburgh, a juryman, was objected to, on the ground that there existed a deadly feud between the Kers, the town of Jedburgh, and the "hail name of Turnbull." A testimonial was produced under the hands of George Douglas, clerk of the Presbytery of Jedburgh, bearing that Turnbull the panel was excommunicated for slaughter, mur-der, incest, adultery, &c. His right hand was struck off at the cross of Edinburgh. Next month he was tried for the crimes of incest and adultery with Marion Turnbull, spouse to Jock Turnbull, his brother's son, for which he was excom-municated by the Presbytery of Jedburgh; and for stealing horses, oxen, and cows, he was found guilty and hanged. In 1604 Hector Turnbull, Lilliesleaf, was declared rebel for the slaughter of Thomas Ker of Crailing. In the same year, Hector

---

* Pitcairn, vol. iii. p. 265.

Turnbull of Barnhills, his brother George, Gavin
Turnbull, their father's brother, and Hector Turnbull of Stanyledge, were denounced rebels for not
appearing to answer to the indictment against them
for the cruel slaughter of William, James, John,
Robert, Andrew, and Thomas Grahamslaw of Little
Newton. Old Barnhills and Douglas of Cavers
were fined in 1000 merks, 400 merks, and 400
merks. Robert Hume of Carolsyde, Hector Turnbull of Belses, in 400 merks each. In the month
of March, 1606, Hector Turnbull of Wauchope,
George Turnbull, his son, Adam Turnbull in
Bullerwell, George Turnbull in Howa, John
Turnbull, son to Wauchope, Hector Turnbull of
Stanyledge, Andrew Turnbull, brother to Bullerwell, Hector Turnbull in Clairlaw, and Thomas
Turnbull in Hoppisburne, were charged with taking
from Margaret Turnbull, Lady Apotside, forth of
the town and lands of Hairwood, 200 kye and oxen,
30 score of sheep, 30 horses and mares, with the
whole insight plenishing, worth the sum of £1000;
from Apotside 130 cows and oxen, 200 sheep, with
the insight plenishing, worth £500; also with
burning the place of Apotside, and destroying several houses and two horses, and slaying three persons; as also for cutting down 1000 birk trees, 500
great oaks, 300 allers, and 400 hazels, within the
woods of Apotside. William, Earl of Angus, appeared at the trial, and claimed the laird of Wau-

chope, George and John Turnbull, his sons, and
Thomas Turnbull of Hoppisburne, dwellers within
the regality of Jedforest. The justice admitted
Angus's right to repledge and ordained him to find
caution to try Adam Turnbull of Bullerwell, at
Lyntilees, on the 15th of April next. The diet
was deserted against the others, and it does not appear whether further proceedings were adopted
against them. It is probable the proceedings were
suppressed. In 1668 Thomas Turnbull of Bedrule
was retoured heir to his father William in the lands
and barony of Bedrule.* Before 1678 the barony
seems to have been in possession of Andrew Ker
of Cavers. At that date Thomas Ker was retoured
heir male of tailzie and provision of said Andrew.†
Part of the barony was purchased from that family
by Sir Gilbert Elliot of Gateshaw, and was afterwards acquired by Elliot of Wells, to whose representative it now belongs. Of all the possessions
of the clan no part now remains the property of
any one of the name. With the exception of the
small estates of Knowe, Standhill, Firth, Over
Tofts, Langraw, and part of Swanshiel, which were
possessed by Turnbulls to the end of last century,
the whole seems to have passed into other hands
during the seventeenth century. The first three
properties fell to female heirs and were disposed of,
the last two fell into other hands, upon a failure of

---

* Retours, vol. ii. No. 243.   † Ibid. No. 272.

heirs male of the last lairds.   The last Turnbull of Langraw was William, some time provost of Jedburgh, who died near the close of last century. This family were the representatives of the outlaw Turnbull of Barnhills.   In 1667 Thomas Turnbull of Standhill incurred forfeiture for his adherence to the Presbyterian cause, but the forfeiture was rescinded by the Act of William and Mary in 1690.*

In 1532 William, son and heir apparent of Thomas Turnbull of Minto, sold the lands of Greenwood and Line, part of that barony, to Walter Scott of Branxholm.   Thomas Turnbull of Minto, who led the affray in 1601 against Ker in Jedburgh, married Barbara Home, and died about 1626.   His son succeeded him in the lands and barony of Minto, Town Mains, Mill, and Kaimes.   His eldest son John appears to have been the last Turnbull of Minto.   He married Elizabeth Elliot, daughter of Sir Gilbert Elliot of Stobs, called " *Gibbie wi' the gowden garters*," and of " Maggy Fendy" a daughter of "Auld Watt of Harden" and Mary Scott, the Flower of Yarrow.   William Turnbull was their eldest son, and a daughter, Alison, married Douglas of Timpendean, in 1655.

---

* His successor, Captain Robert Turnbull, was governor depute of Dumbarton Castle in 1727.   The property was purchased by Lord Minto in 1799.   Walter Turnbull of Beulie also incurred forfeiture in 1665, but which was also rescinded in 1690.

The barony was in the end of the 17th century the property of Walter Riddell, second son of Walter Riddell of Newhouse, who left four daughters who sold the lands to the predecessors of the present proprietor, the Earl of Minto.

From the house of Bedrule sprang William Turnbull about the beginning of the 15th century. He was educated for the church and entered into holy orders in 1440, when he was appointed prebend of Balanrick. The degree of Doctor of Laws was conferred upon him, and he was made Archdeacon of St. Andrew's within the bounds of Lothian, a Privy Councillor, and subsequently Keeper of the Privy Seal. When Bishop Bruce was translated from Dunkeld to Glasgow in 1447, Dr. Turnbull was elected Bishop of Dunkeld, but Bruce dying in the same year, Turnbull was then created Bishop of Glasgow and consecrated in April, 1448. On 20th September, 1449, he said his first mass in Glasgow. In 1450 he procured from Pope Nicholas V. a bull for erecting a college for literature within the city of Glasgow. Upon the institution of the university he was created chancellor. From James II. he obtained a charter erecting the town of Glasgow and the patrimonies of his bishopric into a regality. It is thought that this good bishop restored several portions of Jedburgh abbey. The chapel on the south of the chancel, used for a long time as a Latin school, is believed to have been repaired by him. On a buttress of the south wall of that part of the abbey are the arms of the Turnbulls. It is probable that he also built the whole of the north transept. He died at Rome on 3rd September, 1454.

. RUECASTLE, or ROWCASTLE.—A territory of this name seems at an early period to have been comprehended in Bedrule barony. The town of the territory was situated on the top of the bank overlooking the valley of Teviot, near to where the present farm onstead of the same name stands. It was possessed of two strong towers, which were destroyed, along with the town and all the corn in it and around it, when Lord Dacre's brother visited the locality in 1513. The property belonged to Lady Bethoc and her husband. The family of Cumyn enjoyed it till their forfeiture. A person of the name of William of Ruecastle swore fealty to Edward I. It was the same William, it is thought, who for years received a pension from King Robert Bruce. In the 14th century the whole lands of Ruecastle belonged to Thomas Dickinson of Ormestoune, who resigned them into the hands of King James IV. for the purpose of a new grant of the same in favour of John Rutherfurd of Hundole. When the rent-roll of the abbey of Jedburgh was made up in 1626, a person of the name of Storie possessed a five-shilling land in

Ruecastle.   In 1629 Andrew Lord Jedburgh was retoured in the lands and forest of *Rowcastle*. The lands are now possessed by George Pott, who is also the possessor of Knowsouth, with its beautifully situated mansion, in the vale below.

On the same high ground are several entrenchments, and in a hollow ground at the head of a burn is a spring called the Lady's Well, so named, it is said, from the supply of water it afforded to a fish-pond belonging to the monks of Jedburgh. NEW-TON is situated near to the foot of the rising ground, and within a little distance of the river Teviot. In ancient times it also was the property of Lady Bethoc, and was included in the barony of Bedrule. During the beginning of the 16th century it seems to have been possessed by a family of Grahamslaw. Adam Grahamslaw of Newton was one of the lairds of Roxburghshire, who submitted to the king's will at the Jedburgh raid in 1530.   In 1604 six of his sons were slain by the Turnbulls of Barnhills, and Hector Turnbull of Stanyledge.   The fort of Barnhills stood on the opposite side of the river Teviot from Newton.   But the Turnbulls spared no man in their wrath.   In 1607, Newton with its mills was possessed by the Kers of Ancrum.   It was afterwards acquired by the family of Ogilvie of Chesters, and is now the property of Thomas Scott of Peel.   Like all other places of any consequence in the border district, Newton had its safety peel, the foundations of which can only now be traced.

FULTON.—This place is situated at the extremity of the parish. It derives its name from the foul state of the land in which it is placed—the *Fouletown*. The walls of its square keep standing in the rough waste are all that remain of the town or hamlet of a family of the Turnbulls.

HOPEKIRK.—This kirk obtained its name from standing in a hope, or little valley. The former site of the church is said to have been at the town of Roull, in early days the principal town of the locality. At the beginning of the 13th century the church belonged to the canons of Jedburgh, and was one of the subjects of difference between them and the bishop of Glasgow in 1220. The result of the conference at Nisbet was that the vicar should receive ten marks, or the whole altarage, with its lands and all pertinents, paying therefrom to the canons half a stone of wax yearly at the festival of St. James, and that the whole of the residue should go to the uses of the canons.* In 1496 the town of Rule, Hallrule, Hallrule Mill, Deanside, Apothside, and Titus formed part of the grant by James IV. to Janet, daughter of Archibald Earl of Angus.† As already stated in the notice of the clan Turn-

* Reg. of Glas. p. 98.   † Reg. Mag. Sig. lib. xiii. No. 234.

oull, Wauchope, Howay, Bullerwill, Hawrull, Hoppisburne, Hairwood, and Apothsyde were in
possession of the Turnbulls during the 16th and
the beginning of the 17th centuries.   In 1502, a
town called *Wyndis* (Weens?) was possessed by a
person of the name of Alexander *Wyndis*, designed
of that ilk.*   It is now in the family of Cleghorn.

WAUCHOPE.—The name of Wauchope, or Walch-
ope, it is thought, is derived from the Irish *uagh*,
signifying a *den*, and the Saxon *hope* or *ope*, a
short valley running into a height.   The mansion
stands upon Wauchope burn, which takes its rise
in the Cheviot mountains.   This manor was an
ancient possession of the Turnbulls, from whom
it passed to the Cranstounes, and from that family
to the great-grandfather of the present possessor,
Thomas Macmillan Scott.   The family who now
possess this property are descended from Walter
Scott, second son of Walter Scott of Crumhaugh,
and are now the only representatives in the male
line of the old Scotts of Goudielands, afterwards
of Crumhaugh.   The first of the family was
Walter Scott of Goudielands, natural son to that
Sir Walter Scott of Buccleuch, who was slain by
the Kers in Edinburgh in 1552.   He was born
in 1532; he had the tower of Goudielands built
for him by his father, as the "watch-tower of

* Pitcairn, vol. i. p. 37.

Branxholm." He is a witness to the testament
of Sir Walter Scott of Branxholm, in April,
1574. In 1575 he appears to have led the clan
Scott to the battle of the Redswyre, and is referred to in the ballad as

> " The laird's Wat, that worthie man,
> Brought in that sirname weil beseen."

Scott of Satchells, in his history of the name
of Scott (written in 1688), states that the *Wat* of
the ballad was Walter Scott of Ancrum, a natural son of Walter Scott of Buccleuch. Sir Walter
Scott, in a note to the ballad, says that he thinks
Satchells mistaken in this particular, on the
ground that the Scotts of Ancrum, who are
descended from the Scotts of Balwearie in Fife,
did not settle in this district till the reign of
James VI., and that the person meant must be
the young laird of Buccleuch, afterwards distinguished for his surprise of Carlisle Castle.
While it is clear that the *" laird's Wat "* of the
ballad could not be one of the Scotts of Ancrum,
as that property was possessed by the Kers at the
time, there are no grounds for arriving at the
conclusion that the person who led the clan to
battle was the young chief; on the contrary,
there is every reason to believe that Buccleuch
was not present. Had the young Buccleuch led
the clan, he would not have been mentioned as
the *" laird's Wat,"* but by his own name. The

" *laird's Wat* " is not the laird himself; and when the battle of the Redswyre was fought, there was no lawful son of the house of Buccleuch to lead the clan. Sir Walter Scott, father of the chieftain who rescued " Kinmont Willie," died the year before the battle, leaving his son and heir a pupil. Satchells, however, who may have mistaken the place where the leader of the clan dwelt, states that he was a natural son to Walter of Buccleuch. Now, *Walter* of Goudielands was a natural son of the laird of Buccleuch, by whom he was greatly trusted, and no one so likely to be selected to lead the clan to the field during the infancy of the heir of the house. Besides the name, the age (43) and qualities all point conclusively to Goudielands as the leader on that occasion, so as to leave little or no room for doubt. In 1592, James VI. granted " full power and commission, express bidding and charge to *Walter* Scott of Goudielands, and Mr. Gideon Murray, to demolish the palaces, houses, and fortalices of Harden and Dryhope, their owners having been art and part of the treasonable fact perpetrated against the king's person at Falkland." * A *Walter* of Goudielands was with Buccleuch at the release of Kinmont from Carlisle Castle, in April, 1596; † but it is doubtful whe-

---

* Pitcairn, vol. i. p. 276.   † Tytler, vol. ix. p. 223.

ther it was the " *laird's Wat*," or his son, Walter Scott. The Wat of the ballad would then be sixty-four years of age. He died in November of that year, and was buried in the aisle of the old church of Hawick. His son Walter succeeded. In March, 1612, he subscribed a contract at Jedburgh between the king and certain barons and lairds, for the maintaining of better rule on the borders. In a charter, dated March, 1620, of the lands of Goudielands and Westcotrig, he is designed Sir Walter Scott of Goudielands. He had two sons, Walter and Charles. Walter died without issue, and was succeeded by his nephew, Walter Scott, son of his brother Charles of Crumhaugh. The estate of Goudielands was acquired from him towards the close of the 17th century. He died in 1700, leaving two sons—Charles, who enjoyed the estate of Crumhaugh, and Walter Scott, the first of the Wauchope branch. He married Christian, a daughter of Robert Bennet of Chesters, and by her had Walter Scott, who acquired the estates of Howcleuch, Borthwick Mains, and Wauchope. Robert Bennet was the son and heir of Raguel Bennet of Chesters, and nephew of William Bennet of Grubet and Marlefield, rector of Ancrum. Walter Scott died in 1786, and his son, Walter Scott of Wauchope, succeeded, and married Rachel Elliot, daughter of Elliot of Falnash, and by her had two sons, Walter and

Charles. Walter was twice married, but left no issue. His first wife was Elizabeth Rutherfurd, daughter of David Rutherfurd of Capehope, advocate. This lady was the correspondent of Burns the poet. While on his border tour, in 1787, the poet visited Wauchope, and in his "Memoranda" says that she possessed all the sense, taste, intrepidity of face, and bold critical decision which usually distinguish female authors.* At the death of Walter Scott, in 1794, Charles Scott of Howcleuch succeeded, and had, by his marriage with Elizabeth Dickson of Hassendeanburn, a son Walter, who married Marion Macmillan, a daughter of Thomas Macmillan of Shorthope, Selkirkshire. Walter died in 1857; his son, Thomas Macmillan Scott, now possesses the estate. He is also proprietor of the estates of Pinnacle-hill and Easter Wooden in the parish of Kelso.

In this manor the evidences of the struggles of former races are abundant. In Wauchope rig are two forts or camps. One of these is on the crest of the hill overlooking the *Catlee*, at the pass between Wolfhopelee and Hyndlee. Immediately below it are parallel earthworks extending to the *Catlee*. These earthworks may be seen from the public road, looking like " parallel roads." They

---

* Memoranda of Tours.

terminate on each flank in what is still boggy ground, but previous to hill-draining must have been morass. The other is about a quarter of a mile lower down, and is planted with trees. A breastwork and deep ditch surround it. It is in good preservation. On the north-eastern descent from *Winberg*, the *battle-hill*, to the Rule, are numerous *tumuli*, or cairns, of various sizes, and mostly covered with a thin layer of turf. The two largest are on that part of the mountain embraced within the lands of Wauchope common. Oval seems to have been the prevailing shape. The *Catrail* passes through this district. It was the war-ground of the ancient peoples.

WOLFLEE, or WOOLE, lies on the right bank of Wauchope burn. In early times it was the property of the Abbey of Jedburgh. In 1625 the Rutherfurds held *Woole*, as appears from the rent-roll of the abbey. The Turnbulls possessed portions of the estate in 1621. In 1627, Lord Cranstoune seems to have owned it, from whom it passed into the family of Elliot.

ANCRUM or ALNECRUMBE.—The name of this place has been conferred by its British inhabitants, and intended to point out a town situated at the *crumbe*, or bend of the river Alne. This river, for eight miles from its junction with the Teviot, is remarkable for the many curves or bends in its course. The town stands upon the right bank of the stream and within one of its crooks. On the north is the precipitous bank of the river, honeycombed with the caves or dwellings of the ancient Britons.*   On the south the land slopes down to the rich vale through which the river Teviot flows, and on the east the woods of Mounteviot, one of the mansions of the Marquis of Lothian, bound the prospect.   The town consists of a single street of the form of a triangle, starting from near the building popularly known as the Malton or Mantel

---

* In the first volume, p. 295, it is stated, on the authority of the statistical account and other works looked upon as of authority, that one of these caves was called *Thomson's Cave*, from its being a resort of the poet Thomson while staying with his friend Mr. Cranstoun, the incumbent of the parish, but which I am now satisfied is incorrect.   The poet never tuned his lyre in any of these caves.   One of them, of difficult access, was the resort of Mr. Cranstoun for meditation and prayer.   Into this cave Thomson, one day, managed to go, but after he was there he became so nervous and frightened that he durst not leave till a chair was got with ropes attached, into which he was placed, and hauled up the steep bank.   In a number of works it is said, that while he frequented this cave he carved his name upon the roof, where it is still to be seen.   The statement is without any foundation.   The name was cut by a son of the Rev. Dr. Campbel, a late incumbent of the parish.   I think it right to state that I make this statement on the authority of a clergyman resident in Jedburgh, whose father was parish schoolmaster of Ancrum, and to whom Mr. Cranstoun made the communication.

Walls on the east, and widening in its course westward. It seems to have been fortified by a number
of towers or peels. One tower stood at the east end
of the north row of houses near to the old ruins; a
second at the head of the same row; a third, known
by the name of Rankin's peel, was placed near the
west end of the south row, intended no doubt to
protect the approach from the south; and another
strong house stood in a garden a little to the east
of Rankin's peel. At the head or west end of the
town a strong tower stood upon a piece of ground
lying between the *gait* or road to the present
church, and a burn which runs over the bank into
the Ale. It was called the Parson's Knowe Peel,
and from its naturally strong position capable of
being defended against a powerful force. A little
south from this strength stood the old manse of
Ancrum, in which the good Livingstone dwelt. The
old approach to Ancrum was through the river
near to the Coatlands or Copeland ford, along
what was of old called the *Cappit* road and Causey-
end, to the south-west corner of the town near
Rankin's peel. A beautiful cross, said to be as old
as the days of Alexander III., stands in the middle
of the village green.* The stones forming the
cross are of the same kind as those used in the old
building called the Malton Walls. It is said by

---

* Vol. i. p. 328.

the writer of the old statistical account of the parish, that the town once contained about twenty malt barns. Ancrum is one of the oldest towns in Scotland. So early as the *Inquisitio Davidis* in 1116, the church and territory appear as belonging to the bishop.* Before 1216 several popes had confirmed the lands and church to the bishop of Glasgow. At a very early period the lands were erected into a regality, confirmed in 1490 by James IV.† The barony of Ancrum remained with the bishops of Glasgow till the Reformation, when it passed first to the Duke of Richmond and Lennox, and afterwards to the Earl of Roxburghe, in whose family it now remains. It was at first called the barony of Ancrum, afterwards the barony of Nether Ancrum. Although named differently, the territory remained the same.‡ The bishops of Glasgow had a rural palace at Ancrum, from whence many of their charters are dated.§ Considerable difficulty exists as to the site of this house. It is said by the editor of the Origines Parochiales that the remains of the bishop's palace form part of the castle of Sir William Scott, and that the bishop's house is styled by Lord Dacre, in his letter to Henry VIII., shortly after the battle of Flodden, the "castle" of Ancrum.|| The like statements are to be found

---

* Reg of Glas. pp. 5, 6, 7.   † Ib. pp. 466-7.
‡ Acta Parl. vol. v. p. 395.
§ Reg. Glas., Lib. of Calchow, Lib. of Dryburgh.
|| Origines Parochiales, vol. i. p. 305.

in the introduction to the Chartulary of Glasgow, with the addition that the gardens in which the early bishops practised horticulture were within the present century to be seen at the back of the castle. In support of these views the editor refers to the New Statistical Account of the parish, and to Morton's Monastic Annals. But on turning to these works it will be found that they contain no warrant for the statement. It is true that Morton quotes the letter of Lord Dacre to his sovereign, in which it is stated that the castle of Ancrum was burned, but it is not said that the castle was the bishop's palace, and no information is given as to its situation. It appears to me that the views of the learned editor of these works on this point are wholly untenable. The present castle of Ancrum stands in the territory of Over Ancrum, and never was comprehended in the bishop's barony of Ancrum. Over Ancrum belonged in property to the monks of Jedburgh, and was by them let in feu farm to Robert Ker, third son of the celebrated Dand Ker of Fernieherst, about the year 1542, and who, on his marriage with Margaret Home of Wedderburn, built a tower which now forms the centre of Sir William Scott's castle. At the Reformation the Kers were the owners of this tower or castle, and in 1603 Robert Ker of Ancrum was retoured heir to his father William Ker of Ancrum, of the lands of Staw-waird and Braidlaw in the lordship of Over Ancrum.* Now the *Staw-waird* is the steep ridge on the east end of which the castle stands. No doubt the rocky ridge derived its name from the strengths constructed at its west end. It is popularly known at the present day by the Castlehill, which is just a modern translation of *Staw-waird.* The lands and town of Over Ancrum, with the mills and cottages thereof, formed a part of the grant by King James to Alexander, Earl of Home, in 1610.† Had any part of Over Ancrum been the property of the bishops of Glasgow, it would have appeared in the grants by the crown of the whole estates of that church to Lennox and Roxburghe. The fact that the gift includes only the barony of Nether Ancrum, conclusively shows that the property of the bishops did not extend beyond the territory known as Nether Ancrum, which is now enjoyed by the family of Roxburghe. The castle or palace of the bishops of Glasgow must be looked for within the barony of Nether Ancrum. After the most careful consideration I am inclined to think that the ruins popularly known as the *Malton* or *Mantle Walls,* lying within the bend of the river, formed a part of the bishop's house or castle.‡ A more lovely place could not have been

---

* Retours, No. 20.
† Extract of Charter, in possession of the author.
‡ Vol. i. p. 260.

found in the locality, while the high banks of the Ale on the north and east would afford a complete shelter from the winter storms. It is said that the name is derived from the place having been at one time the property of the knights of Malta, but I do not think it probable that the order ever had any property in Ancrum. If they had, it could only have been obtained from the bishops of Glasgow, of which there is no evidence. It is more than likely that the name originated the popular belief that the place was the property of the knights of Malta. The name Malton or Mantle seems to denote a mansion-house or principal residence, forming a part or in the immediate vicinity of a religious house. The original mansion-house of the Erskines of Shiel-field stood adjacent to the abbey of Dryburgh, and on ground fined from the commendator, was called the *Mantle House.** The same name is to be found at Melrose abbey : *" Viridaria sub lie Mantle Wall."* † It may therefore be fairly presumed that the Malton or Mantle Walls was the mansion of the bishops in the immediate vicinity of their chapel. The place is within the barony of Nether Ancrum, and was undoubtedly a part of the estate of the church of Glasgow, and included in the grant to Lennox, and afterwards

---

* Book of Dryburgh, p. xxxi.   † Retours, No. 251.

to Roxburghe. In addition to what is stated in regard to the buildings which once existed here, in the first volume, to which reference is now made, it may be noticed that I have information from old persons who were told by their parents that in *their* youth a high gable, and in it a beautiful window, stood next to the tower. The last portion of the walls fell in 1837, and the plough has gone over the whole building. Scarcely an old dyke or house in the neighbourhood but has been in part built out of these remains. It is certain that William de Bondington, a native of the borders, who succeeded to the bishopric of Glasgow in 1333, usually resided at Ancrum. The place was, even at that early day, celebrated for its gardens, in which the bishop studied horticulture. During the latter period of his life, Bondington made Ancrum his chief residence. He died here in 1258, and was buried in the abbey of Melrose, near the high altar.* Before 1232, Radulph Burnard of Faringdune granted to Bishop Walter of Glasgow and his successors peats out of his two mosses of Faringdune, for the use of their house at Alncrumbe. This deed was confirmed by Radulph swearing on the holy

---

* "Item venerabilis pater noster Willelmus episcopus Glasguensis migravit ex hoc seculo in vigilia Sancti Martini (Nov. 10), et in die Sancti Bricii (Nov. 13) apud Melros juxta magnum altare sepelitur."—Chron. Mail. p. 184.

evangels and the relics of the bishop's chapel.*
The witnesses who saw Radulph subscribe the
deed, and heard him confirm it by his oath, were
Richard, the parson of Ancrum, and dean of
Tevidale; Adam and Robert, chaplains to the
bishop; Pauline, chaplain of Faringdune; William
of Avest, seneschal to the bishop; Warino the
butler, Peter the dispensator, Robert of Hertford, clerk; Walter the treasurer; and Yvone
of the chapel.   Between 1252 and 1406, there
were several persons of the surname of Alncrumbe.

While the chapel of the bishops stood at the
east end of Ancrum, the church of the parish
occupied a quiet secluded nook on the right bank
of the river, at some distance to the west of the
town. The present church was built in 1762.
About 1660 the godly John Livingstone was
minister of the parish.   He was banished to
Holland in 1662, and a Mr. James Scott, a person
under sentence of excommunication, presented to
the charge. On the day fixed for his settlement
in the parish, several people met to oppose it, and
particularly a countrywoman desiring to speak
with him, with the view of dissuading him from

---

* " Et ego pro me et heredibus meis, super sacrosancta
evangelia et reliquias capelle episcopi juravi, quod sine malo
ingenio et reclamatione vel impedimento elemosinam su-
pradictam in perpetuum."—Reg. Glas., pp. 99, 100.

intruding himself upon a reclaiming people, pulled him by the cloak, entreating him to hear her a little; on which he turned and beat her with his staff. This provoked a number of boys to throw a few stones, but which did not touch him or any of his company. The occurrence was, however, magnified into a great offence, and the sheriff and justices fined and imprisoned some of the people. But the punishment being deemed too lenient, the offenders were taken to Edinburgh, and dealt with as criminals.· The boys admitted throwing the stones, and were sentenced to be scourged through the streets of Edinburgh, burned in the face with a hot iron, and then sold as slaves to Barbadoes. Two brothers of the woman, named Turnbull, were banished to Virginia, and the woman was ordered to be whipped through the streets of Jedburgh. The bishop of Glasgow, when applied to for a mitigation of the sentence, lest the woman should be with child, *mildly* answered that he would make them claw the itch out of her shoulders. In 1639, Mr. William Bennet of Grubbet was rector of Ancrum.

The town of Ancrum was burned by Dacre in 1513. In 1544 it was burned by Sir Ralph Evers, and also Ancrum 'Spital. Both towns were burned to the ground by Hertford, in 1545. Ancrum Spital was also destroyed. Morton identifies this Spital with the Malton Walls, but it is· clear that the Spital here meant stood at Harestanes. In the list of places destroyed, Ancrum Spital is classed along with the Nisbets and Bonjedworth, while the towns of Over and Nether Ancrum appear in the list after the towns of Bonjedworth, and along with Barnhills, Minto, &c. Had the Ancrum Spital of the list stood at the east end of Ancrum, it would have appeared along with the town. I am satisfied there never was a Spital at Ancrum town. Blaeu, in his *Theatrum Scotiæ*, properly places Ancrum Spital on the north bank of the Ale.

ANCRUM CASTLE.—On the left bank of the river Ale lies the *manor* of Sir William Scott, baronet. The Watling Street forms the eastern boundary. The barony of Longnewton is on the north, while on the south and west the river is for several miles the limit of the property. The castle stands on the north bank of the river, in an extensive and well-wooded park. The present building has been erected at three different periods. The oldest portion is in the centre, and is said to have been built by Robert Ker, youngest son of Dand Ker of Fernieherst, about 1558. The eastern part was added after it came into the family of Scott, and the present proprietor made an addition at the west, in which, says Sir Thomas Dick Lauder, " he has contrived to employ a large mass of masonry, which now looks to be the oldest part of the castle."* The view from the castle is full of beauty. On the south, the fertile vale of Teviot and the sloping sides of Lanton Ridge are spread out as on a map, while westward the eye rests on

"Dark Rubieslaw that lifts his head sublime,
Rugged and hoary with the wrecks of time."

On the east is seen a beautiful and fertile tract of country, and far away in the distance appear the green summits of the Cheviot mountains. Within the park itself are a number of lovely scenes, which would require a more glowing pencil than mine to portray. The park is full of old trees, many of which are of large growth. A lime-tree in front of the castle measures fully twenty-seven feet in circumference, and several others of the same kind only a little less. On a ridge a little to the north of the castle is a magnificent weeping ash. Its girth is about twenty-one feet. The beeches are very fine, but begin to show symptoms of decay. One of these trees measures above ten feet in circumference. A willow is nearly fourteen feet. On the west of the castle are two beautiful walnut-trees, one of which is about ten feet in girth. The park contains many trees of various kinds, scarcely inferior to those particularly noticed;

* Tait's Magazine, vol. xiv. p. 743.

and, taken altogether, the trees may truly be said
to be the finest in this part of the country. From
what information I can gather, I think the oldest
trees cannot be less than 300 years of age. It is
probable that the trees about the castle were
planted after Sir Robert Ker came into possession
in 1542. The town of Over Ancrum stood a little
to the north of the castle, but no part of that
monkish town now remains. To the west of the
castle are vestiges of extensive strengths on the
point of a steep ridge overlooking the church
called the "*Staw.*" Although it is always difficult
to assign any period for the formation of such
strengths, owing to the alterations made by different people, it may with certainty be stated that
the British people first occupied this place. The
whole summit of the hill has been taken in and
encircled by a wall of large boulders according to
the custom of the ancient Britons. But it appears
to me that the strength has been made to suit the
warfare of more modern times. In one of the
large stones which had at one time formed a
jamb of the entrance gate, I noticed the grooves
for the portcullis to slip down. I doubt not
a strong fort has existed here in comparatively
recent times. The position is one which from its
nature was certain to be seized upon in all times
of strife. Some years ago a cannon-ball was
found in one of the forts, and is now in the pos-

session of the owner of the land. It is possible that this place may have been the "*castle*" referred to by Dacre in 1513. A remarkable bridge stretches across the river at the foot of the *staw*, the half of which seems to be as old as the 12th and 13th centuries, or it may owe its erection to a much earlier period. It appears to me that a road from the west has crossed the water here and ascended the steep or *staw* near to the strengths on its way eastward. On this manor is Lilliard's Edge, or "dark Ancrum's heath," where "fierce Latour and savage Evers fell," and where "Scott and Douglas led the border spears." The place where the battle took place is on the farm of Heriotsfield near to the Watling Street, along which it is thought the English army retreated from Melrose. Evidences of the deadly struggle are occasionally turned up by spade and plough. A very fine sword found on the battle-field is in the possession of Sir William Scott.*

The family in possession of this manor is of ancient origin. The name of Scot appears at a very early period in the courts of the kings and among the nobles of the land. Uchtred the son

* A full account of this as well as of the other battle-fields of the district will be found in a subsequent chapter. I understand that Sir William is about to erect a suitable monument to the fair maid of Maxton, who tradition says fell fighting in the Scottish ranks.

of Scot is a witness to the Inquisitio Davidis, in 1116.* Uchtred Scot and Herbert Scot appear as witnesses to the foundation charter of David I. to Holyrood, in 1128. They also appear as witnesses to a charter of the same king, founding the abbey of Selkirk. In 1158 Richard the son of Uchtred is witness to a charter of Robert, bishop of St. Andrew's, to the abbey of Holyrood. Between 1174 and 1199 Simon Scot is witness to a charter of Alan, the son of Walter the steward of Scotland. In 1177 Gilbert Scot is witness to a charter of the Lady Eschena of Molle, the wife of Walter the steward of Scotland. In 1178 John Scot was elected bishop of Dunkeld.† Matthew Scot was chancellor of Scotland during the reign of William the Lion.‡

Uchtred had two sons, Richard and Michael. The former was the stem of the house of Buccleuch, and from Michael the present family of Ancrum is descended. So early as the latter part of the reign of Malcolm IV., Michael was a person of property and influence in the county of Fife. He married a daughter of Syres of that ilk. He had a son, Duncan, who made a considerable donation of lands in Fife, which was confirmed by his widow and heir. His son Michael had the honour of

---

* Reg. of Glas. p. 5.   † Chron. Mail. p. 88.
‡ Acta Parl. vol. i. pp. 75-77.

knighthood conferred on him by Alexander II. In the beginning of the reign of Alexander III. he married the daughter and sole heiress of Sir Richard Balwearie, by whom he got the lands and barony of Balwearie in Fife, which was long the chief title of the family. He had one son whom he named Michael, who became celebrated as a philosopher and reputed magician. After residing several years in France he went to Germany, where he studied medicine and chemistry. On leaving Germany he visited the court of England, and was graciously received by Edward I. After returning to his native land he was knighted by Alexander III., by whom he was employed on several confidential missions. On the treaty of marriage between the prince of England and the heiress of Scotland being concluded at Brigham, in July 1290, Sir Michael Scot and Sir Michael Wemyss were sent by the guardians of Scotland to Norway to conduct the Princess Margaret to Scotland, but she sickened on her voyage from Norway, and died at Orkney in September of that year.* The exact period of his death, as well as his place of burial, seems doubtful. By some he is said to have died in 1291, while others have him living in 1296. Some say he was buried at Holme Coltram, in Cumberland, while others contend for Melrose being the last resting-place of the wizard. Many a legend of

---

* Rym. Fœd. ii. 1090 ; Math. Westminster, 381.

the magical deeds of Sir Michael and his familiar spirits lives in the memory of the peasantry of the border land, but the limits of this work preclude further notice of them.*   Sir Henry, the heir of Sir Michael, swore fealty to the English king.   Sir Andrew, his son and heir, was slain at the siege of Berwick in 1365.   His grandson, Sir Michael, was one of the hostages for James I. in 1424.   The grandson of this Sir Michael was possessed of great influence, and was the owner of vast estates in the shires of Fife and Perth.   His estates in Fifeshire were erected into one barony by James IV. in 1509. He followed his indulgent sovereign to the disastrous battle of Flodden, where he was taken prisoner, and, being known to be the possessor of immense wealth, his ransom was fixed at so exorbitant a sum that he was forced to sell part of his estates to redeem himself from bondage.   His successor, Sir William, married a daughter of Lord Lindsay, by whom he had two sons, William and Andrew, and a daughter. His eldest son, Sir William, continued the line of Balwearie, while the second son, Andrew, was the head of the house of Ancrum.   The Balwearie family was greatly injured by the great-grandson of Sir William being engaged with the Earls of Angus, Errol, Huntly, and others, at the battle of Glenlivat, and shortly afterwards as an accomplice of the Earl of Bothwell.   His grandson, Colonel

---

* Vol. i. p. 243; Notes to the Lay of the Last Minstrel.

SIR MICHAEL SCOT.

BODLEIAN LIBRARY.

CANONICI MISCELL. 555.

Walter Scot, was the last of the male line of Balwearie. The succession then devolved upon the
family of Ancrum, descended from Andrew the
second son of Sir William as already mentioned.
He was proprietor of the lands of Kirkstyle in
Perthshire. Sir Patrick, his great-grandson, sold
these lands and purchased Longshaw, and afterwards the manor of Ancrum. His son Sir John
Scot obtained a charter under the Great Seal of
the lands of Ancrum, and was created a baronet by
Charles II., by patent to him and his heirs male,
dated 1670. Sir John was a person of great influence in the kingdom.

In 1670 he was one of the commissioners appointed by parliament to make a valuation of the
five parishes in Eskdale, united to the county of
Roxburgh by the act in favour of James and Anna,
Duke and Duchess of Buccleuch.* In 1689 Sir
John and his son Sir Patrick were appointed commissioners for ordering out the militia in the shire
for the protection of the Protestant religion and
the peace of the kingdom, threatened by the papists
of Ireland. Both were appointed commissioners
for levying money to maintain the troops.† In 1690
Sir John was one of the commissioners for raising
a month's cess to enable his majesty to carry on
the war. In 1693 a disposition by Lord Rutherfurd in favour of Sir John Scot of the barony of

---

* Acta Parl. vol. viii. p. 91. † Ibid. vol. ix. pp. 28, 69.

Scraesburgh or Hunthill, comprehending the lands
of Nether Chatto, Capehope, etc., and the right of
patronage of the parish church of Hownam, was
ratified by parliament.* He married first a daughter
of Scot of Mangerton, by whom he had five sons and
five daughters; secondly, a daughter of Sir William
Bennet of Grubbet, who bore to him two daughters; and thirdly, the daughter of Ker of Littledean,
by whom he had no issue.   He died in 1712, and
was succeeded by Sir Patrick, his eldest son, a
lawyer of eminence, and greatly esteemed for his
integrity.   In 1689 Sir Patrick, and Sir William
Elliot of Stobs, were commissioners to parliament
for the county of Roxburgh.   Both commissioners
subscribed the act of parliament declaring that
they were a free and lawful meeting of the estates,
and would continue undissolved till the Protestant
religion, laws, and liberties of the kingdom were se-
cured.† In the same year he was one of those who
subscribed a double of the letter which was sent by
the parliament to the king of England.   He also
sat as commissioner for Roxburghshire in the first
parliament of William and Mary, June 5, 1689.
In 1690 he was one of the representatives of the
shire.   In 1693 Sir Patrick Scot of Ancrum, Sir
William Scot, younger, of Harden, and a number
of members of parliament were ordered to appear
and sign the oath of assurance, with certification

---

* Acta Parl. vol. ix. p. 344.   † Ib. p. 9

that their places would be declared vacant. In consequence of Sir Patrick not appearing as ordered, he was fined £600, his place declared vacant, and the sheriff of Roxburgh ordered to convene the freeholders to elect a qualified person in his place.* Sir William Elliot of Stobs also failed to appear, and was fined in the same sum, and his seat declared vacant. The freeholders met and elected James Scot of Gala, and John Scot of Wells. Sir William Scot, younger of Harden, was also fined, for the payment of which Sir Patrick became bound. He married twice, but had no issue by the first wife. The second, who was the daughter of Sir William Scot of Harden, bore him four daughters and two sons, the eldest of whom, Sir John, succeeded, and married a daughter of Nisbet of Dirleton. His eldest son dying, William, his second son, succeeded, but leaving no issue he was succeeded by his nephew John, who, in 1792, married Harriet, a daughter of William Graham of Gartmore, by whom he had the present baronet, Sir William, and four daughters. Sir William was born in 1803, and married Elizabeth Anderson, by whom he has several children. In 1827 Sir William represented the city of Carlisle in parliament; and during the struggle for Reform he stood forward on the popular side, and advocated with energy and

* Acta Parl. vol. ix. p. 250.

zeal what he thought the interests of the people. His three eldest sons served with credit in the Crimea, and the third son is now serving in India.

KIRKLANDS, the seat of John Richardson, stands on a fine terrace on the right bank of the river Ale. The house, which is of the Elizabethan style, was erected in 1834. It commands a beautiful view eastward, including both banks of the river, and the well-wooded park of Ancrum. It is a place where the proprietor may forget the bustle of a great city and spend the afternoon of life in the calm enjoyment of that repose which a meditation on the works of creation never fails to produce.

CHESTERS, or GRANGE.—On the banks of the Teviot, at a short distance from the town of Ancrum, stands Chesters, now possessed by the family of Ogilvie. For more than two centuries this manor was the property of the Bennets, a branch of the family of Grubbet. In 1588 Adam Bennet of Wester Grange granted a charter of the lands to Andrew Bennet, his father. Raguel Bennet, the son of Adam Bennet, designed of Chesters, possessed the manor from the beginning of the 17th century till about 1636. He acquired Rawflat in 1622. In 1635 the right was confirmed by the Bishop of Glasgow. He also got Tronyhill about the same time. He was succeeded by his son,

Robert Bennet, who was a remarkable man in his day. He was a stern presbyterian, and for maintaining his principles was repeatedly fined and imprisoned. In 1662 he was forced to pay £1200 before he could get the benefit of the act of indemnity. His offence was desertion of his parish church, and refusing to attend the conforming clergyman. In 1670 he attended the open-air ministrations of John Welsh, Blackadder, and others. In 1676 he was charged with being at a conventicle, held on Selkirk Common, and, failing to appear before the Privy Council, he was outlawed, and his goods confiscated. On his being apprehended some time after, and carried before the Privy Council, the charges were referred to his oath, and on his refusing to swear, he was sentenced to be carried to the Bass and imprisoned till further orders. He was, however, detained in Edinburgh Tolbooth and again taken before the Council, charged with attending field conventicles, at which Welsh, Blackadder, and others preached, and also with harbouring and resetting in his own house Welsh and others. On being examined he admitted the charges, but refused to promise to refrain from attending conventicles, or to attend his own parish church. For his contumacy he was fined in 4000 merks, and ordained to be imprisoned in the Bass till the fine was paid. In February, 1678, a petition was presented by Mrs. Bennet, praying that her husband might be liberated from prison to attend her upon her deathbed. Interest having been made with the Duke of Lauderdale and the Bishop, leave was granted him to go to Chesters till 18th March following, on which day he was to re-enter the Bass, under the penalty of 4000 merks. In 1680 he was again imprisoned in the Bass, because he would not forbear attending covenanting preachers. After suffering imprisonment for eleven months, he was liberated upon paying 1000 merks. Bennet was alive in 1701. His descendants continued to possess the manor for four succeeding generations. It was sold about the close of last century by the three sisters of Robert Bennet, the last male proprietor of that name, to the family of Ogilvie.

BELSES.—This manor and barony belonged to the monks of Jedburgh. It included the town, mill, and common of Belses, Rawflat, Peelquarter, Ryeknowe, Abbotsmeadow, Raperlaw, Parkquarter, Milnacre, Pinnacle, Milnrigquarter, Loanenrig, Myrequarter, and Frith. Ker of Cavers was the proprietor about the middle of the 17th century. The name of the barony is thought to be derived from the river Ale forcing back the waters of the rivulets which flow into it upon the land at that bend of the stream where Belses is situated.

NISBET.—This name is derived from the Saxon, and means the *nose-piece* or *bit*. There are four places which go by the name of Nisbet, all lying on the left bank of the Teviot, and on the slope of Penielheugh. The first owner of this barony was Ranulph de Sules, a Northamptonshire baron, who accompanied David from England. He obtained a grant of land in Liddesdale, and Nisbet in Teviotdale. He granted to the Abbey of Jedburgh half a carrucate of land in *Nasebith*.* On the forfeiture of William Soulis, Robert the Bruce granted the barony to Walter the Stewart of Scotland.† During the reign of David II. it became the property of Sir Robert Erskine and Christiane Keth, his spouse, by grant from Robert the Steward of Scotland, afterwards Robert II. The grant includes mills, multures, patronage of church and hospital, and the men on the property bond and free. The territory was afterwards divided into Over, Nether, East, and West Nisbet, and possessed by the Marquis of Lothian.

In the little church of Nisbet, in 1220 and 1228, all the differences between the bishop of Glasgow and the canons of Jedburgh were adjusted. The church has long since ceased to be, but its little graveyard is still used by the men of Teviotdale, who love to lay their ashes with their forefathers.

---

* Charter of David I. † Robertson's Index, 10, 21.

B B

In 1612, the parliament appointed Crailing to be the parish church.*

CRAILING.—The name of this place is from the British speech, signifying the passage of the stream over a rocky bed, *craig lyn*. Between Crailing and Oxnam the bed of the water is full of rocks. The village which formerly went by the name of Lower Crailing is situated at the turn-pike-road leading from Berwick by the way of Jedburgh and Hawick to the west, but now little used. Oxnam water flows close by the village, driving a cornmill in its course, and joins Teviot a short way to the north of the town. The ancient cross of the barony is yet to be seen standing in a field to the south of the road near the centre of the village. In the days of David I. Sheriff Gospatrick possessed Crailing. He conferred on the abbot of Jedburgh the churches thereof. Berenger de Engain, a noble Norman, granted to the same abbot a mark of silver from the mill of Crailing, and two oxgangs of land with one slave—*cum uno villane*—with other property near the church, for sustentation to the chaplain of the chapel of Crailing. Crailing was long possessed by the Cranstounes. It is now the property of a family of the name of Paton, whose beautiful seat

* Acta Parl. vol. iv. p. 500.

overlooks the banks of the Oxnam, the rich vale of Teviot, and the fruitful slopes of Penielheugh.

CRAILING HALL, known in the early days as the "other Crailing," and afterwards as Uvyrere-lyne, was in the days of Prince David of Cumberland the property of Orm the son of Elav. He granted to the canons of Jedburgh a ploughgate of land in this manor, which was confirmed by William the Lion and Alexander II.* The lands of Over Crailing and the half of the lands of Samieston were erected into a barony before 1370, and were possessed by John Scroupe. Robert II. granted the same to Adam Wawayne. In the end of the 15th century the barony was the property of the Humes, from whom it passed into the family of Ker, ancestors of the Marquis of Lothian. In the beginning of the 17th century, the lands formed a part of the barony of Hownam-mains and were possessed by the Humes, but again returned to Lord Jedburgh. The little mill which served the men of the barony stood on a bend of the Oxnam water close to the road to Jedburgh. For fifteen generations this mill and a small piece of ground was rented from the Kers by a family of Scotts, who left about forty years ago. A malt steep which was built for brewing the ale for the use of

---

* Robertson's Index, p. 22, No. 5.

the masons and workmen employed in the erection of Cessfurd Castle was to be seen at this place till within a few years ago. Modern improvement has nearly destroyed all traces of the mill and its pertinents.

ULSTON.—This old monkish barony bounded both Crailings on the north. David I. granted the territory to the canons of Jedburgh, which was confirmed by his son Prince Henry, William the Lion, Alexander II., and Robert Bruce. The canons possessed the barony till the Reformation. It comprehended in the parish of Jedburgh, Stewartfield, Chapmanside, Tolnerdean, Ulston, Hyndhouse, Hyndhousefield, Aickiebrae and its haugh, Castlewood, the burn thereof, Woolbetleyes, Plainespott, Hardentounehead, and Wells; in Oxnam, Broomhills; and Fleures and Ruecastle in the parish of Bedrule. In 1487 Stewartfield was held by a family of Stewart.* In 1590 Adam Kirkton was laird of Stewartfield. He was one of the barons and lairds of Roxburghshire who, on May 18th, 1530, found surety to enter before the justices and underlye the law for all crimes imputed to them, and for which they put themselves in the King's will.† In 1607 Adam Kirkton of Stewartfield was retoured heir to William Kirkton of the lands

---

* Act. Dom. Aud. pp. 58, 59.   † Pitcairn, vol. i. p. 147.

lying beyond Chapmanside and Tolnerdean, with common pasture and all easements in Ulston, and the office of steward in the hall of the monastery of Jedburgh, within the barony of Ulston.* About the end of the 16th century the barony was divided among a number of proprietors.

In the end of the 17th century the lands of Thickside within the parish and lordship of Jedburgh, the lands of Heartrig (formerly called Stewartfield), Chapmanside, Castlehill, and Howmeadow (formerly called Priormeadow), parts of the lands of Ulston, in the barony of Ulston and parish of Jedburgh, were erected into a barony under the name of Heartrig. The barony was then the property of Francis Scott of Mangerton. In 1700 Elizabeth Scott, his sister, was retoured as heir of line to her brother Francis Scott of the lands and barony of Heartrig.† In 1721 it was in the possession of Colonel Scot. The barony of Heartrig now belongs to Lord Chief Justice Campbell, who has lately erected a mansion on it, in the style of the baronial halls of the 15th century. The situation of the mansion commands an extent and variety of beautiful scenery seldom to be met with in any district. From the park a fine view is obtained of the ancient burgh of Jedburgh with its ruined abbey, in the vale below, environed with rock and wood. An extensive forest of firs existed

---

* Retours, No. 46.   † Retours, No. 326.

on this estate, but is now nearly exhausted. The trees still remaining are said to be the largest and of the finest quality in the south of Scotland. In 1839 a storm of wind from the south-west destroyed a great number of the trees. The Chief Justice has effected great improvements upon the park since he acquired the barony.

BONJEDWORTH, which obtained its name from standing at the foot of the Jed, is thought to be the *Gadanica* of the Roman Itinerary. The Watling Street passes close by it. It was included in the grant by King Robert Bruce to the good Sir James Douglas in 1320. In 1356 Edward III. conferred it, along with the other two Jedworths, the Forest, and Hassendean, on Percy. A person of the name of Pringell possessed it previous to 1358. After that date David II. conferred the subjects forfeited by Pringell on William Pettilok. In 1398 the lands became the property of George Earl of Angus. In 1407 Thomas, the son of John Douglas, and his wife Margaret, got a grant of the lands from Isobel the Countess of Mar, which was afterwards confirmed by Albany. In 1575 the Laird of Bonjeddart was present at the battle of the Redswyre. The family of Douglas was still in possession of the property during the 17th century. TIMPENDEAN, a part of the territory of Bonjedworth, remained in the family of Douglas from 1497 till the present

Sold Jerdon - of Bonjed estate in 1845 to J. of Loth

century. It is said that the Douglases of Bonjed-worth were descended from a natural son of George Earl of Angus. The whole territory now belongs to the Marquis of Lothian. The castle and town of Bonjedworth suffered their full share of the miseries of border warfare. The castle was converted at a later period into a gaol. In 1683 Sir John Riddell of that ilk and another were tried at the court of justiciary at Jedburgh for their religious opinions, and sentenced to be confined in the prison of Bonjedworth. There is now no vestige of this important fort. Two farm onsteads and a few scattered cottages occupy the site of this ancient town. On the right bank of the Jed, nearly opposite to Bonjedworth, is a large *tumulus*, part of which was laid open about thirty years ago, and a number of kestvaens exposed containing bones and beads and other personal ornaments. It is on the west side of the Roman way. About the middle of Lanton Moor, within the territory of Bonjedworth, is a large encampment, near to an old road which once passed along the hill. The crown of the causey of the road is occasionally to be seen.

END OF VOL. II.

J. F. HOPE, 16, GREAT MARLBOROUGH STREET.

OPINIONS OF THE PRESS AS TO VOL. I.

From the London Critic.

Mr. Jeffrey's work consists of two small octavo volumes—only one of which is at present before us—containing a series of essays on the geographical features, the geology, the early inhabitants, and the Roman occupation, and a description of the abbeys and old crosses of the county. The chapters devoted to a description of the geography of the county are made very interesting by anecdotes, and illustration, and pleasant gossip, which each locality suggests, and what under other treatment would have been a very dry subject, is made very readable and entertaining. The long chapter on geology, contributed by another hand, appears, so far as we are competent to give an opinion, carefully and well done. Considerable space is devoted to the history of the county during the Primæval and Roman periods. The author, it is sufficiently manifest, has bestowed diligent study upon the works of the standard writers on such subjects, and has digested their bearing and his own local observations into a history of Roxburghshire under the Britons and the Romans, well calculated to interest all the men of Roxburghshire who have a liberal curiosity as to the early history of their native place. . . The latter portion of the volume is occupied with a description of the architectural remains of the religious houses of the district—Jedburgh, Dryburgh, Kelso, and Melrose —whose literary histories we are promised in the second volume. We are glad to find also an enumeration and description of the crosses of the district—a beautiful class of antiquities, which as yet have hardly attracted the notice which they deserve. On the whole, we can sincerely recommend the volume to Scotsmen in particular, and to our archæological readers generally.

From the Gentleman's Magazine.

The author explains in his preface that, though he has placed the words " second edition " in his title-page, no part of the contents of the present volume were included in the book which he published in 1836, except a small portion of the descriptions of the Abbeys in Teviotdale. The chapters are six in number, describing:—1st, the situation and outline, boundaries and extent, declination and climate of the district, which is distinguished as lying in the centre of the British island, and being the southernmost division of Scotland ; 2nd, its hills and valleys ; 3rd, its lochs and rivers ; 4th, its ancient appearance ; 5th, its geology ; 6th, its antiquities. The chapter on geology is contributed by the Rev. James Duncan, of Denholm, who will also furnish the botanical and zoological chapters to the second volume. Under the head of antiquities, the principal subjects discussed by the author are :—The early inhabitants, their religion, their modes of burial, their forts and caves ; the Roman remains and roads ; the Saxon era ; and the abbeys and crosses.·

Altogether the information is full and satisfactory, the result of the author's devotion to his subject for the term of five-and-twenty years. It has in front a good map of the county, and in a second map its British and Roman features are neatly delineated. It is altogether a very useful handbook for the Border.

From the Hawick Advertiser.

We can safely affirm that it is admirably got up, and far superior to any previous published description of our county. And as the time has gone by when persons can be considered as entitled to assume the character of gentlemen who are unacquainted with the history of their own county, we entertain no doubt that all the " pleasant men of Teviotdale " will lose no time in studying Mr. Jeffrey's most creditable performance, to which we for a short time bid adieu.

From the Kelso Chronicle.

We are glad to find that this work is now before the public. We have ourselves been much gratified and instructed by the perusal of it ; and we are anxious, therefore, to introduce it to the notice of our readers, and make them acquainted with some of the many claims it has on their attention. The plan which has been followed in the present work embraces all departments of the subject, from the earliest inhabitants, through the period of Roman dominion, and the varied struggles of which this Border land was the scene, down to the most recent times. The physical features of the county are delineated at considerable length, and numerous interesting anecdotes are introduced illustrative of the manners of the times, and which vary and enliven the descriptive details. The author has managed to throw much light on many parts of his subject, by tracing the names of places and people to their original sources; and although differences of opinion may well be admitted on topics which are often speculative and uncertain, he must be allowed to have shown no small degree of learning and argument in the use he has made of this means of knowledge. A prominent and interesting feature of the present volume is an account of the geology of the district, from the able pen of Mr. Duncan of Denholm, well known for his intimate acquaintance with the various departments of natural history.

From the Berwick Advertiser.

We have extracted enough to show the interest which the chapter on antiquities has for residents on the Border. On a future occasion we may return to the volume, and run over the five chapters which are devoted to the physical aspects and the geology of the district. The work is the result of five-and-twenty years' attention bestowed on the history and antiquities of the Border, by a gentleman whose profession habituates him to patient investigation, and to careful analogies of evidence. The professional training is manifest in nearly every page. A writer unused to dusty tomes and minute criticism might have dashed off with a more glowing pencil the physical beauty of the districts and the aspects of the human life, richly varying as they ever are ; but what the pages would have gained in picturesqueness would have been dearly purchased in the sacrifice of that scrupulous fidelity which in local history and antiquities is above all price. The volume, which is remarkably well got up, is illustrated with a map of the county, a British and Roman map of the district, and about twenty lithographs, chiefly illustrative of ancient remains.

From the Border Advertiser.

If every county could supply a man who would labour with as much assiduity as Mr. Jeffrey has done to describe the present aspect of places, and snatch from oblivion, or dig out of neglected tomes, the facts relating to each locality, something might yet be done towards obtaining a descriptive history of Scotland, complete in all its departments, and worthy of the country we live in. . . . We beg to assure the author that his volume is a most creditable acquisition to the Border press, and one which reflects the highest praise on himself. We shall look with great eagerness for the next volume, which, if possible, will be more deeply interesting.

From the Gateshead Observer.

The details of Scottish history are scanty, and it is probable that Mr. Jeffrey examined the whole that were open to him in the course of his labours. Nearly all had to be gleaned and garnered by his own hand. Hence we ought to be lenient in alluding to any error or omission he has made. We therefore award him our approval freely, trusting that when the second volume is published he will not desist from gathering still more matter connected with the district, and making either an addition to his history, or in the end leaving his collections as a public bequest to all who may hereafter wish to know more of that remarkable county. . . . Meantime we congratulate Mr. Jeffrey on what he has accomplished; his work is a starting point in the right direction ; and we hope successors will arise to labour in the same field, till Roxburghshire can affirm her historians are as accurate and comprehensive as those of any county in England.

From the Kelso Mail.

The work now before us will, when finished, supply to some extent the desideratum so long felt by those who know the richness of the field and lament the poverty and want of faith of the labourers in it. It will not place us on a footing of equality with our southern neighbours, but it will bring us nearer them. The first edition, which appeared in 1836, was favourably reviewed at the time in this journal, but since then "the work has been entirely re-written, and, with the exception of a small portion of the description of the abbeys of Teviotdale, no part of the contents of the first volume are included in this edition." The author, who is a man of more than common energy and profes-

sional activity, tells us it now contains the cream of the information he has been able to gather during a period of twenty-five
years in relation to the history and antiquities of the district.
We have gone over the whole carefully and with much pleasure,
and, though we have detected a few trifling mistakes on comparatively unimportant points of detail, we feel assured that no one
who has the slightest idea how difficult is the task of collecting
and arranging such a multifarious mass of local information as
Mr. Jeffrey presents to his readers, will be disposed to carp and
cavil with him on that account, as they do not in the least affect
the substantial authority of the book. We regret that our limits
do not permit us to give an analysis of the work, or to make
extracts from it; but we recommend such of our readers as feel
an interest in local history and antiquities, or in the geology of
the south of Scotland, which is treated of here in a fascinating
popular style, by the Rev. James Duncan of Denholm, to add it
forthwith to their private collections, or at least get an early
reading of it from the nearest library.

Encyclopædia Britannica, vol. xi. p. 246.

Its origin (" *Hawick Mote* ") is entirely lost, but Mr. Jeffrey,
whose acquaintance with the historical memorials of the Scottish
Border is perhaps unparalleled, throws out the conjectures in
his History and Antiquities of Roxburghshire, that "the children
of the Gadeni may have used it as a burying-place for their dead,
and their descendants afterwards have converted it into a moat-
hill; or it may have been used from a very early period as a
place for enacting as well as administering laws. . . . There
can be no doubt," he adds, " that in later times the flat top of
the Hawick Moat was used by the judge of the day for hearing
the rude suitors of the district."

Paper by John Alex. Smith, M.D.
(Read before the Royal Physical Society, Edinburgh, May 29,
1856.)

He might mention that a very good general sketch of the
geology of the district, by the Rev. James Duncan, Denholm,
was recently published in a work on the " History and Antiquities
of Roxburghshire," by Alexander Jeffrey, Esq., Jedburgh.

Extract of Letter from John Collingwood Bruce, Esq.,
Author of "The Roman Wall."

With great industry and skill, you have brought together and
arranged a considerable quantity of valuable matter. I am much
pleased with the Roman part of it.

From the Testimony of the Rocks, page 452.

Since these sentences were written I have seen a description
of both the plants of the upper old Red to which they refer in an
interesting sketch of the geology of Roxburghshire, by the Rev.
James Duncan, which forms part of a recent publication devoted
to the history and antiquities of the shire.

DR. PUSEY REFUTED.
In post 8vo., 4s. cloth (Ready).

The Doctrine of the Holy Eucharist Investigated: Modern Innovations of its Purity Examined and brought to the test of Scripture, the Testimony of the Ancient Fathers, and the Declarations of the Church of England. By the Rev. John Duff Schomberg, B.A., Vicar of Polesworth.

London: J. F. Hope, 16, Great Marlborough-street.

Just published, Vol. I., price 7s. 6d.; Vol. II., price 10s. 6d. Beautifully Illustrated.

History and Antiquities of Roxburghshire and Adjacent Districts, from the most remote period to the present time.   By Alexander Jeffrey, Esq., Author of " Guide to Antiquities of the Borders," &c.

London: J. F. Hope, 16, Great Marlborough-street.

In 1 vol., post 8vo, price 10s. 6d. (Shortly.)

The Odd Confidant ; or, " Handsome is that Handsome Does." By Dot.

London : J. F. Hope, 16, Great Marlborough-street.

In 2 vols., post 8vo, price 21s. (Shortly.)

The House of Camelot. A Tale of the Olden Time. By Miss M. Linwood.

London : J. F. Hope, 16, Great Marlborough-street.

Post 8vo, price 3s. (In December.)

Anecdotes of the Bench and Bar. By W. H. Grimmer.

London: J. F. Hope, 16, Great Marlborough-street.

Fcap. 8vo, price 2s. 6d.

On the Search for a Dinner. By W. R. Hare.

London: J. F. Hope, 16, Great Marlborough-street.

Post 8vo, price reduced to 5s. (In January.)

Travels and Recollections of Travel ; with a

Chat upon various subjects. By Dr. J. Shaw, Author of "Rambles through the United States," "A Tramp to the Diggings," &c.

London : J. F. Hope, 16, Great Marlborough-street.

STARTLING NEW WORK.

Vol. I., post 8vo, price 5s. Second Edition. (In January.)

Holland : its Institutions, Press, Kings, and

Prisons; with an awful Exposure of Court Secrets and Intrigues. By E. Meeter.

"This is just the book that people would like to read."—*Saturday Review.*

London : J. F. Hope, 16, Great Marlborough-street.

---

1 vol., post 8vo., price 10s. 6d. Illustrated. (In the Press.)

Juvenile Crime : Its Causes, Character, and

Cure. By S. P. Day, Author of " Monastic Institutions," &c.

London : J. F. Hope, 16, Great Marlborough-street.

Lately published, in one vol., post 8vo., price 2s. 6d., cloth 3s. 6d.

China : a Popular History, with a Chronolo-

gical account of the most remarkable events from the earliest period to the present day. By Sir Oscar Oliphant, Kt.

London : J. F. Hope, 16, Great Marlborough-street.

Post 8vo, price 4s. (Just ready.)

Wild Notes. By E. Passingham.

London : J. F. Hope, 16, Great Marlborough-street.

Second Edition, Second Series, now ready, price 5s.

Brameld's Practical Sermons. (Second series.)

" Full of earnest thought and genial feeling."—*Athenæum.*
" A book of a thousand merits."—*Press.*
" The claims of personal religion are enforced with singular earnestness."—*John Bull.*

London : J. F. Hope, 16, Great Marlborough-street.

Ready, Second Edition, much improved, price 6s.

Thirty-four Practical Sermons.

By G. W. Brameld, M.A. Oxon, Vicar of East Markham, late Curate of Mansfield.

"Truly spiritual."—*John Bull.*
"Brief, earnest, and forcible."—*English Churchman.*
"These discourses are truly what they are termed in the title-page, practical. Mr. Brameld does not command belief, he persuades and convinces."—*Critic.*

London: J. F. Hope, 16, Great Marlborough-street.

Just published, price 7s. 6d.,

Thirty Sermons, on Jonah, Amos, and Hosea.

By the Rev. W. Drake, M.A., Lecturer of St. John Baptist Church, Coventry; Hebrew Examiner in the University of London; and late Fellow of St. John's College, Cambridge.

London: J. F. Hope, 16, Great Marlborough-street.

Just published, price 6d.,

The Prophecy of Khoshru, &c. Translated

by J. D., and Edited by M.D.

London: J. F. Hope, 16, Great Marlborough-street.

Just published, price 4d.,

Christian Fear. A Sermon preached by

desire of the Congregation. By John Barton, Curate of Rivenhall.

London: J. F. Hope, 16, Great Marlborough-street.

Post 8vo, price 3s. 6d.,

The Sea. Sketches of a Voyage to Hudson's

Bay; and other Poems. By "The Scald."

London: J. F. Hope, 16, Great Marlborough-street.

Post 8vo, price 7s. 6d.

Mess-Table Stories, Anecdotes, and Pasquin-

ades, to Promote Mirth and Good Digestion. By Hoin Sirmoon.

London: J. F. Hope, 16, Great Marlborough-street.

In 3 vols., post 8vo, price 31s. 6d.   (In the press.)

Annette Doyne : A Story from Life.
By E. D. Fenton.

London : J. F. Hope, 16, Great Marlborough-street.

Post 8vo, price 3s. 6d.

Reflections on the Mysterious Fate of Sir
John Franklin.   By James Parsons.

London : J. F. Hope, 16, Great Marlborough-street.

Post 8vo, 1 vol., price 6s.

Voyages to China, India, and America.
By W. S. S. Bradshaw.

London : J. F. Hope, 16, Great Marlborough-street.

Post 8vo, 1 vol., price 8s.   (Ready.)

Dearforgil, Princess of Brefney : A Historical
Romance.   By the Author of " The Last Earl of Desmond."

London : J. F. Hope, 16, Great Marlborough-street.

Post 8vo, 1 vol., price 4s.   (Ready.)

Italy's Hope : A Tale of Florence.
By John Ashford, Author of " The Lady and the Hound."

London : J. F. Hope, 16, Great Marlborough-street.

Post 8vo, price 2s.

The Lady and the Hound.   By John Ashford.

London : J. F. Hope, 16, Great Marlborough-street.

Post 8vo, price 7s. 6d., Illustrated.   (Just ready.)

Poems.   By " Sir Oscar Oliphant."

London : J. F. Hope, 16, Great Marlborough-street.

Price 1s.,

A Day on the Downs, by the Vale of White Horse.

London : J. F. Hope, 16, Great Marlborough-street.

Price 3d. each, or 20s. per 100.   (Third Edition.)

An Elementary Religious Catechism ; being

a Compendium of the chief Truths and Events revealed in the Holy Scriptures, as expounded and commemorated by the Church of England.   By the Rev. Henry Kemp, M.A., Head Master of Cleobury-Mortimer Endowed Schools.

London : J. F. Hope, 16, Great Marlborough-street.

Post 8vo, price 4s.,

Poetical Romances and Ballads.

By R. V. Sankey, Author of " Sir Hieram's Daughter."

London : J. F. Hope, 16, Great Marlborough street.

Post 8vo, price 1s. 6d.,

Sir Hieram's Daughter and other Poems.

By R. Villiers Sankey, Author of " Poetical Romances and Ballads."

London : J. F. Hope, 16, Great Marlborough-street.

Post 8vo, pp. 332, price 1s. 6d.,

The History of England in Rhyme, from the Conquest to the Restoration.

"A delightful book for children and young people."

London : J. F. Hope, 16, Great Marlborough-street.

Demy 8vo, price 12s. 6d.,

Switzerland in 1854-5 : A Book of Travel,

Men, and Things.   By the Rev. W. G. Heathman, B.A., Rector of St. Lawrence, Exeter, late British Chaplain at Interlaken.

London : J. F. Hope, 16, Great Marlborough-street.

2 vols., post 8vo, price 14s.   Second Edition.

Frirwin : A Novel.   By Octavia Oliphant.

"Has a spirit about it which serves to carry on its personages and events with all the ease of conscious power," &c.—*Weekly Dispatch.*

London : J. F. Hope, 16, Great Marlborough-street.

Post 8vo, price 8s.,

Julia ; or, The Neapolitan Marriage.
By Margaret Tulloh.

" This work should be read by all who wish to possess a thorough knowledge of Neapolitan Life."

London : J. F. Hope, 16, Great Marlborough-street.

Price 3s.   Second Edition.

The Young Lady's First French Book, with
a Vocabulary of the French and English, and the English and French, of all the words used in the book.   By R. Aliva.

" This work is decidedly the best we have yet seen of the kind, and we observe that our opinion is backed by our numerous contemporaries."—*Courier.*

London : J. F. Hope, 16, Great Marlborough-street.

Post 8vo, price 2s.

Manual of Confirmation.
By Rev. C. Henxman, Incumbent of St. Andrews, Dunmore.

London : J. F. Hope, 16, Great Marlborough-street.

Demy 18mo, price 3s.,

Duty to Parents : Honour thy Father and
thy Mother.   By a Clergyman of the Church of England.

" A useful companion to persons newly confirmed."—*Guardian.*
" Excellent in its purpose and contents."—*Spectator.*
" This excellent little volume may assist the parents above alluded to.   It is a well-planned, well-executed book."—*Leader.*
" This little book, placing the duty on its true scriptural basis, would be a useful present to most young gentlemen, and even to some young ladies too." —*Churchman's Magazine.*

London : J. F. Hope, 16, Great Marlborough-street.

Post 8vo., price 2s. 6d.

First Steps in British History, for the use
of Schools and Private Families. By the late Tutor to the Earl of Glamorgan.

"The 'young nobleman' is the Earl of Glamorgan, and whoever his tutor is, we feel, on the perusal of these pages, that he is a man worthy to be trusted. The leading facts of British history are thrown into the form of a narrative, so simple that a child of six years may understand it. Taking this excellent nursery-book from beginning to end, we should say that the main facts are truthfully stated, and the great religious and constitutional principles guarded with a vigilance that would have done credit to the authors of many more pretentious books."—*Christian Times.*

"A concise and well-written summary of the history of England, from the invasion of Julius Cæsar to our own times. The language is simple, and, as the title premises, adapted to the comprehension of very young children; and the author, not satisfying himself with the bare recital of historical events, seizes every opportunity of inculcating good principles by pointing out those actions worthy of admiration and imitation, and those which should, contrariwise, be shunned."—*Britannia.*

"*First Steps in British History* is that rarest but most valuable of all educational works—a really simple and intelligible composition, adapted to the capacities of children. It is the best English History for schools we have yet seen."—*Critic.*

"*First Steps in British History*, being letters to a young nobleman by his tutor, is a summary of the leading events of the history of England, written in a plain, familiar style."—*Literary Gazette.*

London : J. F. Hope, 16, Great Marlborough-street.

---

1 vol., demy 8vo, price 10s. 6d.

Travels through the United States, Canada,
and the West Indies. By John Shaw, M.D., F.G.S., F.L.S., Author of "A Tramp to the Diggings," &c.

"This is a most valuable work at the present time," &c. "This book is remarkable."—*Press.*

London : J. F. Hope, 16, Great Marlborough-street.

Post 8vo, price 5s.,

Christian Politics.
By the Rev. Henry Christmas, M.A., Author of "The Cradle of the Twin Giants," "Echoes of the Universe," "Shores and Islands of the Mediterranean," &c.

London : J. F. Hope, 16, Great Marlborough-street.

Post 8vo, price 2s. (Ready in January.)

Family Interests : A Story taken from Life.
London : J. F. Hope, 16, Great Marlborough-street.

Post 8vo, price 1s. 6d.,

Arnold : A Dramatic History.

By Cradock Newton.

" There is exquisite beauty in ' Arnold.' "—*Glasgow Commonwealth.*

" ' Arnold ' is a book of real poetry. It is full of beauty, and will be felt to be so by all who have a lover's passion for the great and small things both of nature and of thought, and whose delight is to see them dressed in poetic fancies again and again."—*Inquirer.*

" In toiling across a wide desert of arid verse, we are too delighted to meet with the sound of a spring or the fragrance of a flower not to give it a welcome. Of the kind have we found in ' Arnold.' There are evident touches of poetry in it. The stream of the verse has a gleam of gold. The author is apparently very young, but has undoubtedly shown that he possesses the poetic temperament. An unusually pure tone and purpose in the book argue well for the future of the writer. The various lyrics show a sense of music in verse. The patrons of our minstrels will do well not to pass this little pamphlet by."— *Athenæum.*

London : J. F. Hope, 16, Great Marlborough-street.

Price 1s. 6d.,

Thoughts on the Revision of the Prayer-

Book, and of the Terms of Clerical Conformity. By the Rev. J. R. Pretyman, M.A., late Vicar of Aylesbury, Bucks.

London : J. F. Hope, 16, Great Marlborough-street.

Demy 8vo, price 7s. 6d., Illustrated.   Second Edition.

Lays of Love and Heroism, Legends, Lyrics,

and other Poems. By Eleanor Darby, Author of " The Sweet South."

" The authoress is already well and favourably known to the British public by her previous publication, under the title of ' The Sweet South.' The appearance of the present volume will but call forth a repetition of those high encomiums which were so plentifully bestowed upon her former effort. The ' Lily o' Dundee ' is of itself sufficient to show the distinguished abilities of the authoress, displaying, as it does, in a very high degree, her power, pathos, and poetic skill. The volume, as a whole, cannot fail to contribute very materially to the popularity of the accomplished authoress; and it deserves a very extensive circulation."—*Morning Advertiser.*

London : J. F. Hope, 16, Great Marlborough-street.

Demy 8vo, price 1s.

Gems of Thought, on the Principal Subjects

of Life. By James Badnall, of Bishop Cosin's Hall, Durham.

London : J. F. Hope, 16, Great Marlborough-street.

Post 8vo, price 4s., Illustrated,

The Sweet South ; or, a Month at Algiers.
By Eleanor Darby.

For the excellent Reviews of this Work see *Athenæum, Observer, Literary Gazette, Critic, Courier,* &c.

London : J. F. Hope, 16, Great Marlborough-street.

DR. E. LEE ON NICE AND MALAGA.
Demy 12mo, price 2s. 6d.,

Nice and its Climate. With Notices of the
Coast from Genoa to Marseilles, and Observations on the Influence of Climate on Pulmonary Consumption.

London : J. F. Hope, 16, Great Marlborough-street.

Price 1s. 6d.,

The Nurse and the Nursery ; being a Digest
of Important Information with regard to the Early Training and Management of Children ; together with Directions for the Treatment of Accidents apt to occur in the Nursery, and which every Nurse, Nursery Governess, and Mother ought to know.

"The instructions which he conveys are expressed in plain and intelligible terms, and no nurse or mother ought to be without them."—*Morning Post.*

London : J. F. Hope, 16, Great Marlborough-street.

WORKS BY THE REV. WILLIAM DUFF SCHOMBERG, B.A.,
Vicar of Polesworth.
Price 3d. (Just Published.)

The Pretensions of the Church of Rome to
be considered Older than the Church of England, examined.

London : J. F. Hope, 16, Great Marlborough-street.

BY THE SAME AUTHOR.
Price 1s.

Protestant Catholicism; or, the Characteristics
of Catholicism as inherited, and maintained, under Protest, by the Church of England.

"The reader will find that he has at his fingers' ends a mass of information and argument."—*Church and State Gazette.*

London : J. F. Hope, 16, Great Marlborough-street.

In 2 vols., large 8vo., price 10s.

The Theocratic Philosophy of English History,

Showing the Rise and Progress of the British Empire. In which the events of history are traced to their proper origin, the characters of persons whose actions have influenced the progress of society delineated, and the overruling providence of God vindicated.

"In this age of ephemeral publications, seldom does it fall to the lot of a reviewer to enjoy the privilege of calling public attention to a work of such profound research, written in such powerful and concise language, and presenting the result of years of patient investigation of an almighty power unravelling the entangled web of human affairs. If to justify the ways of God to man—if to exhibit Divine benevolence educing ultimate good out of apparent evil; making 'the wrath of man to praise him,' and overruling every event to subserve the grand designs of Providence; if such an attempt, executed by an author possessing in combination mental powers of no common order, has long been a desideratum, we are enabled to announce the completion of a task which will continue an imperishable memorial of the talent, and genius, and perseverance of Mr. Schomberg."—*Church Intelligencer.*

London: J. F. Hope, 16, Great Marlborough-street.

In demy 12mo., price 2s. 6d. cloth. Second edition, with copious additions.

Elements of the British Constitution, containing a comprehensive View of the Monarchy and Government of England.

"It is precisely what it professes to be, an exposition of the 'Elements of the British Constitution;' and as such it is deserving of a place in every Englishman's library, and should be early placed in the hands of every English schoolboy. It is comprehensive without being diffuse; clear in its statement of principles without cumbering the mind with details."—*Liverpool Courier.*

London: J. F. Hope, 16, Great Marlborough-street.

Price 6d.

Political Protestantism, designed for the First Forms at Schools and for Young Men leaving their Homes for the engagements of Public life.

*** The Profits of this Work are devoted to the Society of Church Missions in Ireland.

"The work consists of 78 pages of well-selected matter, drawn from valuable historical resources, and puts the question of Church and State, and the aggression of Popery, in its proper light."—*Shropshire Conservative Journal.*

London: J. F. Hope, 16, Great Marlborough-street.

Price 1s.

Claims and Responsibility of the Christian Ministry.

London: J. F. Hope, 16, Great Marlborough-street.